WHERE WE COME FROM

Aniefiok 'Neef' Ekpoudom is a writer from South London who documents & explores culture in contemporary Britain. In his work, Ekpoudom tells stories about the people, voices and communities shaping the country as it exists today. He writes for publications including the *Guardian*, *GQ* and *Vogue*, and has previously worked with music platforms such as GRM Daily, Link Up TV and SBTV. Ekpoudom has also contributed essays to *SAFE: On Black British Men Reclaiming Space* (2019), *Keisha The Sket* (2021) and *A New Formation: How Black Players Shaped The Modern Game* (2022).

He is a British Journalism Awards winner and was named on the *Forbes* 30 Under 30 List in Media & Marketing.

Further praise for *Where We Come From*:

'A stunning exploration of a genre, a movement and a world. It's every bit as lyrical as the rap Ekpoudom has documented.' Candice Carty-Williams

'Ekpoudom has written the book I've been waiting to read. Charting the history of migration of communities to south London, West Midlands and South Wales, and the sonic expressions which emerge from these places, the writing is intimate and illuminating. Ekpoudom's prose is rhythmic and deft but also crackles with joy. I know I'll be reading it for years to come.' Caleb Azumah Nelson

'In this engaging, erudite, sweeping social history of grime in Britain,

Ekpoudom focuses on three regions: south London, South Wales and the Midlands. He takes us to the unfashionable places – Neath, Croydon, Walsall – that created these fashionable sounds. He documents a mostly working-class, male, minoritised experience raised in the shadow of Britain's industrial collapse that weaves their parents' migrant identities – Caribbean, African, Greek – into the racially, ethnically and stylistically hybrid fabric of the music scene to create a uniquely and determinedly British genre . . . The writing is sublime.'
Gary Younge, *New Statesman*

'Rigorously researched, beautifully written and deeply moving. *Where We Come From* is a landmark work that will undoubtedly shape conversations about not just UK rap and grime, but British music for years to come. It is impossible not to learn from and I recommend it highly, whatever your music taste – this long-needed book is one many of us have been waiting to be written.' Yomi Adegoke

'A work of supreme cultural diplomacy from the disregarded and much demonised margins. *Where We Come From* reveals the deep, meaningful roots of UK rap and grime and, while not shying from uncomfortable realities of gatekeeping, systemic inequality, and the pervasive violence the genre is often marred by, illuminates its fundamental keystones of family, representation and belonging.'
Graeme Armstrong

'A (long overdue) social history of UK rap and grime. It's both moving and invigorating to read about Black British music with such a thorough depth of research, literary elegance and a palpable love for the art, and Ekpoudom importantly highlights the power of Black musical culture as a force for upliftment that is in constant battle with the heavy hand of the state.' Diana Evans, *Granta* (Books of the Year)

'A rich, vivid account of the wild and turbulent journey UK rap and grime has been on, told with characteristic wit and passion. Black British music is finally getting the platform it has long been denied, and Ekpoudom has created a truly captivating chronicle of the world it came from.' Dan Hancox

'Phenomenal – this is the book we've all been waiting for. Like the heroes he chronicles, Ekpoudom acts as torchbearer, his book a beacon, for the story that follows.' Guy Gunaratne

'It's no small feat to immortalise the lives, minds and words of one art form into another, never mind rap, a form that's rarely afforded the literary rigour it deserves. Ekpoudom not only illuminates the lives often ignored by those outside the culture, he gives them a gravitas and understanding many have yearned for. I read these pages with great pride, hefty emotion and often a smile. I turned the final pages and thought to myself, "At last. At last."' Courttia Newland

'A singular account of the rise of the genre, focusing on a careful selection of the people and places that shaped the music . . . this is a highly original, almost subversive project, full of personal stories and small-scale experiences. None of its main characters changed the world. Yet the changes they made in their own lives – spurred on by the rebel force of underground rap music – really are remarkable when studied in painstaking, loving detail.' Oliver Keens, *Guardian*

'Aniefiok Ekpoudom's illuminating, eye-opening social history traces the remarkable ascent of Black British music . . . An ambitious and unusual social history, it steps far outside the east London postcodes usually associated with the music to visit Walsall in the industrial West Midlands, Newport in South Wales and "deep south" London . . . The delicacy and empathy of Ekpoudom's writing shines.' Miles Ellingham, *Financial Times*

'The propulsive lyricism of *Where We Come From*'s prose is one of its most persistent pleasures.' Jimi Famurewa, *Evening Standard*

'*Where We Come From* traces the meteoric rise of British rap and grime music over the past ten years . . . Ekpoudom's extensive knowledge of the genres and the communities that created them shines through this book.' *Sunday Times*

'Remarkable . . . *Where We Come From*, like Jeffrey Boakye's *Hold Tight*, feels long overdue as a corrective to the white middle-class mainstream's reductionism about the recent revolutions in UK music . . . An untold history by someone who knows. Essential.' Neil Kulkarni, *The Wire*

'Each page enhances our understanding of the broader political context in which rap and grime operated – from the earliest Black pirate radio stations in Birmingham to a chapter dedicated to London rapper Dave . . . *Where We Come From* emerges as more than just a historical account; it's a mixtape and a comprehensive journey through Britain told from the perspective of the people who have spent the past seventy years shaping the culture.' Angel Lambo, *Frieze*

'[An] assured and humane study of overlapping generations of MC endeavour . . . pioneering.' Ben Thompson, *Mojo*

'Ekpoudom is, hands down, one of Britain's best music writers, as attested by his new book, *Where We Come From*, a kaleidoscopic, state-of-the-nation social and cultural history.' Craig McLean, *The Face*

'A journey down memory lane, from one of the most trusted voices of our time. Ekpoudom guides us through points of history, tragedy, and celebration – *Where We Come From* is a triumph.' Yomi Sode

ANIEFIOK EKPOUDOM

WHERE WE COME FROM

Rap, Home and Hope in Modern Britain

faber

First published in 2024
by Faber & Faber Limited
The Bindery, 51 Hatton Garden
London EC1N 8HN

This paperback edition published in 2025.

Typeset by Sam Matthews
Printed and bound by CPI Group (UK) Ltd, Croydon, CR0 4YY

A CIP record for this book
is available from the British Library

ISBN 978–0–571–36326–1

Printed and bound in the UK on FSC® certified paper in line with our continuing
commitment to ethical business practices, sustainability and the environment.
For further information see faber.co.uk/environmental-policy

Our authorised representative in the EU for product safety is
Easy Access System Europe, Mustamäe tee 50, 10621 Tallinn, Estonia
gpsr.requests@easproject.com

2 4 6 8 10 9 7 5 3

For Mum. Thank you for everything.

And for those who paved the ground,
who built something from nothing.
Without you there is no us.

The manor:
Throwing bricks at glass ceilings,
Do or die,
He who dreams with open eyes is alive.

KANO

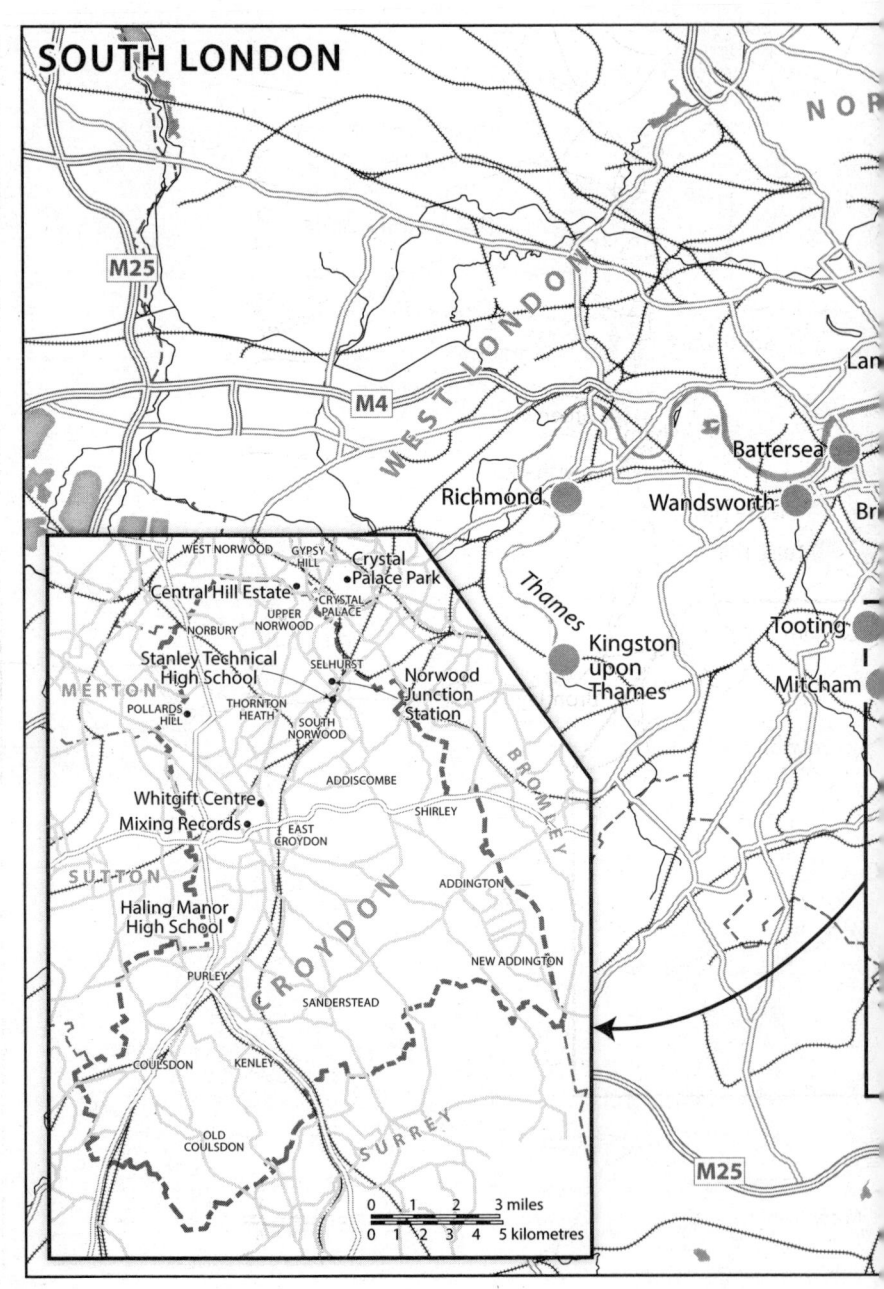

SOUTH LONDON

M25

M4

WEST LONDON

NOR

Lan

Battersea

Richmond

Wandsworth

Br

Thames

Kingston upon Thames

Tooting

Mitcham

WEST NORWOOD

GYPSY HILL

Crystal Palace Park

Central Hill Estate

CRYSTAL PALACE

UPPER NORWOOD

NORBURY

Stanley Technical High School

SELHURST

Norwood Junction Station

MERTON

POLLARDS HILL

THORNTON HEATH

SOUTH NORWOOD

ADDISCOMBE

Whitgift Centre

SHIRLEY

Mixing Records

EAST CROYDON

SUTTON

BROMLEY

ADDINGTON

Haling Manor High School

CROYDON

NEW ADDINGTON

PURLEY

SANDERSTEAD

COULSDON

KENLEY

SURREY

OLD COULSDON

M25

| 0 | 1 | 2 | 3 miles |
| 0 | 1 | 2 | 3 | 4 | 5 kilometres |

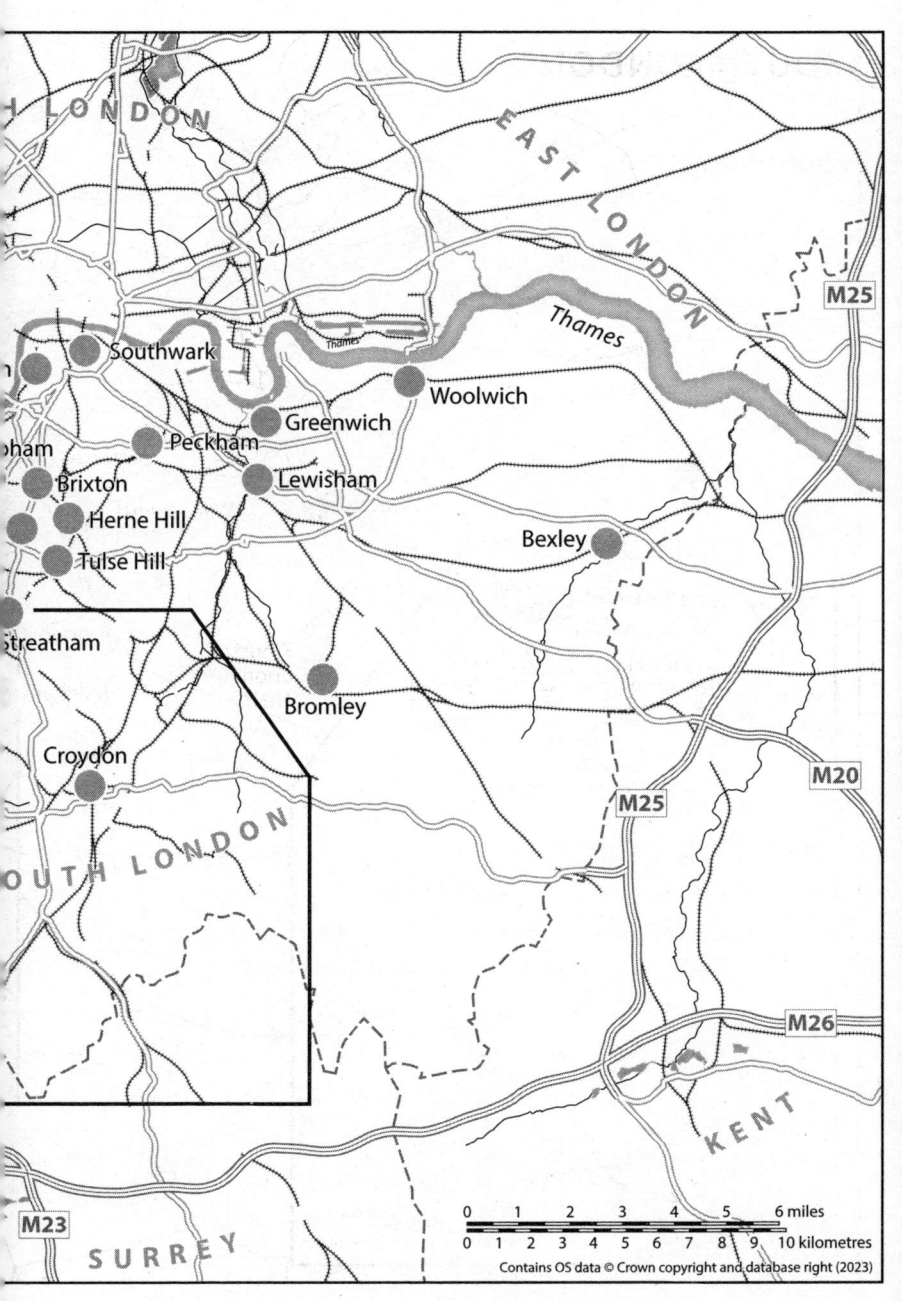

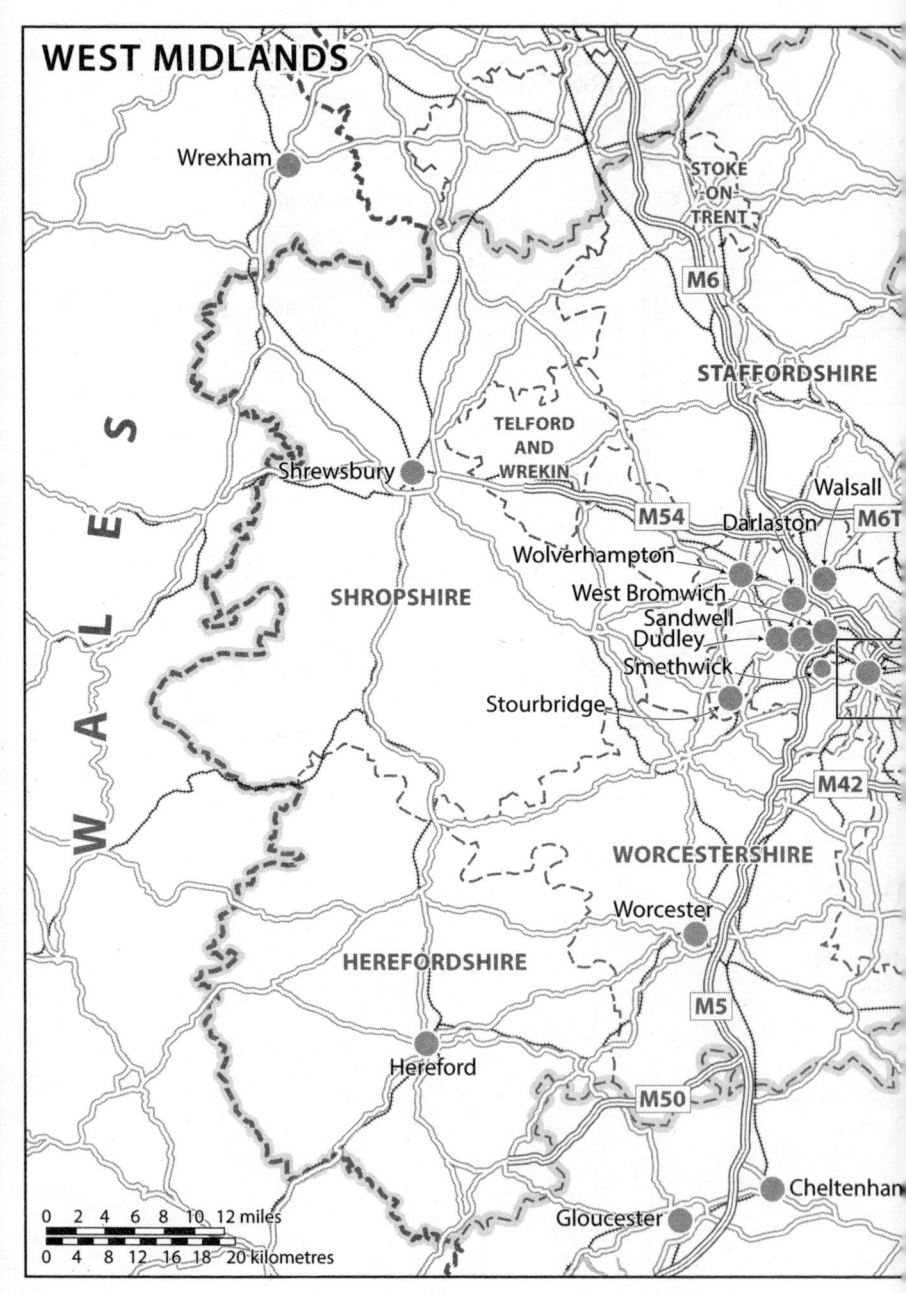

WEST MIDLANDS

Wrexham

STOKE-
ON-
TRENT

M6

STAFFORDSHIRE

W
A
L
E
S

TELFORD
AND
WREKIN

Shrewsbury

M54

Walsall

Darlaston

M6T

Wolverhampton

West Bromwich

SHROPSHIRE

Sandwell

Dudley

Smethwick

Stourbridge

M42

WORCESTERSHIRE

Worcester

HEREFORDSHIRE

M5

Hereford

M50

Cheltenham

Gloucester

0 2 4 6 8 10 12 miles

0 4 8 12 16 18 20 kilometres

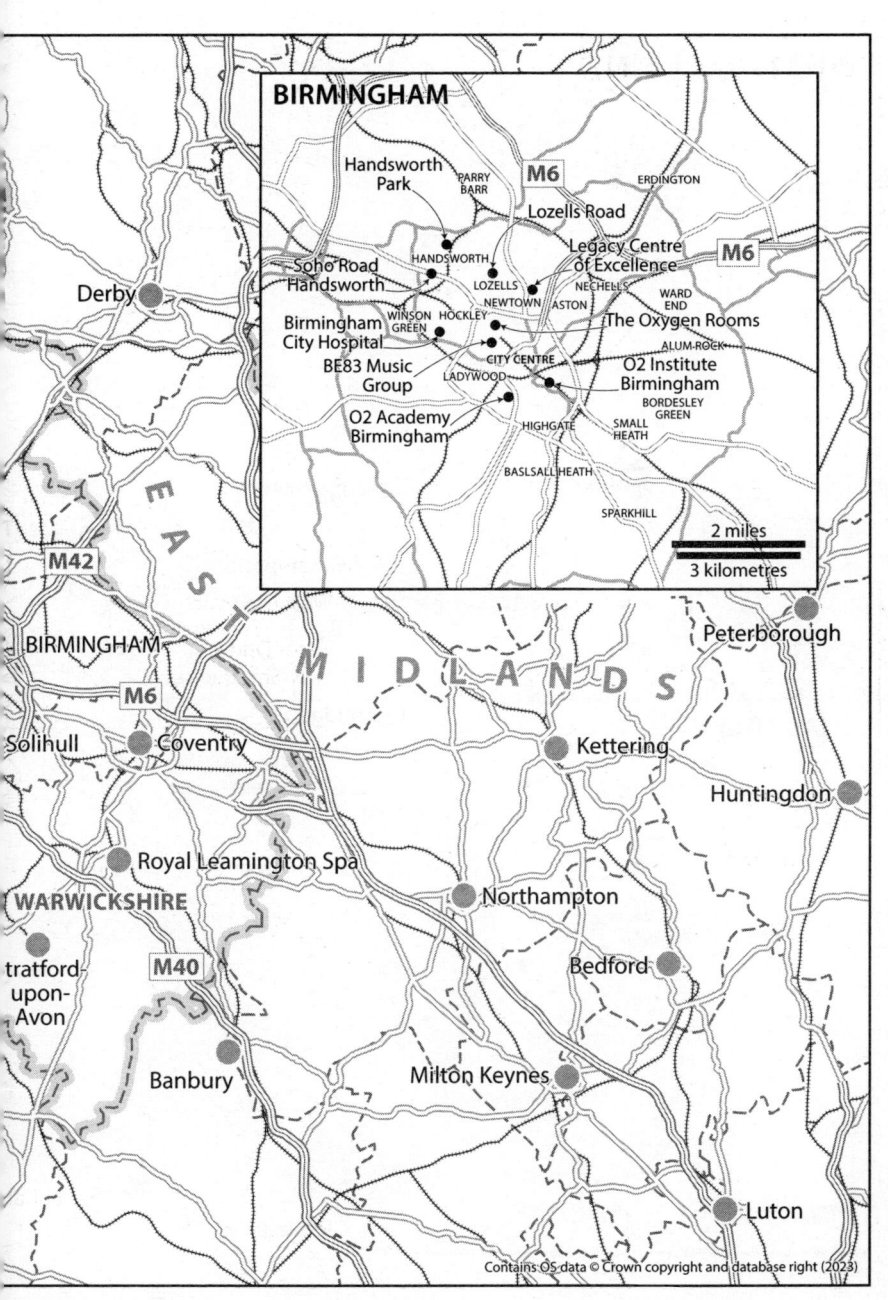

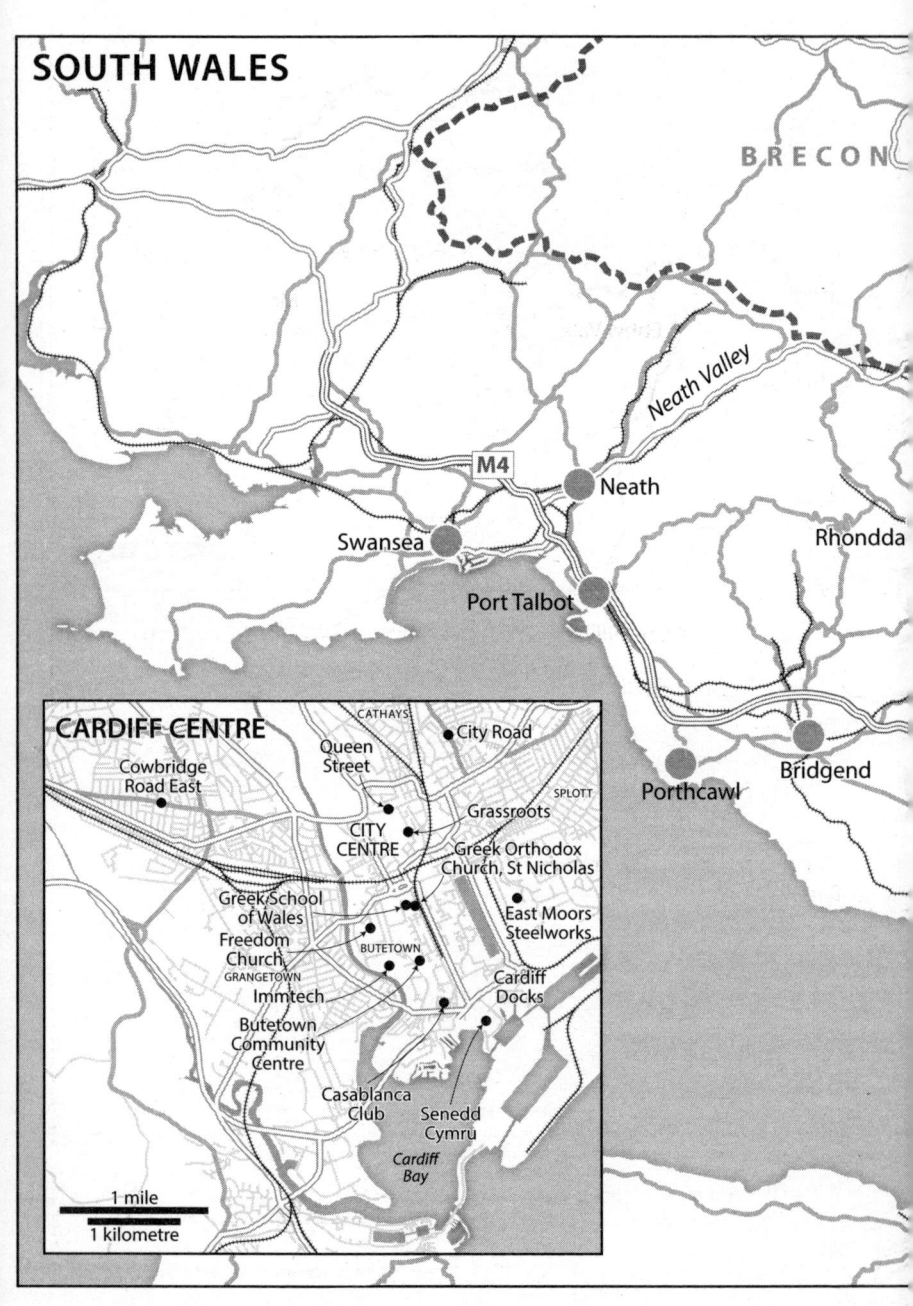

SOUTH WALES

BRECON

Neath Valley

M4

Neath

Swansea

Port Talbot

Rhondda

Porthcawl

Bridgend

CARDIFF CENTRE

CATHAYS

City Road

Cowbridge
Road East

Queen
Street

SPLOTT

CITY
CENTRE

Grassroots

Greek Orthodox
Church, St Nicholas

Greek School
of Wales

Freedom
Church

GRANGETOWN

BUTETOWN

East Moors
Steelworks

Immtech

Cardiff
Docks

Butetown
Community
Centre

Casablanca
Club

Senedd
Cymru

Cardiff
Bay

1 mile

1 kilometre

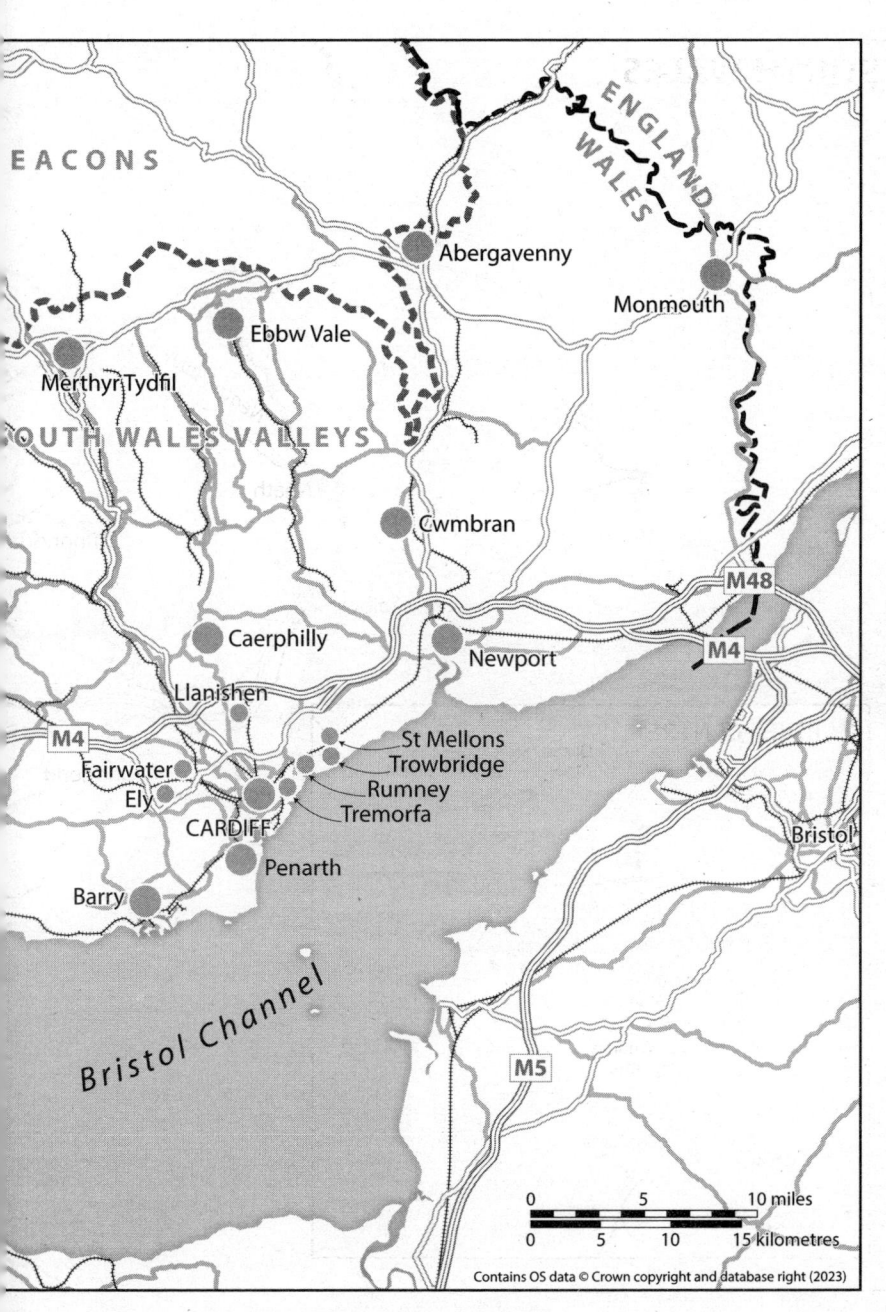

CONTENTS

FOREWORD

In his landmark book, *What is History?*, the late, celebrated scholar E. H. Carr unpacks how central the role of the historian is in deciding what is worthy of record. 'The facts speak only when the historian calls on them: it is he who decides to which facts to give the floor, and in what order or context,' he writes. 'It is the historian who has decided for his own reasons that Caesar's crossing of that petty stream, the Rubicon, is a fact of history. Whereas the crossing of the Rubicon by millions of other people before or since interests nobody at all.'

Where We Come From by Aniefiok Ekpoudom is a book rooted in the experiences of the kind of people who crossed the Rubicon that we are interested in, but too rarely see represented. It tells the stories of working-class men, most of whom enjoy attention and acclaim, but not quite fame, in grime. He shows how they take the strands from their parents' migrant identities – Caribbean, Greek, English, African, Welsh – weave them with their own sensibilities and experiences and create a unique British sound. We see their joy and confidence grow as they break through into the music business and then fade as success turns their passion first into a profession and then to labour, with all the monotony and obligation that comes with it. We see them commute between their twenty-first-century music genre and late-stage capitalism with jobs in call centres and Apple stores. And we witness them grow up as men, from catching cases and getting patched up in the emergency room to raising children and committing to relationships.

This may be non-fiction. But it is not journalism as we have come to know it; that time-efficient practice where someone sweeps in, finds whatever misery or derring-do they were sent to find, and then sweeps out again. This kind of work takes however long it takes to grow the kind of trust and honesty that will allow a subject to build a relationship with the writer, open up to them and allow the narrator to witness them at their most vulnerable. Often, though not always, quality non-fiction writing demands 'quantity time' spent listening, watching and engaging.

This would be valuable writing at any time. But the book lands in a moment when its findings are both particularly useful and hopeful in two main ways.

First, it emerges at a time when British people are keen for a more hopeful narrative but find precious little evidence of that in their political culture, after an election with pitifully low turnout which returned a government with the lowest ever percentage of the eligible popular vote and one of the largest parliamentary majorities ever. A month following the election there were huge racially motivated riots across the country, many in the kind of areas Aniefiok writes about. A general sense of alienation and ennui compounded, and to some extent driven, by growing levels of inequality and economic disadvantage, has led some to either lose hope, turn on each other or scapegoat minorities. But our mainstream political culture does not adequately represent the aspirations of the country we live in. A British Social Attitudes Survey from September 2024 found the proportion who felt that you had to be born in Britain to call yourself British fell by 25% over the previous decade – roughly the same fall was found in those who say they are 'proud to be British'. Meanwhile, more than three quarters were proud of Britain's achievements in arts, literature and sport.

In the most gentle and unintrusive way, Aniefiok features a

multiracial group of young people who emerge from a youth of austerity, war and economic collapse, often in depressed areas, who find themselves, and some kind of future, in music. Multicultural Britain, to them, is not an ominous threat but a banal fact of life, which they leverage creatively. The hardships that they experience, be they emotional or economic, are not particular to any race, ethnicity or citizenship status. It offers us a country enriched and improved by migration and difference rather than impoverished and diminished by it. Describing the mourning of one rapper, Cadet, Aniefiok writes: 'How does South London mourn one of its own? There is an Islamic burial, and there is a Christian church service. There is a Jamaican Nine Night, the traditional wake where the family and the friends of the bereaved come together in memorial of their loved one . . . By doing so, they honour the many sides that made him whole.'

Second, it emerges at a time when many young men struggle to find a role in a society where norms and expectations are shifting, with roughly half believing society expects them to 'man up' when faced with challenges and that crying in front of others makes them less masculine. Aniefiok manages to get to the frailty behind the machismo as the people he writes about struggle with a range of familiar rock and roll demons – drugs, alcohol, aggression – but nearly all mature into responsible, caring parents or partners.

Aniefiok achieves all of this by showing, not telling. Trusting the reader to make their own conclusions, he pens portraits, not polemics. The primary characters are not cautionary tales in a morality play but real people. The kind of people we are interested in, but rarely hear about. With great humanity and eye for detail, what Aniefiok offers us here is both an understanding of social history through grime and of grime through social history.

Gary Younge

INTRODUCTION

They mark this night with a prayer.

In the green room of the O2 Forum Kentish Town, North London, they are gathered. There are more than twenty of them, huddled in a loose circle, arms over each other's shoulders, spare hands carrying liquor in plastic cups. Dim spotlights glow over bowed heads as they listen quietly to the blessing being spoken aloud. Many of them are musicians: rappers and MCs, sums of a long line of sound and resistance and migration in working-class cities across Britain.

They carry these stories in their songs. They come from the south of the country and from the north, young British men tracing roots back to family lines in Jamaica and Guyana, Ireland and Nigeria, Grenada and Ghana, a people moulded anew, fused together by this island on the edges of north-western Europe.

Here, on this evening in November 2016, they are gathered to celebrate and support one of their own.

Giggs is a rapper from Peckham, South London. He stands with his head lowered. He has called them all out tonight for his first ever London headline show. A black cap covers his eyes. A gold chain dangles from his neck, and he listens quietly as his manager, Buck, leads the group in prayer. 'We just want to give thanks and appreciation because this is a big moment for us. We've been shut down for many years. This is a blessing.'[1]

Since Giggs first picked up a microphone and dared to dream of music he has been walking the heavy path towards tonight. Many here have made the walk with him. His music bears the scars of those journeys. It has been a long road, a long road for him, a long road for the gathered, a long road for their genres.

Buck continues: 'There are many people over the years that have died, in jail, that can't be with us here today. There's many that have started our journey and won't finish our journey. But they're here in thoughts.'

Outside, a few thousand are waiting in the arena. They have walked the road with them too. They were there when Rap was only a pipe dream for British kids, a hobby that blossomed in the souls of the inner cities, but never really paid. They were there when Giggs's voice first began to push out from South London council estates, drifting across the country region by region. They were there when he met resistance, stayed with him on an uncertain course. They bought tickets for the shows police cancelled at short notice, listened when he was banned from national radio, and sought out his music when he spent six months inside, awaiting trial for a gun charge. They listened as he has shared his story, shed his traumas, used music to leave a permanent account of his existence here. They have followed him into the light, into this moment where the genres they hold close have reached the tipping point, where Rap and Grime fantasies are starting to mean something more concrete. A few thousand are waiting out there for him, waiting for all of those here gathered. They are waiting to see what it looks like when a sound emerges out of the fire.

———

Something has been happening in Britain, and British music. Over the past decade, underground, connected genres like UK Rap and Grime have leaked out from the inner cities. In that process, they have become among the most popular sounds in the country, forcing themselves onto the stages of mainstream pop culture. They are entrenched on the biggest, most traditional platforms, are a major presence at awards shows like the BRITs and at festivals like Glastonbury, are widely seen on newspaper front pages and magazine front covers, are debated in parliament, are shaping new legislation in the country, and have left permanent fingerprints on streaming services and the Official UK Charts. They are the soundtrack for popular film and TV productions. They regularly play out on morning radio shows and prime-time adverts, and they are even used as learning devices in schools, their existence finely woven into the casual, day-to-day running of this country.

This uprising is not an accident. This is not a beginning, is not the emergence of something unexpected. This commercial conquering does not define their history, or their legacy either. There is more here. For decades, genres like UK Rap and Grime, children of British MC culture's tight family tree, have been tuning in Black and working-class communities across the country. They are sounds whose existence has been shaped and sculpted by waves of migration, by forebears adapting to the terrain, the politics, the culture of this foreign land.

As generations of these people made sense of themselves in these new places, giving and feeding off the land, slowly turning British soil into home, they have documented their experiences in music, using sound to mark and catalogue their individual and collective presence. UK Rap and Grime are contemporary pieces of this wider musical legacy that stretches back over a period of seventy years to the earliest stems of British-Caribbean Sound System culture. They are products of these older genres, products of Reggae and 2-Tone, Jungle and Garage, as well as American Hip Hop. And, as time passes, newly fruiting, MC-led sounds and subgenres like UK Drill and Afroswing are a product of them too.

Grime has its roots in East London in the earliest years of the new millennium, a genre that evolved out of Garage, as well as wider influences from Jungle, Ragga, Drum & Bass and wider Sound System culture. Formed by MC Wiley and other teenagers from council estates across Tower Hamlets and Newham, it became a sound unto itself, and eventually spread across the rest of the city, and then into other Black, and working-class pockets of the country. Alongside it, a specific strand of British Hip Hop known as UK Rap began to chart a similar course. Emerging a few years after Grime, it was a less localised sound with its originators in the many corners of the capital.

The two diverged at points. Grime beat along at a rapid pace of 140 bpm, while UK Rap was slower. Grime's spiritual home was Pirate Radio stations in East London council estates, freeform sessions called sets where MCs went to war over instrumentals in a direct lineage from their parents and grandparents who ran Sound Systems. UK Rap instead thrived on mixtapes and full songs with an emphasis on visceral storytelling.

Despite these differences in tone and in practice, the two share an essence. Wherever there was UK Rap, there was Grime also, both existing side by side in marginalised pockets of the country. They are close siblings. They were born of the same conditions, in the same estates, towns and areas, and as the years passed, they coalesced into a shared musical scene, collaborating with one another, building infrastructure, each subgenre still maintaining their distinct uniqueness.

UK Rap and Grime, who together form this musical movement, have become an oral canvas for the writing of an alternate history of modern Britain. Deep in their texts are connected stories of community and identity, personal accounts of sacrifice and loss, of hope and pride, of violence and family. They are a social commentary from the margins, a vessel and a voice for the disregarded and overlooked. This book is an excavation of these stories and the sounds they have underpinned, the music they have forged and been forged by.

————

Over this past decade, as the rappers, MCs and other participants in these genres have carried these sounds into a new era, they have transformed their own lives in the process. These quiet and loud, personal and community legacies have been written into the day-to-day lives of people across the country. They are still being written at this moment.

This is an account of this history and current reality, a tracking of this movement from underground into mainstream, and, most importantly, a documentation of the lives so powerfully altered by the journey. This is about what lies at the soul of British Rap's boom and blossom.

I have been writing about, reporting on, and interviewing members from this musical movement for eleven years now, first working with grassroots platforms like Link Up TV, SBTV and GRM Daily, and then, as the music began to take off and intrigue from wider Britain began to peak, writing profiles and essays for national newspapers and magazines. In this time, I have witnessed first-hand the impact music was having on artists and managers, producers and DJs, supporters and their wider communities. I wanted to write a book that captures this legacy.

Where We Come From is the result of more than five years of reporting. To offer a detailed look at the country, I centred my reporting on three different regions: South London, South Wales and the West Midlands. In these places, I found an alternate history of modern Britain scribed into song. I found people whose experiences growing up in this country had pushed them to the brink. In music, many of them had found salvation.

During my travels it also became clear that these music scenes, and the environments and circumstances that accompanied them, especially in their earliest years, were largely dominated by young men. As a result, this skew is reflected in the contents of this work.

This book is not intended to be an exhaustive chronicling of UK Rap and Grime. Instead, this is a book about the connected realities that have birthed these genres. It is about the communities and people who drive the music, the conditions that have formed them, their sounds, and now, in this era, the landscape of contemporary culture in the UK. By writing *Where We Come From*, I hope to place these communities and an overlooked history of place, Grime, Rap and resistance into the national story of modern Britain.

PART I
TOUCH ROAD

1 BABYLON
WEST MIDLANDS

This is how they arrived here.

There are stories about the Britain that existed in the imaginations of those early West Indian settlers arriving through the forties, fifties and sixties. Fantasies held close by young men and women setting out for the supposed promised land of 'milk and honey' where the roads were rumoured to be paved with gold. But the reality of this place was different than they had imagined. The West Midlands was grey with bitter winters that stripped leaves from the trees, where the skies screamed hail and rain through the long cold evenings. There were factories unfurling black smoke for as far as the eye could see and there was isolation, a loneliness among solo travellers who had left family and friends behind. They were men and women taking brave steps into a cold new world, building new lives in a land so different to back home, pouring themselves into a country that would, at times, resent their presence. Some struggled to find housing. Some struggled to find work. Some noticed hostility in a region and a wider population angered by, and ignorant about, its growing Black communities.

For these early settlers to survive Babylon, they would have to walk through fire.

This is how they arrived here.

The line from the Caribbean to the West Midlands, from Jamaica and Trinidad and St Kitts and other islands to Birmingham and Coventry and Walsall and Wolverhampton, has its beginnings in the ashes of war. In the 1940s, when the Second World War had finished and Europe sank back into a tense peace, Britain began a slow emergence from the wreckage. Soldiers returned home. The elderly resumed retirement after taking up vacant civil responsibilities to help with the war effort. Housing developments were planned in bombed-out towns and cities. Slums were cleared and a National Health Service was announced. The war had worn on the economy and the workforce, and a country needing to rebuild itself couldn't do so alone. So, in 1948, three years after the war had ended, the British Nationality Act was introduced. Residents of British colonial territories and independent Commonwealth countries were recognised as British subjects, and were in theory granted the right to settle in the UK; free to find work and housing, to vote and raise families.

In the aftermath of the act, a steady wave of West Indian immigrants arrived. They came to be known as the Windrush generation, named after the HMT *Empire Windrush*, which docked at Tilbury in 1948 carrying 1,027 passengers-turned-British-citizens on its voyage from Jamaica. By 1970 more than half a million immigrants from the Caribbean had arrived here. They settled in places like Newport in Wales, Notting Hill and Clapham in London. They slowly fanned out across the West Midlands too: Birmingham, Wolverhampton, Walsall, Coventry, West Bromwich and so on, erecting the early stems of large Black communities in these towns and cities across the region. The settlers were the forefathers and foremothers of a UK Rap and Grime generation, Caribbean people moving across North Atlantic waters, laying down their roots in new homes, readying the soil for a generation of Brit(ish) children to emerge.

This is how they arrived here.

These families often came to the West Midlands in staggers. A husband first, then a wife and the children. They first worked as bus drivers and as nurses, as factory and construction workers, a growing Black enclave in the heart of the country, building Britain up from the rubble.

Their early experiences in a foreign West Midlands are collated in Birmingham Museums Trust's Black Oral History Project, where the lives and memories of the city's first generation of Caribbean immigrants were orally recorded and set permanently into stone. In these accounts, their growing presence encounters early aggression, racism ranging from the subtle to the overt. Frank Scantlebury, who moved to the UK from Barbados in 1955, told the project, 'Very early on after we arrived, we didn't notice any racism. But after a while, after we'd settled in, we realised that some people were rather hostile to us. We found it very strange, we never expected to encounter that sort of thing. We were always taught that it was a fair society.'[1]

Another recording comes from Esme Lancaster, who arrived from Jamaica in 1950, joining her sister who had settled in the country years prior. Esme's early memories of Birmingham and Britain are of a deep winter moving over the city and a homesickness that lasted for months, reducing her to long spells of tears. She fell into the Church to find comfort. She found a job doing office admin on the weekends, and in doing so, brushed up against a white community hostile to her people. Racism at work was whispered, communicated in gestures unspoken, hinted in low tones behind closed doors. Sometimes Esme's boss would bring her the work unfinished and set aside by white colleagues. They had spent the afternoon slacking off, their leftovers now hers to complete.

One afternoon, while in the cloakroom, she overheard colleagues tell one another how they couldn't stand the sight of her. In response she told them, 'I am here. We are here. We are coming, and we are increasing. One day we will be like the children of Israel in the land of Egypt, and if you don't like it, you can go, or die.'[2]

Then she walked away.

This is how they arrived here.

2 HANDSWORTH SONGS
WEST MIDLANDS

Tower blocks bloomed on West Midland skylines. In the sixties and seventies, after the war ended, and reports like the 1946 Housing Survey in Birmingham revealed a city where half of its homes lacked a separate bathroom, slum-clearing programmes were announced. The local councils levelled communities, reducing city streets and their tightly packed terraced housing to rubble. They began to buy up disused green lands on the edges of towns, earmarking these outskirts for regeneration and development.

On the bones of the old terraced rows, tower blocks and mass housing estates were drafted and then slowly assembled. Across the region, long streaks of grey concrete began to sprout on the skyline like beanstalks, new council flats in their hundreds scratching at foggy heavens. The Castle Vale estate, built on an abandoned Second World War airfield in North Birmingham, housed 20,000 people. The Bromford Bridge estate in the east of the city housed around 10,000, its ten high-rises constructed on what was once a racecourse. Further east, on the edges of the city, 1,500 acres of greenbelt in Solihull were cleared for the Chelmsley Wood housing estate, population 12,000.

It was a handful of towns and areas like these, anchoring new housing estates to the earth, that became the centre point for the region's Black and immigrant communities. The inner cities of North Birmingham, in towns like Handsworth and Aston, Nechells and Newtown, were a home away from home for Caribbean immigrants. In Coventry it was Hillfields, north of the city centre. In Darlaston, near Walsall, terraced housing was flattened and two fifteen-storey blocks of flats were erected in replacement: Great Croft House and John Wootton House welcomed their first residents in 1965.

The early seeds of the Black community and Black British music scenes in the West Midlands were forged in these post-war housing settlements. By 1961, 17,000 Caribbean people were living in Handsworth, a sign of a growing Black enclave in the region. In response to the racism they faced, those early generations seized fate to build brighter days and better futures for those who would come after. Black-owned businesses and organisations began to blossom in the community: the Marcus Garvey Nursery emerging in the British Black Power movement and setting firm foundations for the young Black kids of Birmingham before they entered the school system. The Harriet Tubman Bookshop on Grove Lane. The African Liberation Day marches in Handsworth Park. The butcher shops, the churches, the theatre groups.

This is how they arrived here.

And when they did arrive, they brought music.

In Newtown, not far from Handsworth, Cecil Morris, part of this early wave of Black enterprise and business, founded one of Britain's first Black Pirate Radio stations. Cecil had arrived in Birmingham from Brandon Hill, Jamaica, in 1962, when he was around fourteen, and found a haven in the high-rises. After running a record shop and throwing talent competitions and managing local singers and Reggae artists like Steel Pulse, he turned his attentions to radio. In the late seventies and early eighties, the airwaves echoing over Birmingham were dominated by two stations, BBC Radio Birmingham and BRMB 94.8 FM, both white-owned, both in possession of the city's only two legal licences, neither catering for a Black population who had by now existed en masse in the West Midlands for a few decades.

'They reckoned what they broadcast was good enough for us,' he says, 'because we speak English.'

Frustrated by the absence of Black music, he set up meetings with both the stations, intending to bring his people's sounds and identity onto national radio. From the stations, he demanded a daily two-hour programme, a show 'presented by us, in our format, with our accent'.

The meetings bore no fruit. In the session with the BBC, he arrived with local soundmen and other musicians who were flattered when the broadcaster offered a half-hour slot on a Sunday. Frustrated at his colleagues, Cecil walked out, 'because they were giving the management strength by showing interest in accepting half an hour when we should be blazing hell'.

A few hours later, at the BRMB meeting, he was told that the station already had an Indian presenter, that said presenter sometimes played a Reggae record or two, that there was nothing more they could do for him, that his request was futile.

He told them, 'Okay, no problem, I will establish our own radio station.' They laughed at him, one of them saying, 'Mr Morris, that's a good idea, don't you think so, guys?'

He left the meeting determined. He went back to his record shop on the ground floor of a five-storey block, bought a radio transmitter from an English friend, set up some records, plugged everything in, went to his bedroom on the third floor where his bed had an inbuilt radio, and switched it on. Music began to play and his resistance in radio began.

By 1981 he was recording programmes in the weekdays and playing them out via Pirate Radio on the weekends, sending songs of Reggae and home comforts out into the ether, notes whining on the wind, waiting to be grasped by whoever had fine-tuned their dial.

1981 was the same year summer riots swept across Black

communities in Britain, a restless storm blowing like wildfire from inner city to inner city. The mood had been tense in the years before the uprisings. Across the country, manufacturing industries were on the decline, inner cities were in decay and the economy was in recession. It was a country where politicians and far-right organisations like the National Front were fixing blame for rising crime and failing economies on foreigners and others. Anti-immigration sentiments were being written into law, and the legislation that freely welcomed Black people into Britain was slowly washed away. The Black Caribbean community in the UK was isolated and antagonised by the institutions governing the nation, by the same country they had helped rebuild.

It was a country where the 'Sus' (from 'suspected person') law[1] granted police the authority to stop and search the public without evidence of a crime being committed, a power disproportionately used on Black and ethnic minorities. Consequently, the fractures in an already strained relationship deepened. In Handsworth, young Black men told a local community survey in 1978 that the police were pushing people around, that the police were treating young Black men like dirt, like 'we are still slaves'.[2] In Handsworth, after the local manufacturing industries had dried up, an estimated quarter of young Black people in the area were unemployed. So when uprisings began in Brixton in the late spring of 1981, and then spread north in the summer to Black communities in Liverpool and Leeds, Manchester and eventually Handsworth, Cecil found himself in the centre of a storm.

On a Friday afternoon in early July, he was in the Black-owned Harambe Bookshop on the Handsworth frontline, the Soho Road that drives through the spine of the suburb. In the shop he was confronted by a man he describes as a 'massive white guy: hippy, beard. He kind of look like a giant.'

The man told him there would be riots in Handsworth that evening. A few hours later, Cecil walked the street in disbelief. He could see about forty police buses on Soho Road, and as he walked deeper into the frontline and on towards the police station at Thornhill Road, he could see hundreds and hundreds of policemen marching down to the main strip. 'Bang. Bang. Bang, like the Zulu going to war.' After the police battalion charged a gathered crowd, he fled, frightened and 'run like hell to come back over to my place'. Over the next few hours, shop fronts were smashed and cars were set alight. More than a hundred arrests would be made. The damage was estimated at £500,000.

When back home, he gathered his broadcasting equipment, pushed his aerial out of his window and when the broadcast went live, he began to speak, 'telling young Black youths not to go out into this thing here because we will get blamed for anything that occur'. Then he played music, hoping to calm bristling nerves of a generation riled by police, state and nation.

This is how they arrived here.

It was the start of something. In the aftermath, people in the local area began writing to Cecil, telling him that a station was what they wanted. Buoyed by their encouragement, he turned his passion into something permanent.

The first station was called Radio Starr. In those days he would record shows onto tapes that held an hour's worth of space on each side. The tape would be connected to a transmitter and then placed at the peak of a tower block. While the station played, he would sit in his studio, recording the next show, then when an hour had nearly passed, he would rush back into the tower block and flip the tape onto its second hour. For years he went on like this, recording talk shows and playing the sounds of the day to the community, basking the Handsworth air in soft Reggae and Soul. As he played, the audience began to swell.

In 1985, riots came back to Handsworth. Little had changed in four years. Unemployment was still cresting in the West Midlands. Policing was still heavy in the area and when a man was arrested for a traffic offence in nearby Lozells, the sparks of a community still on edge again ignited into flame. Shops and buildings were set alight, and police and groups of young men and women jockeyed back and forth in battle on the streets of inner-city Birmingham. There were over a hundred injuries suffered and two civilian deaths.[3] When a hardware store stocked with propane gas caught fire, the sound of exploding cylinders echoed like fireworks into the night. As the sun set on that late summer evening, Handsworth burned.

A community leader would go on to say, 'What we're seeing here today is the result of the type of insensitivity that has been displayed by the police in this area over a very long period of time. A simple road traffic incident escalated into major violence. Virtual anarchy took place as a consequence of the way in which the police decided they could deal with Black people within this community.'

Another would say, 'The general state of the young people here is helplessness, and we need help,' and a young man would remark, 'We have no chance. If we right we wrong, and if we wrong, we double wrong.'[4]

When news of the riot spread, Cecil again took to the airwaves. Now armed with a stronger transmitter, a regular listenership and more professional equipment, he began to play records and speak. Broadcasting on the night of the uprising, he told the young people, 'We understand there may be some big trouble in Handsworth but it's got nothing to do with us, just stay in your house. Let's have a party.'

His second station, People's Community Radio Link, widely known as PCRL, was born on those evenings of unrest, a community stronghold emerging from the ashes of fire.

This is how they arrived here.

PCRL was the pirate station that raised generations of Black families in Birmingham. Throughout the eighties and nineties, parents played the station in their homes and in their cars, mothers with their sons, fathers with their daughters, young men and women gathered under shared roofs, tuning into the frequency with extended family and friends.

In spite of its illegal status, PCRL evolved into an operational radio station with a studio and a management team who met monthly, as well as a revolving roster of presenters and DJs. Together they bound into one, offering their people what the national broadcasters had defiantly withheld.

The station was renowned for playing Reggae. But there was more. They regularly broadcasted Gospel shows, ran Soul shows, ran Calypso and Rock shows, even ran a West African show from a presenter in Gambia. They also ran a weekly talk show titled *Talk Black* where they carved out space to discuss police brutality and educated listeners on Black history, about the revered kingdoms of Timbuktu and the very visible impact the Moors had had on modern Europe.

'We were actually letting people know what *they* perceive us to be is not *us*,' he said. 'They didn't get it in school. They didn't get that portrayal in the radio or the television. We remained a nobody and we would remain a nobody until *us* prove who *we* are.'

The station became a meeting point for a community to reason and reckon with itself, to ruminate on the climate of the time and the path that lay ahead. It was by them and for them, knitting together the fragments of families now spread across other pockets of the inner city and the wider West Midlands. Blues Parties and local businesses were regularly advertised, and when there was a bereavement in the community, PCRL would announce the passing on air, spreading awareness about the loss and impending funeral to distant family and friends. They hired venues to host Christmas parties for children and senior citizens. They gave a platform to local Asian and Muslim presenters who too struggled to find space on the national broadcasters. And when the station began to peak in popularity and young people began finding their way to Cecil's door, begging to be presenters, PCRL would offer them broadcasting training programmes, awarding certificates to whoever stayed the course.

'At one stage I feel like there's nothing I couldn't do,' Cecil says of that time. 'If I think it, I can do it.'

Pirate Radio was prohibited in Britain, a criminal offence for any person or entity pushing out illegal and unlicensed broadcasts on the airwaves. The laws around these terms were enforced by the Departments of Trade and Industry, known as the DTI. In Pirate Radio's second boom during the eighties and nineties, DTI officers would scan the tower blocks and the airwaves, raiding makeshift studios and disconnecting transmitters wherever they found them. When a station was pulled from the air, the DJs would relocate to a new tower block, reassemble their station, and the chase would begin anew.

PCRL came under sustained pressure from the DTI. Cecil was first raided in the early eighties when he was still recording programmes on two-hour tape packs. The station went dead one afternoon and when he went across to the transmitter in the tower block to seek out the problem, he found four DTI and police apiece, standing at the bottom of the stairs with his aerial and equipment in hand.

'I looked at them. I said, "Where you going with this?"'

When he said that the equipment belonged to him, the officers took him to the police station and locked him in the cells for the night. In court he was fined £180.

It was the beginning of a long tug of war between Cecil and the DTI, between PCRL and the authorities, an eternal loop of cat and mouse playing out on the concrete beanstalks of Birmingham. Some days he would be sitting in his office, the transmitter and aerial stationed on a fifteen-storey tower block across the road, when he would notice the DTI officers on the roofs, wrecking and dismantling his equipment. On occasion, he would go out and challenge them. At other times, when he had live court cases due to the station, he would just sit and watch, powerless as the DTI took the station to pieces, because showing his face would jeopardise his trial.

Whenever the station was pulled from the air, Cecil and the team would scramble to set up in a new tower block, roving across the city to bring PCRL back from the dead. With the station's rising popularity, he was able to afford and stockpile aerials and transmitters. In his tenure, he had set up base in hundreds of high-rise council flats across the city and says, 'There's not a tower block or building in Birmingham that we don't use.' In his head he counts around three hundred.

When the early morning DTI raids took the station apart, PCRL would be back on air by the late afternoon. Noticing this stubborn streak, the authorities began to expand their efforts. They barricaded doors leading to tower-block roofs, and began raiding six days a week, twice on some days, steaming the station in the evenings too, just as Cecil and his team had reassembled and recovered from the morning ambush.

But Cecil found an ally in the community he served. Council block caretakers could be bribed for the keys to the roof. Tenants moving out of their flats would give him their keys, leaving him a scatter of empty apartments in a single high-rise. They loved the station. When the DTI installed a covert camera by a door leading to a roof, and a resident in a flat below switched on her TV, the camera feed unwittingly played through her screen. She phoned Cecil, warning him of what had happened.

'They don't get me,' he says.

That tower block was in town, opposite a DTI office. As they hunted him through the span of the city, he was broadcasting from across the road.

Rumour is that PCRL became so popular throughout Birmingham that the BBC and BRMB were growing anxious, unnerved at a Pirate Radio station eating into their listenership. Cecil says they began threatening to take him to court.

The end of the station began when he was abroad. After years of talk shows informing the city's first- and second-generation Black Caribbean community about the old kingdoms of Africa, he decided to go and see the real thing for himself. He ran two trips in 2002 and 2003, taking seventy-five and then eighty people, most of them Jamaican, to Gambia, on the far edges of West Africa. They visited James Island, a fleck of earth floating in the wide mouth of River Gambia, the rumoured birthplace of the folklorish character and freeman-turned-enslaved Kunta Kinte.

'I wanted to know where I'm from,' Cecil says. 'I'm born in Jamaica, I'm from Africa.'

When he arrived back in England and was on the motorway towards Birmingham, he tuned the radio. The static hash of a Pirate pulled from the air came through the dial. Returning home, he discovered that the DTI had raided his office and his studio, his transmitter site and the homes of the core management team.

'They got a lot of information. They got us good.'

He was accused of conspiring to manage, finance and operate an unauthorised station. It was to be his tenth time appearing in court. Apart from the early £180 fine, he had successfully defended himself on each occasion, once leaving the prosecutor so frustrated that he tossed his legal papers in the air.

The tenth trial was different. Originally scheduled for hearing in Birmingham Magistrates' Court, he says they suspended his case for a year, 'then they go in the Houses of Parliament and change the law from my hearing being a magistrate court hearing to being a Crown Court hearing. A heavy court case now.'

In the early weeks of 2004, at a trial in Birmingham Crown Court, allegedly one of the first of its kind, a relentless judge found him guilty on conspiracy charges. He was fined £3,000 and ordered to pay £5,000 in costs. He was given twenty hours of community service and a two-year suspended jail sentence.

The BBC News report read:

> Addressing Morris, the judge acknowledged he was a cornerstone of the black community in north Birmingham and had done much work to help disadvantaged youngsters in the area.
>
> But he added: 'If you are caught and investigated again and convicted within two years of today, I would be amazed if you do not have to serve the nine-month sentence.'[5]

In the aftermath of the trial, Cecil says ten commercial broadcasters and radio stations threatened to put up £2,000 each if he continued to broadcast, telling him that the pot of £20,000 would be used to crush him in court.

Things were coming to an end, a community enterprise shot down from the skies of North Birmingham by the anxious hands of government and big business. With the threat of jail looming, Cecil downed tools.

'That was when I thought I can't go any further.' He called a meeting with the staff and then made an announcement on air, telling loyal listeners that PCRL would be turning off their dial for good.

In his estimates, during PCRL's twenty-year run, the station was pulled off air around 1,500 times, and had its studios raided on over a hundred different occasions, DTI officers grabbing everything: their records, their equipment, their livelihoods.

'We lost so much money, but the station was popular, the station was making money [too].'

It was about more than radio. The presence and enduring success of PCRL was bigger than him. It was, he says, 'a challenge to the government, it's a challenge to the broadcasting authority, a challenge to the BBC, a challenge to the independent radio authorities and all the people like Capital Radio, BRMB Radio, everywhere a commercial radio station is'.

Though no longer lingering over Birmingham airwaves, its legacy lived, a symbol of how Black communities in the West Midlands would provide for themselves in the absence of institutional support, establishments like PCRL preparing the land for those who would come after.

A generation of young children came of age listening to the station, sitting in the cars with their aunts or rolling somewhere with their uncles, PCRL playing loud in the background. When these kids would grow up, and start making music of their own, producing Jungle and Garage, Grime and UK Rap, Pirate Radio would sit as the bedrock of their new sounds. Something had been inherited. The second and third generation of Black British-Caribbean people born and raised in the West Midlands were cast in the station's shadow. What they would eventually carve out for themselves is testament to what was sown into the tower blocks long before they arrived here.

3 LONDON UNDERGROUND

SOUTH LONDON

I n the summer of 1948, 236 of them walked down the *Empire Windrush* gangplank at Tilbury. They stepped out under British skies and started new lives on a gamble. They were not like the others. The vessel had carried around 802 Jamaican and Trinidadian and Guyanese and other people from the wider Caribbean islands into port in deep Essex: Black immigrants in the finest tailoring, bracing themselves for a new country.

Some who made the journey had jobs waiting on the other end. Some had set plans for accommodation and housing. Some planted themselves in Notting Hill and began building close new communities. But some 236 of them, arriving on that first journey, had no housing pre-organised, had no workplace to walk into. They had packed old lives and far countries into small suitcases, gambling on their futures, waiting on the hope of what Britain could be.

For those 236, Britain was first a bus from Tilbury to Clapham, South London; was the tease of finding work opportunities at the Labour Exchange on Coldharbour Lane in nearby Brixton; was a temporary holding hostel deep underground at Clapham South Tube station.

In the war years, deep-level shelters were built in the Tube stations surrounding Clapham Common. They were intended as refuge from the heavy German air raids raining hell on a crumbling city. The shelters had twin parallel tunnels stretching 400 yards, able to accommodate around 8,000 people overall, safeguarding local residents from the carnage that lay above ground. After the war was over and the city was deemed safe, the shelters were used by the army to demobilise. And after the army had moved on, they were reopened to house the few hundred Black immigrants arriving in South London during the summer of 1948, looking for work.

And so for the 236, Britain was Clapham South Station and a reception tent at the shelter entrance where they were checked in. It was the Women's Voluntary Service handing them each a linen bed sheet, a grey blanket and an allocated bed bunk. It was a welcoming with English tea and white bread with meat dripping. It was a lowering of eleven storeys and 180 steps, a plunge into the empty core of Clapham Common.

Some remember how the tunnels were poorly lit, musty and clammy. One arrival described his temporary new home as 'a sparsely furnished rabbit's warren'.[1] They slept on bunk beds, one beneath the other. Their first meal was roast beef with potatoes and vegetables. They wrote letters home to pass the time, thumbed through newspapers, readied their suits, styled their hair in cracked mirrors. They undressed from suits into pyjamas, settling in for a few long nights under South London. Sometimes in the early mornings, they were jolted from sleep by passing Tube carriages rattling the tracks in the overhead Northern Line tunnels. When awake, they would set out into the city to find work, heading over to the Labour Exchange to forage for a first wage, a Black community taking their first steps over South London, seeking to make good on their long gamble.

This is how they arrived here.

A month later, and the shelter was empty. Some had found jobs in the National Health Service, some in local factories and mills. A man called Sam King rejoined the RAF and then, after, became a postman.[2] He settled in Southwark. Another man, John Richards, found work with London Transport, clocking in at Orpington Station in

Kent and a few others around London too. He moved to a hostel in South Kensington, before settling in Kensal Rise.[3]

Many of the others clustered around the Labour Exchange, moving into rented houses and rooms across Clapham and Brixton. They slowly etched their family lines into the city, began carving out a community that resembled home, pulling out space for inbound family and countrymen to join them. What would come after in Clapham and Brixton is an echo of their efforts, those first settlers dropped deep into the South London soil, the cracked seeds from which a community began to flower.

———

Clapham is mapped by Clapham Common, a triangular green, sprawling over 220 acres of parkland, fenced tight by three busy A roads and cleaved in two by the invisible borderline that separates the London Borough of Lambeth from the London Borough of Battersea. Side roads and streets slip away from the green, leading into a scattering of separate estates. These loosely connected territories give sum to Clapham as a whole.

The half of Clapham claimed by Lambeth is defined by parallels. In an area known as Clapham Common Northside, side streets and residential housing bleed from the A3 road that fences the north of the Common. It is a small area of old affluence, of quiet terraces and bilingual private schools and old sprawling Victorian and Georgian mansions overlooking the green. Families of old and new money conceal themselves in timeless palaces of South London, in homes that hint at centuries gone by, ghosts of long-passed aristocrats and businessmen and composers entombed in their walls.

Then as the A3 spans east, further into Lambeth, meeting the A24 at the tip of the Common, there is Clapham High Street and the post-war council estates and packed terraced housing hidden behind its frontline. These are the roads and tower blocks that see Clapham blur into Acre Lane and Brixton, where working-class families settled in estates like Notre Dame, known as Notre, and the William Bonney Estate, known as Redbrick for the scarlet clay bricks that define its set of low-rise flats. Then, further south, in Clapham Park are the large estates that lead into Brixton Hill. Both areas are less than a mile removed from Clapham Common Northside, two faces of a polarised city rubbing up against the Common.

The Wandsworth side of Clapham Common can also be defined by these divides. There is affluence and a middle-class community in the Clapham Common Westside, clustered around Northcote Road and the houses that sit at the residential passage between the Common and the nearby Wandsworth Common. But as the A3 runs north-west towards the Thames, the Common fading into concrete, Battersea and the river leaning into view, Clapham blurs into Clapham Junction, or just Junction: an area defined by the long, overhanging Winstanley and York Road estates. Built in the decades after the war, housing an estimated 10,000 people, they are the scattering of twenty-three-storey and seventeen-storey and eleven- and seven-storey council blocks inscribed on the skyline, looming over the railway station and the river and the wealth of Northcote Road. A city again at odds.

From these many corners of Clapham, the children and grand-children of the Windrush began to emerge. By the west of the Common, nearing Junction, were Debbie Pryce and Susan Banfield, friends and pioneering rappers whose parents arrived in Clapham and South London alongside a generation who migrated as a result of London Transport and NHS recruitment drives in Barbados, Jamaica, Trinidad and other countries across the Caribbean.

In the 1950s, London Transport had set up an office in Bridgetown, capital of Barbados, and then aired news of their recruitment scheme on local radio, in the local Bajan newspapers and on posters across the city. Word spread soon across the island, and before long, applicants were being interviewed. Written and medical tests were conducted, and workers were cleared to start new jobs in London. The Barbadian government covered their travel fees, and the new recruits journeyed across the Atlantic, filling out the London Transport workforce. Shortly after, British Rail and the NHS erected similar schemes, and thousands of Caribbean people slowly dripped from the islands into Britain, starting work as bus drivers and rail workers and nurses in South London. Susan's mother was a nurse, Debbie's father a skilled tailor who also worked for London Transport, among a wave of immigrants drafted into the city's local economy from overseas, many of who were received by family members and friends already settled on the other side.

Together, this new influx rented rooms, they bought property, they sought to build Caribbean communities in South London, weaving among each other in church congregations and Blues Parties and Pirate Radio stations, then raised children in these community cradles. Debbie and Susan grew up among this loosely connected fraternity of families in Clapham.

In the eighties, when they grew up, some Caribbean people's houses were furnished from trips over to Brixton market and the salesmen who would go door to door, hawking to the West Indian families in the area. Susan and Debbie were raised on their parents' record collections, fed on Sunday Reggae shows on Pirate Radio and on British pop music like David Bowie and Dexys Midnight Runners. Elsewhere they were emerging alongside distinctly Black British genres like 2-Tone and Lovers' Rock. Sounds of home and sounds of a far home underscoring their early tastes.

There were influences from further afield, too. In the early stretches of the decade, Hip Hop, born of Jamaican Sound System culture, and fashioned in the housing estates of the South Bronx, began seeping into Britain. Sometimes, a friend would travel to see family in New York, and then arrive back in South London with tales of what they had seen, or would bring back handfuls of records, or tape recordings of documentaries like *Style Wars* (1983) and films like *Wild Style* (1982) and *Beat Street* (1984), which catalogued and then broadcast the early moments of Hip Hop culture.

In this process, the genre's elements: MCing, breakdancing, DJing and graffiti writing jumped from the working-class, Black and Latino neighbourhoods of New York, and into the working-class Black areas of London and Bristol and Birmingham. They travelled on tapes passed between extended relatives, played on Pirate Radio stations like Invicta FM where British DJs began to spin the early records, or were performed on early tours like The New York City Rap tour in 1982, where American breakers, MCs, DJs and graffiti artists delivered their fledgling art forms on a London stage.

Running parallel to the breakers and the MCs and the graffiti artists were kids of the same era, second-generation, British-raised Caribbean young people entrenched in Sound System culture. Many of them were raised around Clapham and wider South London, their sounds the products of music that had travelled along strong family lines stretching between the islands and the UK. There was Smiley Culture from Stockwell, son of a Jamaican father and a Guyanese mother, who, among others, bent Reggae into something of his own. Reggae artists often DJed and toasted on songs, a vocal delivery style where the artist would chant and talk over the cruising melody. In Britain, Smiley Culture and others like Peter King and Tippa Irie took things further, chanting with an increased pace and speed over the records. Some would call it fast-chat, fast-chat Reggae or speed rapping. On his Reggae riddims, Smiley Culture placed Jamaican patois alongside British cockney, bringing the dualities of a young Black Britain onto record, building on the foundations laid by the Sound Systems erected across Clapham and Brixton, Battersea and Lewisham in the seventies.

There was Reggae Sunsplash too, the music festival, first held in 1978 at Jarrett Park in Montego Bay, Jamaica, before spreading into Selhurst Park, South London, in 1984. By its 1987 iteration, over a quarter of a million people crested on Clapham Common, the festival coinciding with a celebration of Jamaica's twenty-fifth year of independence, and the centenary year of the country's deceased, but still influential, political activist Marcus Garvey.

And so, young British-Caribbean people, from South London and further field, raised on Sound Systems and Reggae and Soul and now Hip Hop, began to fuse these scattering of influences into sounds of their own. It's a process they would repeat for the next forty years. Susan and Debbie would hit up Hip Hop nights called The Breakers Yard at a club called Podium in nearby Nine Elms, where teenagers from across Clapham Junction, the Common and Battersea would assemble to practise, and enjoy their new art form. Or in Covent Garden, an early mecca and a meeting point for British Hip Hop, where new crews from across the city and the wider country would link, battle and throw up new graffiti pieces. The girls witnessed a genre on the rise, bound themselves to its ascent by taking on the names Susie Q and MC Remedee, calling their new coalition the Warm Milk and Cookie Crew.

They were among the first Hip Hop groups in Britain, and after practising for hours in Debbie's front room, began taking their gift to youth clubs and early Rap shows, sharing the stage with their UK and New York counterparts, their songs ringing out in nightclubs and on the radio, peaking with the single 'Rok da House' that reached number 5 in the UK charts in 1988, and a debut album

Born This Way that settled at number 24. In their wake came further Hip Hop acts from Clapham and Battersea, rappers like MC Melo, Monie Love and No Parking MCs.

The generation raised both by Rap and Sound System culture marked the beginning of something distinct in South London, their tastes a symbol of music boomeranging across the Black Atlantic: Jamaica into the Bronx, the Bronx into Britain's inner cities, where it began to evolve into something new. In South London, these fusions of cultures were a window into what was stirring on the ground, the sounds a reflection of an emerging and distinct Black British identity in this remote corner of the city. A drumskin was being layered, early rappers and chatters in the ends, and the varied music genres they leaned into, a signal of a distinct and varied strain of MC culture shooting from the seeds their parents had buried.

PART II
ENDZ

4 JUNCTION BOYS

SOUTH LONDON

They were dreamers in South London. They long had visions about the terrains their music could cross; imaginings that genres nurtured on Sound Systems and Pirate Radio stations in the ends would someday push out from South and roam through the world, following the same Black Atlantic lines their influences and ancestors first floated in on.

York Road and Winstanley and the cluster of smaller estates hanging over the river and emblazoned on the skies over Battersea were originally built in the years after the war, a remedy for an area wrecked by heavy German bombing that sought to sever the Clapham Junction train lines linking London with the rest of the country. In the years immediately after, the area was mainly populated by English and Irish families, who were then joined in the 1960s and 1970s by the rising numbers of West Indian families. Some of the Black families suffered racism on their arrival, but eventually created their own community cradles. They threw Blues Parties on Friday, Saturday and Sunday nights, and some of their kids made Reggae bands at the Providence House youth centre. Gradually they mixed in with the other locals.

They lived together in furnished flats with views peering out over the city. Accounts from that time speak of exciting childhoods in London, where kids scampered across the estates, playing run-outs and knock down ginger, carving out their own adventure playground from the concrete.

But in the 1970s through to the 1980s, local industry began to wane. Battersea Power Station went into decommission in 1975, the

Tate & Lyle sugar factory closed in 1980, the Airfix factory closed in 1981, other depots and warehouses following after. The area reeled, and a 1981 Thames News Report filmed on the estates claimed that in the preceding year, unemployment jumped 69 per cent leaving 13,000 people out of work within the borough.

In the decades that followed, extreme poverty and social deprivation and continued unemployment were endemic on the estates, and a young, emerging second generation of British-Caribbean kids stumbled through the flames. So Solid Crew, from Junction and the York Road and Winstanley estates were born out of these embers, local romantics with a vision of what could be.

The crew came out of a dream. It was 1997. Dwayne Vincent, known as Megaman, was sitting in jail. He was around seventeen years old, and alongside his friend Face had been charged with attempted murder. About a month into his time, he had a dream: he could see flashing lights, gatherings of people, and money, lots of money. When he awoke, he turned to Face and told him that they were going to build a crew, that they were going to cash out, that they were going home. Shortly after, their charges were dropped from attempted murder to GBH. They were tried, found not guilty, and released. Two years later the crew had been assembled, and they set about becoming one of the biggest musical groups in the country.

So Solid represented a shift: they were among the first generation of Black Caribbean kids who had parents born and raised in Britain. Megaman's mother was born in London, and his father in Grenada. His brother Swiss had grandparents who came to the UK from Barbados and Jamaica. Another member, Ashley Walters, had a mother who was born in London after his grandparents moved into Britain from Guyana. Elsewhere there was Kaish, who grew up on the estate with Swiss and Mega, all of them meeting at the local Falconbrook Primary School. There was G-Man, who immigrated from Jamaica, Lisa Maffia of Italian and Jamaican heritage, MC Harvey of Sierra Leonean and Jamaican descent, and a wider extended family of young men and women from the flats and surrounding houses.

They were a reflection of a Caribbean presence now entrenched in the city. South London and the community cradles in which they were raised had come to shape their identities, a melding of Caribbean and British culture moving into something distinct. It's why Megaman and one of the crew's MCs, Romeo, from the nearby Surrey Lane Estate, first tasted music at Notting Hill Carnival, rapping and chatting on the Ragga Sound System Killerwatt, run by Mega's uncle. It's why word of their emergence, and the weekend raves they would be appearing at, was spread on a network of Pirate Radio stations they performed and hosted shows on. It's why Mega looked to Sound Systems like Rampage, a Sound with so many members that they could perform at simultaneous bookings on the same night. Mega decided to fill out his crew accordingly.

Their elders had worked their grooves into the city, had pulled scattered sounds into new traditions and identities, leaving a blueprint for them to inherit, a foundation for a new generation like So Solid to build on.

By the early millennium, Mega's generation were making UK Garage (UKG) on the ends, another genre descended from the Sound Systems, combing the finer influences of Jungle and R&B, Dancehall and House into an easy bounce and swing. It had spread through the veins of Pirate Radio stations and raves that stretched from Britain's inner cities to the European party islands in Ibiza and Cyprus, and by doing so, had come to dominate the UK for a few long summers.

So Solid, which at one point numbered almost thirty members, existed on the darker end of the spectrum. There was still the bounce and step that had defined late-era UKG, but where other acts and artists leaned on soft-toned vocalists coasting across the foams of summer-sounding instrumentals, stirring ecstasy in the rave with trancing keys and kick drums, light strings and hypnotic R&B singers, So Solid centred MCs over bleaker, more minimalist productions.

They were influenced by Rap as well as Garage, MC culture as well as R&B. They were coming off the roads and out of estates of South, and their music would reflect this. Mega remembered how, when he was young, 'I woke up to fight every day, there was nothing else on my mind, not money – partly girls – but war.' G-Man was living on his own at fifteen after arriving from Jamaica. He sold weed to get by. Romeo was raised on the Surrey Lane estate with his mum and three siblings in a two-bedroom flat ('Tell me how that works innit?'). In music, they found a space to document and catalogue what they had seen, and through this evolving strain of UKG, a Black, working-class community living in South London again found its way into sound.

There were many So Solid singles that defined their era: the throb of 'Oh No (Sentimental Things)' in 2000 and the murky pulsing of 'They Don't Know' in 2001. But cult classic '21 Seconds' was their showpiece. Released in 2001, it was the brainchild of G-Man, who figured one afternoon that for the extensive array of crew members to be heard on one standard three-and-a-half-minute song, they should each get twenty-one seconds to spit their verse. This was their opportunity to tell their devout listeners and the wider watching audience about who they were, about the lives they'd come from, about what they wanted for their careers and future. And so, after a stripped down, 2-Step instrumental was sliced into fine pieces, ten members emptied their minds, 12 bar by 12 bar, bounding across the soundboard one after the other as if the song were a rally track.

It took hold in South London and the inner cities. Stand on the kerb in any area across Lambeth and Lewisham and Southwark and Battersea in 2001, and you would hear its melody and pulse moving from car speakers and from radio sets. Young kids huddled over vinyl, verse after verse braiding the South London air, knitting together a generation, and eventually breaking the seal of Middle England and washing over the rest of the country too. On 9 August 2001, '21 Seconds' claimed the number 1 spot on the UK Singles Chart, the first ever UKG song to do so, Mega and his crew becoming among the first Black South London MCs to claim national fame.

At the peak of their popularity, they were as famous as footballers. During school tours, where a few members would turn up at schools up and down the country, they'd perform a song or two in assembly halls for screaming teenagers and children. Online footage shows Romeo walking onto stages in Liverpool and Manchester, Birmingham and Coventry, Nottingham and Leicester and Cardiff, greeting his young audience. The kids howl in response, then after the Live PA is finished, swarm him: delirious smiles and screams exposing gap teeth and braces, their hands falling over his shirt as they follow him from the assembly hall to the car, to the school gates as he is driven off the premises and onto the next stopping point.

When Lisa Maffia tried to drop her own daughter at school, she remained trapped for two hours, signing autographs and waving away requests for her to sing. Eventually, the family were forced to change schools, and at the new place, when the school day was over, she sent her sister or her mother in to collect her daughter instead.

In the slipstream of '21 Seconds', So Solid released their debut album, *They Don't Know*, in November 2001. It peaked at number 6, and in the following year, the crew of thirty-plus were at the 2002 BRIT Awards, packed into the exhibition centre at Earls Court and nominated for Best Breakthrough Act and Best Video for '21 Seconds'. They were nominated alongside mainstream artists like

Coldplay and Elton John, Robbie Williams and Kylie Minogue, in a contest decided by the popular vote.

The award for Best Video was presented by American actor Michael Madsen, who stood on stage alongside hosts Frank Skinner and Zoe Ball, waving a white card in his fingers as he read, 'The winner is . . .' before a pause, '"21 Seconds", So Solid Crew.' Shrieks rose in the arena, as the camera panned towards the winners, catching a flutter of gun fingers saluting the evening air. The crew filed from their seats onto the stage, flashing past broadcast cameras in a procession of thick fur coats and cocoa-butter cream blazers, mesh vests and New Era caps, denim skirts and blue bandannas saddled on glistening foreheads. They scattered across the stage and applauded the screaming supporters in the audience. At moments, they extended their arms in a salute, as if reaching through the TV screen to their people watching back home. This win was bigger than them: it was an illustration of what MC culture, of what Garage, of what kids from South could become, of how their music could enchant the ears of a country.

'21 Seconds' opened the door. So Solid's boom years moved in the souls of a generation of kids coming of age in their high tide, new fruits of the South London soil inheriting greater visions of what life and music could mean. Sometimes, around Battersea and Clapham and wider South London, kids would see one of the crew members going about their business, national celebrities who were still local boys and girls, walking the ground on which these kids also stood.

A boy from South Norwood had a neighbour who was friends with Megaman. The kid was a So Solid fan, as were his older sisters, and so whenever the crew's founder passed through on the ends, visiting, the boy would stop and look, stunned, thinking, *Rah, that's Mega you know.* He grew up to be a producer.

The young kids attending Clapham Manor Primary School caught brief glimpses of Asher D, whose partner lived across the road. On the days he appeared, they would shout his name from the school gates, Asher usually responding with a greeting, even taking time out to come and speak with them. One of the kids who glimpsed him from across the street grew up to be an MC, another a DJ.

But outside of the community, So Solid met opposition. In November 2001, at a birthday party for Romeo at the central London nightclub Astoria, there was a shooting. Two people were hit and injured. So Solid released a statement that read:

> So Solid Crew very much regret the violence that broke out at the birthday party show at the Astoria last night, but want to make it clear that they abhor violence and have made it clear on their record that they want the violence to stop.
>
> They were not in any way involved in last night's disturbance and were on stage performing when the trouble broke out. They were ushered off by security and none of the So Solid Crew were hurt or in any way directly caught up in the trouble.[1]

In the shooting's aftermath, the crew were woven into a narrative about the alleged peaking of gun crime across the inner cities of the UK, their music blamed and labelled as a fuel for the violence, scapegoats for complex social issues. They were slandered in newspapers. Their UK tour was pulled. The Metropolitan Police assistant commissioner blamed Garage and Rap music for encouraging young men to carry weapons as fashion statements.[2] And, after a fatal incident in Birmingham, unconnected to So Solid, where two girls were killed in the crossfire of a shootout during a 2003 New Year's party, then culture minister Kim Howells described rappers as 'boasting macho idiots'.

A report from the *NME* at the time read:

> The MP claimed Britain's black music scene 'created a culture where killing is almost a fashion accessory', and claimed: 'The

events in Birmingham are symptomatic of something very, very serious. For years I have been very worried about these hateful lyrics that these boasting macho idiot rappers come out with.'

He continued: 'It is a big cultural problem. Lyrics don't kill people but they don't half enhance the fare we get from videos and films. It has created a culture where killing is almost a fashion accessory.

'Idiots like the So Solid Crew are glorifying gun culture and violence. It is very worrying and we ought to stand up and say it.'[3]

These were among the incidents that served as an example of the venom MC culture and Black British music would have to withstand, sounds beat back against the surge of state censorship and veiled racism. The longevity of So Solid was damaged by the allegations in the media, Middle England warned off a group their kids had just embraced.

There were internal issues, too. Neutrino was shot in the leg after leaving a club in central London. Skat D was convicted of breaking the jaw of a sixteen-year-old girl in a Cardiff hotel lobby. And in 2002, Ashley Walters pleaded guilty to possessing a revolver. He was sentenced to eighteen months.

By 2003, their momentum was on the wane, and second album *2nd Verse* arrived in the charts at number 70. The boom was petering out, the crew beginning to go their own ways. A Channel 4 documentary captured their last stand. In one shot, towards the end, Mega is leaning on a black Mercedes, a bucket hat shading his eyes, a cream tracksuit around his frame, rings hanging from his fingers. Staring into the camera with a steady resilience he says:

The UK needed, deserved something like this, some negativity talk coming from people from the ghetto, to understand that we are living in a dangerous city, you get me . . . I'm just ringing the alarms, ringing all the alarms . . . You put me in this system, you put me down there, you put my parents down there to live, so I had no choice but to grow up around these things.[4]

And then, reflecting on how far So Solid had come, he says, 'We've achieved a lot already, man, broken certain rules, kicked off certain doors so that people can't lock it again.'

Then he continues, saying that their next mission was to break through worldwide. But he was unaware that the real legacy of their movement lay in the estates and communities transformed across Clapham and Battersea and other areas across South London, a spark in the young kids they had encouraged to dream of music.

Among the children who spotted So Solid out and around in South London during the crew's rise were the Johnson siblings, Chandler and Blaine from Clapham, a sister and brother, who one day went out shopping in Vauxhall Market, wandered into a store and saw Romeo and Harvey standing in front of them. They left starstruck. They saw them again on the TV a little while later.

When *They Don't Know* was released, Chandler rushed to Woolworths on Clapham High Street to buy the album, and then, when back home, opened all the windows and let the music play loud, thinking, *Yeah, South London's made it.*

Blaine knew every word to some of the songs, like many boys in Clapham did. He would grow up to be an MC, inheriting a South London tradition that started with Sound Systems and Cookie Crew and pioneers like So Solid. He was a product of all of this. South London is where his story begins.

5 **MIDDLE ENGLAND**
WEST MIDLANDS

When his grandad passed in 2001, Ryan was eighteen and a fuck-up. He was selling weed. He was debt collecting. He was fighting. He was a good-hearted boy lost to a time and a place that demanded a stone-faced camouflage from its young. This is Darlaston, a small town on the edges of Walsall. An old coal town. A steel town. A Blitz survival story. In the decades to come, he would scratch the place from memory, an era best buried, the sufferings in a shallow grave. But it's the early millennium now, and he is eighteen, still here, where he has always been. He is living with his mum. His grandparents live in a house across the road. This is all that he knows.

Darlaston is in the Black Country, the region in the far north of the West Midlands loosely defined in the 1800s when black smoke from the many ironworks stained the horizon with an eternal fog. Here, as he was coming of age, among the ruins of these once booming industrial heartlands, towns like Darlaston were withering, smoke fading into dust, dust holding the ghosts of what once was. His generation were birthed in the ashes. They inherited a home where the population was falling, where unemployment was high, where expectations were low and, as Ryan says, 'almost nobody escapes'. A home where the education system is flawed; where you left school to work, as he says, at the packing plant down the road, to work in retail, to work in a bar, to work in the big ASDA.

Or, if you are him, you sell weed. You work at Burger King for a year. You work at the packing place for a few weeks, filling and moving boxes, then quit. You sell some ecstasy pills. You sell coke for a month.

You spend your savings on a music studio and jelly babies in an era when UK Garage was the sound of the time, and something darker was readying to take its place. You live your days as your town and your generation has determined. You have done so for years now already.

He was around fourteen or fifteen and depressed when he left school. The family had followed a long line from Jamaica to Walsall. They settled in Caldmore in the south of the town, then moved on to Darlaston, and fell apart. There were traumas he buried. The aftershock opened wounds. And when the stress of family and home and looming GCSEs got too much, he dropped out.

His mum was unaware. She left in the early mornings and returned late in the day. And when any letter from school arrived, he would be sitting in the house, 'like "Yeah. Safe. Bin."' By the time school eventually reached her by phone and told of his truanting, it was too late, he was too far gone. He was kicking around the area with other truants, spending their days smoking weed outside school gates or sitting in someone's yard, watching shit films, smoking roll-ups, 'living like feral animals'.

'Most of my friends had fucked-up family homes,' he explains. 'I didn't want to be at home, so I was outside the house . . . If you think about anybody that's on the streets, why are they not at home?'

There was anger in him when he was young. Because when you are born in the ashes of this place, you are taught to fight and never show weakness, taught to conceal the flutters in your stomach with a mask. But then the mask eats the face and you become something you're not.

There was always stuff happening that I always had to be on guard or be quick to lose my temper so somebody would be scared of me . . . You do that for six, seven years, it's now you. Do you know what I mean? You were trying to [pretend to] be somebody at one point, now you *are* that person, you've embodied it and internalised it.

The day his life began to turn was a day like any other. He was still in Darlaston, still making music but shotting, still truanting. He was falling deeper into a crevice that most times bottomed out with jail or death or addiction. It was a normal afternoon, another day out of education, roaming the area with a few friends, smoking weed outside school during lunchtime with the not-yet-dropouts. That is where Bob Szpalek found him, a hulking powerlifter-turned-headmaster who had spotted him hovering by the school gates, and instead of shooing him away, walked him into the school, into his office and asked him, 'What are you doing here?'

Ryan told him about what had happened, how he had dropped out, then sat and watched as Bob made a phone call to Walsall College of Arts and Technology; sat as Bob told them he had a kid he wanted to bring down; sat in his car as Bob drove him there himself, outstretching a hand as he scrambled to crawl out from a Black Country void.

In college he was still shotting weed. But he was studying again, was enrolled on a programme called Achieving Together where he studied Music, was put onto a scheme for Performing Arts and gained an IT GNVQ. It wasn't salvation, but it was a start. And then grief struck. In his second year, his baby brother Aiden died, and then a little while after his big brother Adrian passed too. When his grandad died that changed everything.

Shortly after the passing, Ryan was over the road at his nan's. She and his grandad had raised him since he was a boy. He called himself their fourth son. He inherited music from them, inherited sound. He inherited PCRL playing in their house as a kid, inherited the spirit of a people seeking to forge diamonds from scraps. And now grandad was gone too. He was sat listening to his nan on the phone as she passed the news back along the line to Aunty Pet in Jamaica.

'Despa's gone,' she said down the phone.

Ryan was confused. He knew no Despa, only Grandad.

Eventually, she turned to him and explained:

'That's your grandad's name back home.'

A life can turn slowly on a name and a promise. When his grandad passed, Ryan made a private pledge in his soul, told himself that by the time his own life was over, he would've made his grandad proud. That declaration to the dead marks a line in the sand, a window into what was, and what could be for a young kid stuck out in Darlaston. In tribute, he asked his grandma if he could make his grandad's nickname his own, if Despa could live on through him and his music.

She agreed and, in that moment, a mantle was passed down the Robinson family line, a name crowned on a son reborn, preserving who came before and opening a blank canvas for this new branch of the family tree to write his own future, for a grandson to pull himself back from the brink. The day he became Despa was the day his life began to change.

When you lose loved ones young, the grief sits in you, it bends and moulds the body and mind in ways unpredicted. You can lose your sight or your hearing, your faith in your family and your God, or if you're Despa, you push on into the long days with a nagging voice in your head, telling you that you'll never grow old.

He never thought he would see twenty-five, the age his uncle died. He never thought he would even see eighteen. So much loss, so much grief, so much depression. Those years in Darlaston were dark. He soldiered through alone and smoked himself numb to cope, felt himself coming apart, and on days when the heaviness weighed on his chest and he arrived home, closed the front door and found himself alone with the voice, he thought about it. Thought about ending his life, about succumbing to that whisper, about bringing things to an end. His girlfriend Fallon at the time saved him, because 'having somebody to just love and love you' can sometimes pull you out of the void. She was his rock while his soul wept.

Music saved him too. Music had never left him. Music was there when he was fourteen and dreaming of sound, of someday owning a successful record label, walking the road paved by Eazy-E and Russell Simmons, then Diddy and Master P. Music was there when he started out as a producer, saving his coins and notes to build his own studio. It was there when he first picked up a microphone to MC, and when it wasn't, like the early stint in the packing factory at sixteen, where they told him no headphones during shifts, he quit, and found his way back to sound.

Music was there in dark days when his grandad and his brothers passed and the family withered. In that period the raps he recorded were angry, he says, pained vibrations echoing out into a lonely world, maybe relieving the tension in his chest. Music was his rock, a constant glimmer in a fading night, the lighthouse beam at dead dawn. It saved him and an entire generation growing up in dark times.

———

Where does Grime begin in the West Midlands?

How do you trace a sound that has roots in another, a sound that was crafted quietly in the closed arenas of raves and radio, outsiders only catching on after the fact?

Is Grime a product of East London tower blocks only? Or is there more here, dormant in the West Midlands? Import as well as export? Faint tracks on the road that carried a sound out from the region, not only welcomed it in?

This is how the genre begins here. It begins in Birmingham.

In Birmingham, every elder has a theory about how the violence started. In the late eighties a Rastafari movement had washed the young of Black Britain in a Pan-African dye, and seeded a conviction to reconnect with a history that had roots deep in Africa. There was a hunger to soak in the words of political activists like Marcus Garvey who had preached Black pride, Black unity and Black economic empowerment to a diaspora cleaved and scattered across the continents. The sons and daughters of the Windrush generation bound together around these ideals. Britain had sold their parents a fantasy, and now, birthed in the fire, they were fighting to shatter the lingering illusions of colonialism. They began to question their identity, question their history as a people, question the food they ate and the God they prayed to. They strung up Sound Systems in houses and wet the gathered crowd in Roots Reggae melodies and affirmations from Burning Spear and Bob Marley, then Horace Andy and Steel Pulse out of Handsworth.

In those days, elders told me, you could wander into a dance or a house party in Birmingham, in Manchester, in London, Bristol or Nottingham, light up a spliff with a stranger and speak for hours on revolution and re-education. Back then, they say, they were a tight community bound by common goals and a deepening sense of self. And then the violence came. Some elders in Coventry point to the aftermath of Jamaica's bloody 1981 election, where gangs were tools for political violence and hundreds were killed. When the police cracked down on the gangs, many of them allegedly fled to Britain, settling down in already-established Caribbean communities. In Nottingham they will tell you the same, tell you how these new immigrants stuck up the peaceful dances at gunpoint and bullied the second-generation Black British kids on the roadside, who in self-defence, formed gangs of their own.

In Birmingham, they will tell you not just about 'Yardies', as the media termed them, but about poverty and deprivation, and a crack epidemic wrecking the region, a savage white substance hooking and sinking lives, and how in the scramble for control of the new trade, once-close communities began warring. Gangs formed. Town turned on town. Cousin turned on cousin, the splinters of a golden time and community scattered like ash in the West Midlands dirt.

By the late nineties, North Birmingham was a place divided by two factions. There was the Burger Bar Boys, a gang gathered around Handsworth, Winson Green, Smethwick and Hockley. And further east were the Johnsons, spread among Newtown, Aston and Lozells, Nechells and Erdington. Blood was shed in the street. Many young boys lost their lives to violence and prison. If you were involved, certain areas were no-go, some say. If you weren't, you were sometimes still careful.

These were the conditions from which Grime in Birmingham and the wider West Midlands was born, young kids with MC and DJ dreams, building a music scene around the hazards and daring pulls of an uncertain time. From this era certain names stand apart like diamonds in the earth, the legend of teenagers who toiled on the frontlines of a sound, moving on instinct to shape brighter tomorrows. There were a handful of these people scattered across the region, founding forefathers, teenagers of the new millennium who signalled a changing of the guard and actively tilted a sound away from Garage and into something new. To understand the West Midlands' emergence of Grime that they say ran parallel with the East London origin story, you must understand the MCs and DJs and teenagers out here who helped shape history. Vader, Big Mikee and Despa are among that anointed few.

Many in Brum consider Big Mikee as the first DJ to play this new sound in the West Midlands. Mikee was a kid from Aston with roots in Kingston, Jamaica. His parents and grandparents found a home in Birmingham as part of the Windrush generation. And so, he sits at the biting point of two countries, a family past buried in Jamaica and a family future fanning out in Britain, meaning in the family line anyone, 'who is sort of older than me would be from Jamaica. And anybody younger would be from Britain.

'I was born here in Britain, so I am British, cah this is where I was born, Dudley Road in Birmingham. But my upbringing and my culture is Jamaican.'

He grew up in the days of Acid House and Techno, of Jungle and Drum & Bass, in the days when the elders in Birmingham ran Sound Systems and the younger relatives followed the lead. The elders operated Romantic Bubbler Sound tailed by the kids running Junior Bubbler. Love Injection followed by Young Injection, Love Express by Junior Express. Mikee's uncles ran Now Generation. His cousins ran Young Generation.

In the weekdays, PCRL would waft through his home. At the weekends, he would be out at Blues Parties in Spark Hill or at sound clashes at the community centre in Winson Green, or at a house in the early evening, stringing up a Sound with his uncle, a baptism in Sound System culture echoing through his early adolescence; music seeping its way in. Then he went to prison.

Around seventeen Mikee became a father. Reluctant to tell his mother, his dad already incarcerated and Mikee himself too young for a National Insurance number, he found himself unable to support his child, unable to work, unable to claim benefits. He turned to the streets for a wage and ended up in prison the year after, setting a dangerous cycle in motion and entering a period where for the next seven years, he spent most of his days in a cell somewhere in Britain.

When his first stint was finishing, he told himself he would fly straight. But when a free man once again, he returned to a reality that hadn't changed: he was still a young father, still needed to provide, still needed to care for his child. A reflex kicked in. Thoughts of redemption were buried. He was back on the road now. He was stealing cars. He was out for two weeks before he found himself back inside. A three-and-a-half-year sentence was handed down. Prison became habit.

'The more you go back to prison the easier it is,' he says, because, 'when you first go to prison you need to do enough crime that the judge says, "I've had enough of you", but when you come out you only need to get caught once and you're back down.

'It was becoming a pattern, and it was the same pattern that my dad was going through because he was in and out of prison as well, and God bless his soul he ended up dying in prison. He had a heart attack.'

Mikee served most of that stretch at HMP Woodhill in Milton Keynes, and the tail end at HMP Winson Green. While inside, alone with himself, he began to turn a corner. He thought about his child growing up without him. He thought about what had brought him here and how his life had unravelled and landed him in these four walls. He wanted change. He began to play football and basketball, table tennis and volleyball. He was made gym orderly and in conversations with a friendly prison officer mentioned that he loved sport, that he wanted to pursue work in the field when released, but wasn't sure how. Together they sketched a plan. With his sentence winding down he completed a Life Saving course, allowing him to work in a leisure centre, then started his Level 1 Football Coaching badge.

This time when he was released and went home, he went back to college, began working as Assistant Manager for West Bromwich Albion's women's team and gained his UEFA B badges. He told his mum about his child, and he went back to living in her house again. He was working. He was still shotting on the side, but was careful; rode a bike instead of fancy cars; slipped under the radar and worked a plan centred around football and sport, hoping it would carry him into a life lived fully above board.

Then he came home one day after college and saw a set of decks laid out in the front room. They were owned by a guy called DJ Roots who played sets with Mikee's brother, a rapper who went by

Poverty P. Mikee was curious about the decks and the bag of records on the side, was unaware that this was the start of something, for him and for everyone, that his life was about to take a sharp turn towards music. Curious, he began playing around on the decks, and when he came home the next day and they were still there, staring at him in the front room, he did so again. This went on for three months. Sometimes he would sit quietly and observe Roots on the equipment, noted how he mixed, how he transitioned from one song to another, the old giving way to new; two sounds becoming one for a fleeting moment in his mother's front room.

By 1999 Mikee was a regular on Pirate Radio, following the legacy set in motion by Cecil Morris, PCRL and their peers. PCRL's foundations had been built on by the generations who followed, a new breed of kids scaling the aging tower blocks to connect communities with their music. The sound had evolved from Cecil's day, Reggae passing over to Dub, Dub passing over to Ragga, Jungle and Garage. The set-up was still the same, transistors sinking their teeth into rooftop aerials, covertly infecting their host, and claiming the broadcasts and frequencies as their own. But the stations were different – they were a range of Birmingham-bred local frequencies going by names like Passion FM and Smooth FM, Heat FM and Serious FM, and the London transplants like Choice FM and Kool FM who set up sister stations in the city. These stations were all home to a revolving roster of DJs and MCs, who at that time presented Garage, Drum & Bass and Jungle sets to the young and the restless craving bounce and sound in Birmingham.

In his early years on the circuit, Mikee played sets on legendary Pirate station Silk City FM, first situated on the sixteenth floor of a Nechells tower block, Mikee's Drum & Bass then Garage records slipping through the wires into a transmitter on the rooftop and blowing out over the city.

In any music scene that blooms in the shadows, finding its fleeting

final form in raves and Pirate Radio sessions, the DJ sits at the fulcrum: the DJ is the conductor, binding producer to crowd and crowd
to MC, is the acid test for the record shops stocking vinyl, and the
vibe supplier in the house parties and raves. Genres like Rap, Jungle,
Garage and then Grime were built on these efforts, formed on the
backs of men and women who found divine joy in stirring a dance
to the pulse and rhythm of these electronic music and Sound System
mongrels. Mikee is carved from this same stone.

He started out mixing and blending on Silk FM's Saturday morning slot, then after regular trips to record stores, where he began
filling his bags with Garage records, he was moved to the Sunday
morning slot at 8–10 a.m. He was eager. He was driven. He covered
for whoever could not make their shift, and he often shadowed the
station's more experienced DJs. He got his first booking for fifty quid
at a local pub in Nechells, and when it was all over, and the money
was in his hand, he stared down at it in awe, thinking, *This is actually
honest money for something that I loved, and I only played for an hour.*

It's this kind of relentless enthusiasm that creates scenes from out
of the ether. DJing became an obsession. He hunted records down
the M40 to London, setting out on road trips to the capital and
bringing back treasures, bags of new releases two weeks before they
reached the record stores in Brum. Then he was back on radio again,
Saturday or Sunday morning, firing off his new arsenal on the airwaves, proudly telling the listeners how he was the first in the city to
play these riddims live on air.

The persistent pursuit of sound brought him to a rare vantage
point in the evolution of Black music in Britain; one of a handful of
DJs standing at the vanguard as Garage evolved into something else,
a sound growing darker as a new wave of teenage producers stripped
the genre of its gleam. During his forays into London, Mikee began
to collect records that had severed their ties with Garage, work from

young producers like Wiley and Youngstar who had pushed a sound over the edge into territories uncharted.

And so Garage hatching Grime can be traced through the lost recordings of Mikee's Silk City Radio sets. On Saturday and Sunday mornings, in the tower blocks above North Birmingham, Garage began to wilt and fade from the airwaves, replaced slowly by its bleaker, more skittish descendant, a music vibrating at a tone and an energy that truly reflected and responded to the at times dangerous days of Brum in the early millennium. Grime was a response to these conditions. Big Mikee was one of its first conductors.

Another was Vader. He is known as Godfather Grime MC in the West Midlands.

Vader was born in the Dudley Road Hospital and raised amid the madness of North Brum in the nineties and new millennium. He was a Winson Green boy with a white mother and a Black father, a family beginning anew in Birmingham when his Windrush grandparents came over from the Caribbean island of St Kitts decades before him.

The evolution of Black sound and MC culture in Britain can be traced through his career. Vader came of age in the nineties listening to Ragga and Rap, to Admiral Bailey and Shabba Ranks, then N.W.A and Ice Cube. By eleven he was recording tapes on old stereos, rapping and messing around with friends, flaunting their new skill set at school talent shows, a rugged American art form seeping into the heart of Britain.

The infatuation with music from across the Atlantic was fleeting. Jungle music brought him home. One year, at Handsworth's summer carnival, he walked the road with his dad and heard Jungle wafting off the Sound Systems, a music that blended Ragga and Rap, and opened space for pioneering local MCs like Lenny and Bassman to harry over the instrumentals, Brum accents drizzling from their tongues. It was an awakening. These were sounds where scattered identities found union. Black kids in Birmingham and Britain, fusing all elements of home and reflecting their woven sense of selves back out into the world.

By fourteen, Vader and his friends were Jungle MCs, known locally as 'the Winson Green lot'. They fed off the buzz of the older MCs in the area. They began recording tapes, and Vader performed at under-eighteen raves and local house parties, in record shops and at birthdays, claiming the genre as his own, the same relentless enthusiasm moving through Mikee moving through him also. By fifteen, he had piles of lyric books, filled from margin to margin, verses finding their way to ears on tape-pack recordings, his voice breezing through the local area like a whisper on the wind. His rolling tongue and fast-chat flow saw him gain notoriety which spread through the city, his name ringing out on the roads in a time where kids turned to badness for street fame.

When Vader was on the climb, young boys in the bits pulled themselves into crews. These loose musical collectives, scattered through the ends, were assertions of self, carvings of community, the deepest representations of adolescent home. They raided onto Pirate Radio in numbers, hosting sets, MCing into the dawn, clashing with other crews live on air. MC culture in the West Midlands is defined by these extended families, roaming bands of boys who marked their era. There were Powerhill and NRG who had an infamous clash on Passion FM 92, Lowkey and Vortex, Bass Developers and Devious, all breaching the intermission between Garage and Grime. Together they formed a whole, a wave of second- and third-generation immigrant kids scaling the tower blocks like those who came before.

Many crews only endured a season. Members fell away, banded together with new MCs and other friends, then reformed again, starting out afresh under different banners and crew names, taking new momentum back to the airwaves. After the Jungle era, Vader became a member of the crew Midlands Mafia, who started on Garage with an assembly of MCs ranging from Birmingham to Derby. They canvassed stations like Smooth FM in Aston and Silk City, spitting on Garage first, then following the instrumentals as they got darker.

The role of the MC shifted in this interlude. On radio, in the tower blocks, classic Garage instrumentals sometimes limited the MC to hosting duties. They sprayed light lyrics over instrumentals and gave shout-outs to friends and listeners texting the studio phone lines as one song turned over to another. They were an usher, a tether and support for the DJ supplying songs on the decks, an anchor and a steer for the audience locked in.

Then as the 1990s drew to a close and the 2000s spanned out ahead, the instrumentals at the darker end of UKG, a sound crews like So Solid were known for, began to surface on the B-sides of the genre's popular, bouncy riddims. These secluded corners of the record were brooding, open for the MC to catch the pockets and glide over a riddim for its entirety. In these gaps those like Vader found space to tell stories, to speak at length about what was happening where they were from.

With Jungle and Garage, Rap and Sound System culture in his veins, Vader began to pool these influences into one on these hybrid instrumentals. He was one of the first of a handful in the country to do so, instinctively falling in step and leading the charge of a cultural evolution that was happening concurrently in East London. Knitted together, these elements were the foundations of Grime's earliest iteration. They are the bedrock on which the sound sat and then flowed into other working-class pockets of the country, its existence a consequence of MCs like Vader, who crawled into Garage and Jungle, US Hip Hop and Sound Systems, and emerged into the millennium with a new genre called Grime. And this is why many refer to him as a godfather MC in the West Midlands, among only a handful of individuals from the regions who were with the genre from its start. His friend Big Mikee was one. Despa was another.

———

Walsall and Darlaston, about seven miles out from Birmingham and teetering on the edges of rural Black Country, had isolated Despa from the madness and violence of the second city. In that period, his clamour for the spotlight as an MC drew to an unassuming close, ending quietly with a solitary Pirate Radio session where he realised that throwing words over microphones and instrumentals was not a life he craved.

Instead, he was learning other elements of the game. In that hazy era when Garage was turning over to Grime, he was still shotting. But he was producing too, assembling these mongrel beats for a crew out of Wolverhampton called Higher Stakes. And he still had the studio in the house. When MCs came over, he engineered their records, adding strings to his bow, trying to build doors for the region's artists to run through.

The collective deaths that rocked his early adolescence left in their wake an urge to document, to capture his close friends and family, because in this unsteady life you never know when a loved one will be snatched by the heavens. So he bought a cheap Samsung flip camera and began shooting subtle moments, then became a cameraman in the early West Midlands Grime scene, recording music videos and pirate DVDs, learning as he went, sharpening his skills, documenting the transition out of Garage in real time. But he was still playing both sides, still shotting while going for a dream.

What does it take for a man to make a change?

Is it the day he discovers *The Secret*?[1] The book that teaches how *thoughts become things*, affirming deep within him that a man makes his own destiny, that if you hold your attention on a goal or a destination for long enough, you can ultimately pull it into existence?

Is it the era he hosts a show on Pirate Radio station Smooth FM with a guy called Booski, meeting each other for the first time on the show's debut, then slowly becoming best friends, naming it the 'Despa n Booski' show and gathering a cult audience stretching from Wolverhampton across to Birmingham?

Maybe it's the day a friend from college asks him to start selling crack, teasing promises of money to be made. Despa was unsure but tempted. And then on New Year's Eve, when driving down Birmingham New Road, heading to Brum on a whim for a year-end night out, he passed a red Honda parked on the roadside. It was surrounded by police. Boot, doors and bonnet all open. As he cruised by the scene, Despa recognised the apprehended driver. It was his friend from college. The police had caught him with crack. He ended up serving time in prison.

What it actually takes for Despa to make a change is the night he was jolted from sleep. He was in his flat, the same flat with his studio, the same flat he was selling out of, paraphernalia scattered around the rooms. Noises stirred him from sleep. He could hear police somewhere in the near distance. Awake and on edge, he inched to the window. Recently he had heard whispers about the police looking for him, the authorities closing in, and now, peeking through the glass, he could see a group of officers amassed. They barrelled into the flat next door. The raid was for his neighbour, not him. A divine sign and warning from someone or somewhere. It was time to get out for good.

6 **THE DOCKS**
SOUTH WALES

P hil can show you pictures of himself as a boy. He's lying on a beanbag in his bedroom, a gallery of music posters plastered to his ceiling. There was Tupac and Limp Bizkit and Bob Marley, and all the singers, performers and rappers who inspired his early years as a kid in the east of Cardiff. Even back then, something was moving in him, turning, a desire and a dream burrowing itself in his mind.

While sat in his room, he would close his eyes, shut the world out, lock a vision in, and see himself on a stage, looking out over a 100,000-strong crowd bouncing in rage and rapture to his every word.

These are the promises we make to ourselves when we are young. Vows deep-set in fertile soil. Dreams of what could be pushing at the hard cages of flesh and skull until they are released and realised in the world set out before us. Phil had one of these dreams, a fantasy clawing its way to light.

Through his band Astroid Boys, he would spend the next twenty years trying to breathe those heavy visions into life.

———

There is a philosophy that exists among social and political analysts in Wales that splits the national identity along regional and lingual lines. They are the unseen barriers and frontiers that both fracture and loosely unite a country with a combined population of three million people. The 'Three Wales model' was introduced in 1985 by political analyst Denis Balsom,[1] at a time when the country was wrestling with deindustrialisation and the demands for political independence and devolution from Westminster. Among the social fog, Balsom captured modern Wales as a country splintered into three regions, Y Fro Gymraeg, Welsh Wales and British Wales.

In the north and west of the country lay the Welsh-language area, Y Fro Gymraeg, proud Welsh heartlands like the quiet coastal towns and commuter villages of Gwynedd County where Welsh remains the common tongue, and the rural farmlands and country villages have come to dominate the exported national image.

In the South Wales Valleys, among the post-industrial communities, was Welsh Wales, the cluster of Welsh-identifying but non-Welsh-speaking regions dominated by the former mining towns, ravaged and still reeling from the lingering consequences of deindustrialisation and the country's waning reliance on the coal once birthed from the belly of its green mountains. They are the historical country boroughs like Neath Port Talbot and Rhondda Cynon Taf, Merthyr Tydfil and Bridgend of the South Wales coalfields, where the Welsh language had faded over generations, the kids no longer learning it through school any more, but where a sense of national patriotism remains tightly woven into the Valley air.

Finally, running along the border towns of Wrexham and Monmouth, and then driving along the southern coasts, where cities like Cardiff and Newport meet the blue mouth of the Severn estuary, comprised the area Balsom delineated as British Wales. These were the towns, Balsom argued, who carried an idea of Britain in their self-definition. They were the regions who voted against Welsh devolution when the rest of the country pulled towards political independence in the 1997 referendum, the county towns and cities stretched along the England–Wales border, who spoke English, not

Cymraeg, and who often, when the informal rankings of 'Welshness' arose in casual conversation, were placed near the bottom.

And though Balsom's theory has been challenged in the decades that have passed, if you travel through South Wales today, among the kids raised in the inner cities of Cardiff and Newport, you will hear these loose definitions unintentionally surface in conversation, their ideas and experiences of Wales and Welshness casually repeated in uniform, the connected stories of their lives bearing out political theory.

They will tell you, 'We are Cardiff boys in Wales.' 'We are Welsh but can't speak it.' They are more likely to foray over to Bristol, than they are into the rural north. They are disconnected in character and outlook from the Valley towns, isolated from an idea of farmlands and romantic Welsh villages in Y Fro Gymraeg. They are of the country, but at the same time, sit distinctly apart.

But there is more here, and they are more than Welsh and British, more than political theory, more than their postcodes and loose city borders. They are others. They are Greek and Jamaican and Cypriot and Somali, dual nationals who occupy a grey area, a space overlooked by a Three Wales Model that never quite fitted the frictions and tensions of the country's oldest ethnic communities living out in the heartlands of British Wales.

They are the immigrant families who had lived in minority enclaves in the country for generations now, but who still sometimes felt a gnawing tug between birth cities and the lands from which their grandparents had wandered. They were the grandchildren of those who had journeyed across continents and settled in new lands, the kids who had created identity in sound, subtly seeking out a holding space of their own.

Phil is one of those kids, of that generation who pushed the fragments of these scattered identities into music. He is among the young working-class boys and girls who stumbled out of Wales's forgotten corners in the early millennium, etching their adolescent realities on early Grime productions. They came of age in the youth clubs of south Cardiff and east Cardiff and neighbouring Newport. A generation who grew up chasing music dreams in South Welsh youth centres.

They recorded rookie demos on blank CDs and freestyled on community radio stations: a huddle of boys gathered in the middle of the room like a rugby scrum, an instrumental running in the background, mics passing between palms, everyone taking their turn to shell. Before they were anything else. Before they were fathers and labourers and small-business owners and barbers and incarcerated souls, they passed around songs via Bluetooth on Nokia brick phones. They stood in youth clubs, or in parks or in roads around the city centre, soaking themselves in the songs and sermons from estate kids in cities far away, the hot winds of Grime blowing west into Wales, into postcodes that bore CF10 and CF3 and NP20, a heat wrapping itself around the souls who needed a shoulder, lives briefly illuminated in the trailing headlights of street memoirs.

They were working-class kids, woven together in a tight sequence of small towns and housing estates chained across the Cardiff and Newport seaboard: the looming tower blocks in Bute Town by the old Cardiff docks, hollowed-out estates in Rumney out east, Fairwater and Ely out west. Grangetown, Adamsdown and Tremorfa by the coastal roads in the south. Pill and St Julians in Newport. Terraces and estates and council homes rising up from the same waters that brought many of their ancestors here.

They are of a time when the country was remoulding herself, when the people had pushed fiercely for political independence in the 1997 devolution referendum and tore some sense of freedom from the heavy hands of Westminster. A time when Wales was moving on from an industrial and maritime past, scaling back industry that brought distant settlers in over the waters. Deindustrialisation and a Wales apart. A new future for the old country.

Renewal and regeneration were on the national agenda when they were coming of age in the late nineties and early millennium. But the regeneration never reached them. They are the kids who grew up in the decades after the docks closed by the water and the steelworks were shuttered on the mainland. When the long boom was over, and work fled the industrial inner cities, they were what, and who, was left behind, exclusions from a nation's new chapter, echoes of the darkness that remained. Forgotten. Isolated. Many clung to music to get by. Phil Davies, aka Traxx, was one of those kids.

In the youth clubs in Fairwater and Ely and Rumney and Newport, in freestyles in friends' bedrooms and on streets by Cardiff city centre, a dream turned over in his mind. He glimpsed it in Cardiff night-clubs, as the opening act in under-eighteen raves for famous London MCs who had made their way across to Wales for weekend bookings. When the nights were finished, Phil and the rest of the boys would spill out from the venue, waving their CDs at the icons they had glimpsed from afar, wishing for a big break. He gave his CD to Bashy once, an older MC from north-west London. When Bashy took the disc, loaded it into his car stereo and cranked the volume to maximum as he drove away, Phil and his boys broke out in ecstasy, his fledgling songs echoing out into the Cardiff night. He had worked all week in the youth centre to finish those songs. And when you ask him about it, years later, he will say: 'We were so naïve, but we were grinding. We were all trying to get songs made. We were all trying to buss in music. We didn't know how or why, but we just had this dumb illusion.'

He glimpsed it through his youth, glimpsed it when he first saw the bright lights of a stage show at a Slipknot gig with his mother. Glimpsed it at the Punk shows, the Limp Bizkit shows out in Milton

Keynes; the Newport youth clubs and the Cardiff council estates. Something was pulling him, and he followed. One evening he smuggled across the border to Bristol with his girlfriend to watch a Kano gig. He was around fifteen. After the show finished and the set cleared, he approached the stage and jumped the barriers. He walked through the venue's back alleys, out into the lot and onto the tour bus where Kano and his friends, lounging after the show, stared at the new unannounced arrival, bemused.

'I want to speak to Kano,' Phil said. 'I want to spit you my bars.'

Kano, amused at the young kid who had wandered onto the tour bus, agreed.

When Phil had finished, Kano told him, 'When you're famous, when you're big, come and shout me innit.'

They would cross paths again ten years later.

———

A dream takes root in a place before you arrive. His story here in South Wales and Cardiff starts with the water. In the 1800s, when steam engines began to be used for trains and ships, global demand for the coal that fuelled them surged. The natural coalfields encased under the South Wales Valleys were mined. A railway was formed, linking the Valleys to Cardiff, and allowing space for a previously minor industry to boom. Cardiff is a by-product of this evolution, rising with the tide of the world's demand for coal, transforming itself from a small town by the Welsh coast to one of Britain's major points of export. The first dock was built in 1839, shipping all across the world. By 1913, there were five, and 10.6 million tonnes of coal per year being carried along the Valley-to-Cardiff trail and out over the water.

Cardiff expanded quickly, money flowing in in millions, a city scaling up and sprawling outward around its new trade. Coal moved out on ships from docks in Cardiff and Newport to ports across the world, docking in Europe and Africa and the Caribbean too. When readying for return, they would bolster the crew with local men from these far countries who were keen to find work, Black and Arabic and European seamen tired of life on steady ground. And so, the ships returned to South Wales with pieces of far continents.

The newly arrived men from these foreign countries often stayed in boarding houses around the docks, in a place known as Tiger Bay. Some passed in and out of the city, before taking again to the sea on another voyage to another far place. But many stayed. Some of those who settled ran cafés and shops and boarding houses of their own. In Tiger Bay through the early twentieth century the streets echoed with Maltese and Portuguese, with Malay and with Yoruba. More than fifty-seven nationalities were crammed into its population of 3,000, the streets teeming with foreign seamen. Some married local women and began new lives on a new continent, a home away from home, Welsh with an asterisk coming into life for the first time.

It was one of the early stems of a substantial ethnic minority presence in Britain, people who came from elsewhere. There are wedding-day photos from that period in the late 1800s, and early 1900s, that capture and reflect how a community came into bloom: one with a West African groom and a white Welsh bride. Another showing a Yemeni groom and a Welsh bride, then a West Indian groom and a Welsh bride. A Somali seaman on his big day, flanked by Black groomsmen in black suits, standing in new union with a white Welsh bride and her bridesmaids. Two continents meeting, early couples forging the foundations of a multinational community by the waters, their descendants now spread across the region.

***

In the early 1950s, the Constantinou brothers, Odysseas, Philip and Angelo, left homes in Cyprus to build new lives in Cardiff. On arrival they plied trade as hairdressers, and eventually began erecting salons of their own across the city. The salons were called Constantinou's. Odysseas's branch opened behind a tobacco shop in 1960. Philip opened his salon on the Cowbridge Road East that flows out towards Ely and Fairwater from the town centre. His wife ran a florist next door. The chains expanded as the family grew, until Constantinou's, in their many iterations, were scattered throughout Cardiff: Constantinou King's on the corner of King's Road, west of the city centre. Tino Constantinou Hairdressing and Stavros Constantinou sat minutes apart on Cowbridge Road East. Constantinou was planted in the city centre's Castle Arcade. The hair trade became family business, the shops passing down from generation to generation. And so Phil Davies aka Traxx, grandson of the early Philip Constantinou, and the third generation in a family that has seeped its roots deep into Cardiff, grew up in hair salons with his large extended clan of Greek Cypriots.

That is how his family arrived here. This is where his story begins, in Cardiff, a restless teenager with Cyprus pulsing through his blood, an outsider British Wales never accounted for. He grew up in a Greek house, with Greek food and Greek music. He schooled on Saturdays at the Greek School of Wales on Greek Church Street – until he was kicked out for messing around. His grandma, his yiayia, who worked in the florist, worshipped at Cardiff's Greek Orthodox Church, and the wider Greek Cypriot families gathered for communal events at a Greek venue named Spiros in town.

Phil's mum cut hair in the Constantinou's on Cowbridge Road, and when he was young, she would drop him at the florist's next door, with his yiayia. Then at the close of the day, everyone would gather in the salon, shutter the world out and lock the family in.

They would bring food over. Greek songs would play through speakers, his papou and yiayia moving through the music together, Phil and his older sister bouncing at their feet, this branch of the Constantinou family tree dancing and laughing together as the evening burned towards dawn. They were woven into the fabric of the city, assembling close communities and enclaves that hinted at the lands from which they originated.

By the time Phil was fifteen, and in the trenches of the South Wales youth clubs, hunting down a music dream, the mirage of his home away from home had been shattered. First at school, where he had wandered out of a tight-knit Greek Cypriot community and into a predominantly white Welsh primary, where he and the Somali and Lebanese and St Lucian kids, whose parents and grandparents came from countries far from Cardiff, were outcasts.

At home he remembered how his papou, wide set with a big belly, would sit topless on his chair like a king. So he went to school, a chubby child, took off his top and did the same. Everyone laughed.

'What you laughing at?' he told them. 'This is my belly and my boobs, I don't care.'

Home life was unsteady too. Growing up, they lived in a few places across Cardiff: St Mellons. Llanishen. A one-bedroom bungalow with his older sister and his mum who had begun to suffer with a disability. Growing up, sometimes there would be violent outbursts in the home. There was anger, and resentment and broken family relationships, dark thoughts creeping in alongside his stage-show fantasies:

I'm not loved.

I'm not appreciated.

I'm not valued.

He began to act out, flirting with the roads as a kid, and robbing people on the street.

It was around that time, 2009, when the young divided Cardiff postcodes into street crews. There was the DRG boys from Docks, Riverside and Grangetown by the old docks. There was the ST Mandem from St Mellons in the south-east, and there was MCD – Merk Cardiff Daily – Phil's crew who colonised the roads around Queen Street in the town centre. MCD numbered around fifty: kids fleeing troubles at home, fleeing deportation and wars in Lebanon and Yemen. Kids roaming through Cardiff, partying and fighting, recording songs in makeshift studios. Rebels without a cause in whom Phil found a new family.

Eventually, he ran away from home, roaming across Cardiff, selling things he didn't want to sell. He escaped that darkness by moving into a flat with his friend Marcus in Butetown, where the Muslim calls to prayer from the mosque bellowed from its Tannoy. They lived off Raymond's Fish & Chips, stretching one bag out for four days, eking out a living.

There are decisions we make when we are young, choices that commit us to uncertain paths we cannot come back from. Phil, away from home, robbing and fighting and roaming the city, was hurtling down a one-way road, danger hidden in the fog ahead. A local beef between him and a few other boys had begun to spiral. There were fights. There were boys who came to try to kidnap him from school. There were olders who squashed it all. The beef was dead. Then the beef came alive again. There were confrontations at house parties. There were more fights, and a minor issue turned into something more serious.

When the danger in the fog came for him, he was working part-time at the Constantinou's run by his aunt in the city centre's Castle Arcade. He worked the tills in his early shifts, then began hairdressing: blow dries, one-length cuts, colours, whatever was needed. During one of his shifts, a group of boys who he had trouble with arrived at the salon, looking for him. They dragged him from the shop and into an alleyway around the corner. They mugged him, put a knife to his throat and shattered his jaw.

His face was bruised and swollen. He was fearful. He became a recluse, quarantining in his mum's house during daylight hours, anxious and afraid of the violence outside. Some days, at around 4 a.m., when the city was asleep and the streets were empty, when the night had settled and the roads presumed safe, he would venture out on his moped for food. On one of those early dawns, he was readying to leave the house when his mum woke in epiphany. She came downstairs, concerned and asked, 'Phil, are you going out?'

'Yeah.'

'Put your armour stuff on,' she said, concerned about a warning she had received in a dream.

When Phil refused, she barred him from leaving.

He argued, and argued, but eventually relented. He pulled on the padding and the helmet he had owned for a year but had never worn, saddled onto his moped and began riding through the city. He rode, and rode. Then:

Bang.

He tore into an onrushing car, a stranger on a lonely road. He remembers jolting through the air and his helmet cracking the windscreen, remembers how his legs turned over his torso and how he landed on his foot and his shoulder. He remembers the driver, a local drug dealer, leaping from the car enraged. Remembers being punched until the helmet loosened from his head and rolled across the cold tarmac. Remembers the panic that swept across the dealer's expression when he saw the swelling and the bruising in Phil's face. Remembers gurgling, remembers concussion, remembers rising and remembers crumpling back down onto the cold Cardiff road. The dealer called an ambulance. Phil was in and out of it as he arrived at the hospital, awaiting diagnosis.

He was concussed.

His shoulder broken.

His foot, too.

He had survived.

He was discharged.

He went home.

He returned.

He was in and out of hospital.

He was anxious.

Hyperventilating.

Still wanted.

Still hurting.

He was defenceless now.

Out of options.

He had reached his limit.

He left Cardiff behind and flew to Cyprus.

———

Astroid Boys has its bones in Newport, as much as it does in Cardiff. Newport is around fourteen miles, twenty-two kilometres, twenty-five minutes by car from Cardiff. They are sibling cities, bound by the A48 road and a shared history of dockyards and steelworks. The city is the last major frontier before Wales gives way to England, the Newport concrete fading to a few miles of empty green fields, and then the riverbanks of the flowing Severn estuary, Bristol and the English border waiting on the other side.

A cab driver taking you through the city might tell you that though Newport is smaller than Cardiff, with less than half the population, it has its own sense of identity, with a history of Metal and Rock music, has its own distinct variation on the Welsh accent and a sense of pride and resilience you cannot find elsewhere. Its first docks opened in 1858, slightly later than Cardiff's in 1839, and it too carried iron as well as coal from nearby valleys to countries across the world. On their return, its ships also came back with men from far continents, Newport's own early African and Arabic and European and West Indian settlers building a community in a town by the docks called Pillgwenlly, or just Pill as it is known.

Newport boomed in the age of iron and coal and industrial revolution, like Cardiff. And waned in the decades after the industry's decline. But whereas areas across Cardiff were targeted for regeneration, there is sometimes a feeling in Newport that their city was left behind, that they never received the same care as the capital when work went away and the local industries decayed, and the economic aftershocks tore through their working-class communities.

The working-class kids in inner-city Newport who grew up in the new millennium are an unfolding of this loss. They grew up in a city with one of the worst education records in Wales, with around 16 per cent of the population having no qualifications at all.[2]

In schools, the incumbent Labour government plugged this gap with arts and music programmes, funnelling lost kids towards instruments. But some gaps cannot be filled by note sheets and piano keys.

Some boys from Newport grew up in that era knowing incarcerated friends who could play Grade 7 violin, friends wasting away in prison cells across Wales, rubbing together idle hands that could pull bows and strings into holy melody. They needed more. But still, the community tried.

The soul of the South Wales youth centres was Newport's Urban Circle youth project founded in 2006.[3] It was a focal piece among the community initiatives that braided together to create space for the kids in the city. The centre was based in Pill first. Then after a fire burned the premises, they moved to the city centre and continued their work. Kids from across Newport passed through their doors. Their youth workers ran music studios and opened a radio station, threw community talent shows and curated the Big Splash, the annual family street theatre festival run by young people, where five hundred people attended on back-to-back nights.

Elsewhere, Urban Circle taught teenagers to MC and to DJ, to dance and to produce; helped them gain qualifications on leadership courses and showed them how to push their energies into creative endeavours. Some afternoons, community worker Jamie Winchester would throw cyphers in his studio at the riverfront, and over fifty MCs from across Newport and Cardiff would turn up. On other afternoons, he inspired the kids by bringing down the MC Lady Leshurr from Birmingham for a Q&A and live performance, or famed DJ Charlie Sloth from London, who once sat and watched over ninety Welsh kids spit their best bars. Charlie then picked a handful to grace his coveted Fire in the Booth freestyle session on BBC 1Xtra.

These centres like Urban Circle are the bedrock on which Grime and UK Rap in South Wales were built on. The kids of Newport's new millennium stood on their foundations. The youth workers were the ushers for a curious set of teenagers, leading lights for the young kids from the twin cities who saw Grime emerging and thought to themselves, *Why not?* When a handful chose to chase these questions across South Wales, the Urban Circle would be the rope guiding them into the well.

———

We are tied to the legacies of those who came before us, consequences of how a people push and turn through time and country and continent, the sum of the migrations and ancestral wanderings that move and beat through our blood. Everybody comes from somewhere.

Megalos Brussalis, great-great-grandfather to Elliot Brussalis, was a Greek man. He took his family name from his hometown, Brusa, an ancient Greek town that has since disappeared from the map. His son, Stavros, was a merchant in the Greek navy and travelled the seas, eventually wading into the British Isles and docking in Newport, where he stayed and built a new life on new terrain, the first Brussalis on Welsh soil.

Stavros married a Welsh lady, Beatrice. They fathered Christos, one of four sons, who fathered Elliot's dad Tim, from Pill. Tim left home at fifteen, and later in life he met Elliot's mother. Elliot and his older sister came out of their union, the family line unfurling over generations in a small city by the water. Greek blood. Welsh roots. Newport soul.

Elliot, or Dell as everyone knew him, first walked into the Urban Circle as a twelve-year-old. He would ride the bus from home, or his mum would drop him off, and as he walked in he would see kids from all over the city. Some MCing. Some learning to build beats, teenagers scampering after their own music daydreams. The roots of his music career were set in these Newport youth centres, a child of community music studios and local youth clubs.

His early curiosity was Drum & Bass, so he and a few friends claimed the Wednesday night slot on Urban Circle FM, playing songs to the local community, learning to mix records on vinyl as he went. He was beginning life as a producer, invisible forces pulling him towards Phil and Astroid Boys. It was that curiosity that set him on this path.

At the turn of the millennium, pioneering British electronic music genres Garage and Jungle had descended into a wider family tree of Grime, Dubstep, Drum & Bass and Funky House. The sounds migrated through the country on local club circuits and spread through the veins of the early internet. For some it was a heyday of electronic music and innovation, unconventional sounds emerging out of youthful experimentation. Kids like Dell, in towns like Newport, became disciples of these wider scenes.

The city and the internet were feeding him an expansive range of sound. At the centre he played Drum & Bass. At school he parlayed with the moshers and the Rap kids, a rare example of a kid who crossed party lines. Some evenings he would be at Metal gigs and raves, and on others he would be with friends spitting bars in school, trading songs on Sony Ericssons under the streetlights in the park. And by diving into these two separate scenes, he began to notice a shared ethos, a common energy and rage that connected both Metal and Grime, an impulse for release that pointed towards an unlikely union. This cross-fermentation would lay the drumskin for the Astroid Boys sound.

'The energy that you feel in a venue full of fucking moshers kicking each other's heads in because the music evokes that response that you can't deny, you can't *not* move to it, is unlike anything else,' he says, but, 'flip it, you go to a Grime rave and someone gets a wheel up. That energy is unmatched [too] . . . It's the same energy, it's the same gathering together for common interests.'

Dell is from working-class St Julians, in the north-east of the inner city. He went to St Julians comprehensive and attended sixth form in the area too. When he was young, his father lived an hour away in Neath, in the Valleys west of Newport. So Dell lived in a St Julians three-bed with his sister and his mum and her partner. Then, when his mum and his stepdad split, they moved to an ex-council house on Heather Road on the other side of the park, the three of them banding together in a small place, living pay cheque to pay cheque, his sister picking up shifts at a local shop and his mum working all hours to hold the family together at its seams.

The change forced him to grow quickly, bent him towards adulthood when he was still a teenager, a young boy blooming early into man. He remembers feeling like the older brother to a sister three years his senior, remembers when he could no longer level with the kids his own age, remembers hanging around the older kids instead, remembers older girlfriends, remembers moving through the gears quickly.

Struggle opened him up. It brought people in. The house on Heather Road became a meeting point in the ends, an open door for his carousel of friends to pass through, to sit and make music and feel out the world, their collective presence a welcome diversion from the reality of his fragile home life.

Dell found comfort in music. He continued to spend his money on Drum & Bass records, downloaded Grime where he could, kept track of Dubstep's skittering mutations, and as the developments in digital software and technology removed barriers to entry, he began to produce records on cracked software, learning as he went, going off his own ear, the influences of Grime and Drum & Bass and Dubstep and Metal blending into something new. Whenever he finished with a production, he would sometimes take it to Jamie Winchester from the Urban Circle, who would offer guidance and support, and sometimes even teach an aspiring MC how to vocal over Dell's production.

It was at the Urban Circle where Dell first met Phil. Jamie ran the session where they recorded their first song together. A bond was built. Greek and Cypriot blood, Welsh roots and Newport and Cardiff soul forged their early union.

———

Behind all Rap groups are stories about the moment the members straightened their lives out and decided to give music the full swing, myths told and retold until they become folklore. Astroid Boys was built on these small moments, the metaphorical forks in the road on which entire lives hinge.

When Phil arrived in Cyprus, he stayed with his yiayia, the same grandma who had been a florist in Cardiff. He lived at her house in the village of Dali, just outside the capital of Nicosia. The village was fields and dusty roads, with houses speckled among the deep green. It was a long way from South Wales and Queen Street and youth centres and local radio. A long way from the trouble at home, the bike crash and the violence and the hospital visits.

He spent the days canvassing Cypriot countryside, picking olives in the fields, driving around the dust and the bumpy roads in a one-litre Nissan Micra, playing the two DVDs he brought with him on loop, thousands of miles across the continent, trying to outrun what had happened.

But trauma travels, a restless shadow hounding across time, sea and land barriers. Out in the village, the pounding anxiety that had turned through him after the bike crash, that saw him break out in panicked hyperventilation and pulled him back and forth from hospital, continued to hover over his spirit.

By the second week of his refuge, desperate for his anxiety to relent, he was broken. He wanted out of everything, wanted out of anxiety and the vicious cycle of thoughts playing over in his head.

Desperate, Phil found himself alone one morning by a quiet bay on the de facto border where cliffs stretch their ridges to the skies and blue ocean kisses gold sands in an eternal tug of war. He began to swim out into the sea. Haunted by his thoughts. Alone and afraid.

He swam and swam.

And then he stopped.

He pushed himself under. Waited for his body to give out. Waited for the Mediterranean Sea to drag him down. Waited for whatever sat on the other side of a life that had worn him thin.

I'm gonna go, he told himself.

A quiet fade to black in the expanse of deep blue.

During the course of our lives, we have encounters that no expert can validate, and no science can account for; watershed moments in our most desperate hours; things that hint at something behind the veil, something more here than blood and flesh and birth and death.

He felt something that morning when he was out there in the sea alone. Something more than current, something more than science and ocean and tides; something resisting, pulling and heaving as he pushed himself into the water; some force, some guide who saw more in his life than he did.

And when you ask him about it, his usual poise will melt to a stutter and he'll say with a whisper, '. . . like an angel on me.'

Whatever or whoever it was that met him out there in the ocean that morning, God or ocean currents or angels, it moved something in him, changed him.

Feeling some force guiding him back from the edge, pulling against his push, he burst into tears, spilling himself into the sea. In that moment, he felt the anxiety leak and lift from his body, like a plug had been pulled and a sink had been drained. An overwhelming sense of love spread through his spirit, seeped through his veins, an ecstasy of celestial highs.

All his life he had never had faith, never believed in God, never considered something else.

But now. Out there . . .

He began to wail, praising a God he had never known.

'Yo God, you're real!'

Still floating. Still crying.

'You're with me.'

Still breathing. Still here.

'I'm with you!'

Alive.

Phil swam to shore, to cliffs and gold sands.

He sat by the water, a deep sense of love coursing through his body, saved by something, some force, some divine intervention. There was a soft voice in his head now, a whisper, an intuition unearthed from anxieties drained.

Go home, make music.

And so, Phil left Cyprus.

Back to South Wales. Cardiff.

He started Astroid Boys on the day he returned.

7 **DIRTY SOUTH**

SOUTH LONDON

The Johnson family history stretches beyond these few miles of Lambeth and Battersea. Chandler, Blaine and their half-brother Dillen's maternal side of the family were Johnsons from St Catherine's, Jamaica, their grandparents among that generation who moved across the Atlantic to start new lives in Britain. Their grandmother was a nurse, who lived on Concanon Road, just off Acre Lane in Brixton, before moving the short distance to Clapham. Her daughter Janice Johnson, raised here, went to Pimlico School, out by the river, where she met Paul Johnson, of no relation, whose mother lived in Wandsworth and then a place on King's Avenue, not far from Acre Lane too. He also had a family from Jamaica – St Ann's on the island's north coast. Chandler and Blaine are a product of their union.

The siblings grew up among an extended family of Johnsons and other relations rooted across this corner of South. They went to Clapham Manor Primary School, where their mum sometimes worked as a teaching assistant. Other times she was a childminder, so their house would be flooded with kids from around the area. When she got a nursing role at a place across the road, their uncle would come over and babysit.

Fridays were short walks to Morley's to buy wings and chips, then settling into watch *Top of the Pops*, and *EastEnders* thereafter. In those early years, their dad struggled with addiction and so was not around as much. But the family was still present. Weekends meant sleepovers and parties with close cousins, the kids breakdancing and body popping on the floors. Both nans eventually left Brixton, one moving close by to Wandsworth Road out by Vauxhall, the other moving to Harlesden in North-West London, where Chandler and Blaine would spend their summers. When the whole family were at the latter's on Sundays, they would play songs and she would get up and dance.

Music was a constant. Their Uncle Danny used to be part of a group, their dad and their grandad used to enjoy singing, playing vinyls together while Nan cooked her famed Sunday dinners with gooseberry juice. Music tastes were staggered down the generations. Their parents, raised in South London, had music reflecting their own coming of age: their dad was a Jungle and Garage head, their mum a fan of Soul. When Chandler and Blaine cleaned the house on Saturday mornings, their mum's music would be playing, the song choice reflecting her mood, meaning sometimes you may hear Whitney Houston, other times Aretha Franklin.

Chandler and Blaine were raised on these sounds, on Michael Jackson and Bobby Brown, Reggae and Soul. But they were kids of the new millennium, had glimpsed So Solid roaming around the ends, and had watched them grace stages on TV. Every generation has the genres and albums and musicians that they cling to, and eventually, if music becomes their calling, build on and evolve. Chandler would remain out of music, listening in as a supporter. But Blaine would put his life into art, stretching and crafting these sounds of South London into something new.

Blaine was always different, even as kid. Different because his body had teething problems, eczema and allergies so bad that aged three or four he reacted violently to almost everything, flaky skin breaking out into sores when touched. He was allergic to peanuts and dairy and couldn't even be in the kitchen on Good Fridays when the family cooked fish. Instead, his go-to meals were often dry cornflakes with a sprinkle of sugar or, when the family ordered in, seaweed from the Chinese takeaway.

He was different because he was born with an unnaturally curved arm, so was in and out of Great Ormond Street Hospital as a kid, until the doctors inserted a pin to straighten the bone. When he made his first friends in the early years at Clapham Manor, they were introduced to a kid with metal wedged into his skin.

He was different because of his slick way with words, so slick that his grandma thought he'd grow to be a lawyer or a Casanova when older. Different because, where he grew up, in the roads around Red Brick just off Clapham High Street, some of his closest friends were a handful of Ghanaian brothers and cousins: Tech, Rich and Diogo. With Blaine, and another boy, Ash, they looped together into a childhood clique they termed the Brotherhood, playing football out on the concrete for hours, or in Tech's flat watching cartoons like *Dragon Ball Z*. While anime trailed on the TV, Blaine would overhear Tech's parents speaking Ghanaian Twi, and then attempt to repeat the words and accents himself, his broken recitals pulling the whole group into laughter.

He balanced his banter with a serious side. He wanted to be a lawyer when he was young, an early promise to make his mum proud, even though she would've been happy seeing him fulfilled in whatever path he followed. In secondary school days, he was placed in 'Gifted and Talented' classes for English, and then during the late afternoons, when he and Tech would be walking down Clapham High Street after school, past the chicken shop Shalamar where the owner used to hand out free food to the kids, past the supermarkets and the Ladbrokes where Tech's cousin worked, Blaine's hunger and drive would boil over and he'd say 'someone owns this shop but yet we're going to be employees? . . . Man's working for someone that owns Ladbrokes, these times why can't we own Ladbrokes?'

He always knew he wanted to be someone, to push his efforts into something that meant more. And then he and the Brotherhood found MCing.

They were making Grime on the ends in those days, during the middle stretch of the 2000s, after the genre had migrated out of East London into the sealed pockets of South. The evolution from So Solid and darker Garage into South London Grime and a genre detached was carried on a number of vessels. There were Pirate Radio stations like Bassline FM, Delight FM, Lightning FM, Vibes FM and On Top FM, the latter of which roamed across Brixton and Oval and Peckham and Thornton Heath and Lewisham, allowing local MCs to build cult local followings via radio sets and shows. There were the intense, legendary early raves like Eskimo Dance in Wandsworth, with Wiley, Ghetts, Kano and the genre's early East London hood-stars all on the bill.

There were Street DVDs like *Lost Tapes of Brixton* capturing a genre and its participants in early bloom. The DVD is shot in the summer of 2002, when the open plains of Brockwell Park, just south of Brixton, scaled into a funfair and rides and carnival stalls for the Brockwell Park Country Show. In one scene young boys and girls from around the ends swarm in a large cluster, one person beatboxing, one recording on a grainy video camera, then members of the flock taking turns to stare into the lens and spit lyrics, chains dangling from necks, silver-capped teeth glimmering in jaws, their voices carried by the backing choir behind them screaming '*BRAAAP!*' and rising gun fingers into the afternoon air.

And there were the early music videos, aired on Channel U. Posse cuts like *Rep Your Endz* and *Southside Riddim* assembled MCs from across the region, Lewisham to Clapham Junction, Peckham to Gipsy Hill, and placed them together on one long song. The videos were shot across the region, scenes cutting from estate to estate, alleyways to the roadsides, flocks of teenagers in hoodies and New Era caps gathered around the MC selected to put their corner of South on front street.

These early iterations of the genre in South were a signal of Grime dispersing, a sound spread on the wind, taking root in communities seeking new vessels of expression. For the locals, the genre felt different in South, a distinct street element woven into the music. Many of the early MCs came out of recognised and established gangs from the roads. They pulled a ruggedness into their lyrics, the at times jovial nature that accompanied the more buoyant Grime in East London replaced by an aggression and a realism that hinted at true stories inspiring their street sermons.

There were crews in Peckham like 187. There were crews in Wandsworth like Red Alert Crew with early MCs like Blade Brown from Battersea. There were Essentials from estates across Lewisham borough, Big Narstie from Acre Lane, and a collective from Brixton named the Roadside Gs, whose song 'Come 2 Da Roadside' acted as a signpost of this subdivision. The members – Alan B, Dan Diggerz, Smiley, Elmz, Den-Den, RA and Drz – came from differing pockets of Brixton, discovering each other on Pirate Radio sets and old childhood crews like 2 Darkk, some of them playing with Jungle and Garage at first, some influenced by Dancehall, and then everyone eventually uniting into one, and tying these sounds into Grime.

By the time 'Come 2 Da Roadside' was released around 2006, Roadside Gs had grown a reputation for brutal portrayals of life on the roads. The video trails around the council blocks in Brixton, the boys encasing uncomfortable realities in their lyrics.

There are shootings.

There is shotting.

They never sugar-coated.

RA spits:

'I rep SW9 on the road
Broken niggas from homes on the road.'

Den says:

'There's bare man with no hope
Kids with kids who can't cope
No joke, it's dog eat dog, cut-throat on the road.'

The video was barred from Channel U, allegedly on the orders of a hyper-surveillant Metropolitan Police force. Roadside Gs' debut mixtape was called *Gangsta Grime*. And RA, which stood for Real Artillery, would eventually spend ten years in prison after being jailed under the controversial 'Interest in Public Protection' (IPP) sentence.

At their peak, the crew carried an aura that spread through South. Blaine and the rest of the Brotherhood, growing up a few roads away from Brixton, were pulled into their orbit. Sometimes they would see Dan Diggerz cutting through the manor. Elsewhere, they were taking in their videos and songs, so much so that RA became one of Blaine's favoured MCs as a kid. When Blaine himself started to make music, spitting in school days, the fingerprints of RA's swift, skippy flows found its way into his sound.

Blaine was adopted into Grime, a local calling and rite of passage for working-class South London kids leaning into music. He built himself on a few fronts. At his secondary school, Chestnut Grove a few miles away in Balham, all the kids would gather on the football pitches to relay their bars. Blaine attacked instrumentals with pace, became known for his ability to MC fast, eventually carving out a reputation as the best spitter in school.

Then, with the rest of the boys from the Brotherhood, he would head over to Ash's house, and record in a makeshift studio, or they would come over to his, lock themselves in his bedroom and make music for hours. When he had any tracks he wanted to be heard, he would log on to instant chat messengers like MSN and send his music to whoever he could reach, eager to prove himself as the best.

This process is how reputations were built in this era, songs and status rippling out from schools and early corners of the internet, South London kids defining their sound.

Elsewhere, he would make music with his cousin Casyo Johnson, who lived in Gipsy Hill. They were born less than a month apart, were raised together, a relationship bonded in family functions and parties where they breakdanced and jumped about in the front room, Casyo at Blaine's house in Clapham, Blaine at Casyo's in Norwood, both gathering at their nan's on a Sunday. When Blaine managed to get the music software Fruity Loops on his computer, they began playing around with instrumentals together, crafting beats and experimenting, Grime flowing through the family bloodline.

Every MC needs a name, a calling card that goes before you, its notoriety speaking loud before you have said a word on a set or a song. Casyo had settled on Krept. But Blaine cycled through a few names, tags like MC Fizzy and then MC Bubbly, nothing feeling quite right. One afternoon, the two were sitting on the 410 bus to South Norwood, thinking of a tag. When they reached their stop and dismounted, Krept looked up at the passing 410 and saw printed on the side the specific fleet the bus formed part of. The sign read 'Cadet'. He turned to Blaine, suggesting it as a potential name. Blaine liked it, agreed, and a new MC was born.

———

When he was around fifteen years old, Cadet moved to South Norwood, living with his dad. It was around six miles from Clapham, deeper into South, past Streatham and Tooting, scrambling away from the inner parts of the city, and fanning out into the sprawling residential areas.

Norwood is anchored between the inner and outer city, ranging from the edges of Lambeth and Southwark and into the outer London boroughs of Bromley and Croydon, which until 1965 were classed as Kent and Surrey. The surrounding connected areas are also products of this middling space, gateways between the inner and outer city, meeting grounds for London's opposing tides. Gipsy Hill, where Krept lived, comes under Lambeth and Southwark borough, bordering Upper Norwood and Crystal Palace, where the five boroughs of Lewisham, Southwark, Lambeth, Bromley and Croydon meet. Thornton Heath is in Croydon. Norbury is in Croydon. South Norwood is in Croydon. And Croydon is a place with one of the highest populations of any borough in London. In 1991, the population was 313,510, roughly 20,000 more than anywhere else in London. By 2001 it was 330,587, and by 2011, 363,378, still 7,000 more than any other borough: a city unto itself, supported by a network of schools and football teams and a migrant settlement centre. In the early 2000s, it was still slightly detached from the rest of South, with no Tube stations and a long bus connection to everywhere else. It had its own tram network too, and a skyline blazed with mini-skyscrapers, meaning that at times it felt like its own world entirely.

A Black population fruited and grew in those two decades. In 1991, around 7 per cent, 23,712 of Croydon's population, were Black. By 2001 it had nearly doubled to 13.3 per cent, 44,076. And by 2011, a few years after Cadet had moved into South Norwood, Black residents made up 20 per cent, 73,256; among one of the largest local settlements of Black people in London and wider Britain.

Many were living in the working-class areas in Croydon's northern half that faces out towards Streatham and Brixton and the rest of South, and away from the greener suburban areas that border Surrey. They lived in towns like Thornton Heath and Selhurst and New Addington and Norbury and South Norwood. Towns with relatively new and young Black populations, who were not steeped in the folklore surrounding Black Caribbean migration into places like Brixton and Notting Hill and Tottenham, but who were still, in the mid-2000s, when Cadet was coming of age, facing the similar issues of deprivation and peaking youth violence and social inequality that was strung across South London and the inner cities.

Naturally, Croydon and its surrounding areas adopted Grime in the same way Clapham and Lewisham and Brixton and other areas in the region also had. Sometimes, outside the Whitgift shopping centre in the town centre, or on a bus somewhere else, a boy would start playing an instrumental from his phone, another would start to spray bars, and within minutes a crowd of maybe ten or twelve strangers-turned-participants would have gathered, young kids from around the way tossing the instrumental back and forth like a frisbee, spitting bars with strangers who had become kin.

The swollen youth population fragmented into sets like Laydem Spraydem, Dog Pound in West Norwood, MDS and SMN in Thornton Heath. DSN in Croydon central. Members would usually meet and form crews in ends or while attending the borough's many schools, like Haling Manor in South Croydon and Stanley Tech in South Norwood. A young MC who went by Stormzy attended Stanley Tech, as did a scattering of future Premier League footballers, an array of gifted working-class Black teenagers emerging from testing waters.

Krept schooled there too. He and Cadet became a part of a clique known as Gipset, straddled across Thornton Heath and the grey blocks of the Central Hill Estate in Gipsy Hill. The crew was rounded out with other local boys like Konan, Fret Deezy, Weazy, Bouncer and Redz. They grew up on So Solid, were pulled into the orbit of RA and Roadside Gs, and began to release music of their own: posse cuts over cult Grime instrumentals like the dark, yet celestial strings of Stimpy & Scruface's 'Nutty Violins', or the rough beatboxing of Dot Rotten's 'Beat Box', the boys darting among the oral walls of high-voltage productions, one MC following the other like a relay sprint. Their songs, like 'Gipset Anthem', 'What's Really Hood' and 'Sho Dem Sum Bars', as well as the mixtapes they featured on like *Sly Merkage*, trickled into schools across Croydon as the crew rose to local infamy. Their buzz spread through MSN and LimeWire, seeped into primary schools in Thornton Heath and nearby Pollards Hill where young kids listened with reverence to these local, slightly older MCs.

Teenaged Cadet was a part of this notoriety, well liked and well known in his areas. There was Cadet on a radio set, spitting over a Grime remix of Missy Elliott's 'Lose Control' and earning four wheel-ups in the space of three minutes. There is Cadet on the 'Beat Box' freestyle and 'What's Really Hood' and the other hood anthems from *Sly Merkage*. There was Cadet flanked by Krept in his first video, released in 2007, while they were both students at Richmond College. He is in a red sweatshirt with a matching red beanie leaning over his ears, and is careering over the instrumental, speaking on things they all did back then, punchlines and metaphors pulling out relentless, sometimes exaggerated tales of life on the roads. These themes were pushed through his signature frenzied flow jittering over productions, as well as the howled battle cry 'CADET! CADET!' that announced his arrival on a song like a war drum.

He and Gipset were part of a first wave of a distinct Grime culture in Croydon, and because most of their infamy was contained to rough MP3 tracks and mixtapes passed through the area on Bluetooth and Infrared and MSN, their music and stardom remained local, many of their supporters from across the schools unaware what their favourite MCs looked like.

At a time when young boys began to pull scattered street memoirs into verse, friends became cameramen and DVDs were created for a community to bear witness. In East London, the mecca, DVDs like *Risky Roadz* and *Lord of the Mics* ran parallel to the birth of the genre. Cameramen would move from area to area, filming freestyles and clashes, and MCs hanging on the roadsides, giving an early glimpse into what had only previously been heard.

DVDs travelled along the same lines as the music, filtering across the city and the wider country via record shops and market stalls, raising a young Grime generation, and nudging the kids not skilled or brave enough as MCs, and who had not committed themselves to Fruity Loops or production, into picking up a camera instead.

In the era when Grime and then UK Rap bloomed across South London, street DVDs began to appear, documenting their own early iteration of the culture, bringing faces to names, visuals to estates and areas repped for on songs. There was *Welcome to Borough 6* and *Streetz Incarcerated*, *War Kitchen* and *Streetz Selected*. A friend of Chandler's and Cadet's went round from estate to estate in South with his camera, filming rappers and MCs. He called his DVD *Sticky Business*.

But in Croydon and the deepest parts of South, where Grime was growing a culture of its own, the scene remained largely sealed away from the rest of the city, confined to MP3s and old mixtapes. So a few boys who had once attended Stanley Tech, the school in South Norwood, banded together to film a DVD of their own. They named it *Pixel TV* and set about capturing what they saw unfolding in Croydon and its surrounding areas, bringing the music emanating from a large, slightly new Black British community into focus.

Joey and Shamer and Calum Jacobs, who filmed the DVD, at one point went to school with a lot of the members from Gipset, lived in the same area as them, were growing up on the same music, had cousins out in Battersea running with So Solid, were gassed about RA, had seen strangers on buses break out into collective freestyles, were listening to the *Sly Merkage* mixtapes, and witnessing how a genre had woven itself into the fabric of the region. Joey at the time was thinking to himself, *There's so much talent around here.*

He and Shamer used to grab street DVDs from Vauxhall and Wembley market, watching *Risky Roadz* and *Practice Hours*, *Streetz Selected* and *Streetz Incarcerated*, a subtle inspiration stirring them to start something of their own. Joey began filming freestyles on a Nokia phone with a good camera, starting with Fret Deezy and Weazy from Gipset. Then the boys filmed Cold Boy and YDone from the clique Dogpound out of West Norwood, the two leaning out of a car and speaking on their plans for 2007, how they were going to flood the streets with mixtapes and music. They ended with a freestyle, the two coasting over a thumping instrumental, Cold Boy saying,

'If I don't make pees from rhymes, then I'll make pees on the grind . . . because I've got my mind on my money, money on my mind cos I want a house with a ten-car drive.'

There is a distinct intelligence that shows itself in Rap, an ability for gifted MCs to take in their environment as they see it and then reflect it back via a style that weaves tone, lyrics, cadence and flow into their own signature oral portrait. The artists filmed on *Pixel TV* are an example of this dynamic. Kids who showed up with sixty-four lines of a page diarised and remembered, then spat sixty-four bars off the head, their lines filtering out through similes and metaphors. They jockey the riddims with friends and other spitters as they all crowd on the roadside auditorium, staring straight into a lens, lyrics reeling from their memory, each attempting to make theatre out of words; putting forward an assertiveness and an aura to convince a watching audience they are who their lyrics say they are. Tweaking facial expressions and gestures for charisma, stressing their words on the punchlines and maintaining breath control, all while riding instrumentals that steam ahead at 140 beats per minute. This is how they learned to put words into melody, this is where the future icons of British music learned their craft.

Pixel TV filmed T Block from Tulse Hill, around twenty members of the set mobbing in Tulse Hill train station, letting off fireworks, moving around the camera, shouting and laughing together. They are clothed in the uniform of the days: New Era caps and tracksuits, black winter coats with grey hoodies tucked underneath, thin rope chains hanging from necks and boulder earrings emblazoned on earlobes. There are bandannas on throats, a boy wearing a black T-shirt that reads *R.I.P. Gavin* on the back, smiles and screwfaces, and a freestyle to crown the evening, bars rising into the night, an evening etched into stone.

They filmed MDS from Thornton Heath, and a thirty- or forty-strong gang called DSN in a Croydon park during the dead of night. Roadside Gs in Brixton, crews like Laydem Spraydem, MCs like Charmz, and radio sets with boys gathered in small rooms, cap brims lowered over eyes, hoods over heads, passing a microphone back and forth, capturing a culture in its rawest existence; bringing these secluded areas and estates and the frontlines of a new genre into full colour.

Gipset were filmed on the Central Hill Estate: the rambling blocks in Gipsy Hill everyone knows as the Grey Estate. It has two corner shops, a laundrette, and a long walk from one end to the other. Not just anybody could wander in with a camera and begin to film. But Joey, who grew up on an allied estate nearby, had a pass. When they filmed, the boys gathered under nightfall, pulling in close around the camera as if it were a campfire, Konan first and then Krept and then Reds and back again, young kids tussling and tampering with the English language until they had made it something of their own.

Many of the freestyles were defined by their punchlines, a consequence of a love for New York rappers like Dipset and D Block who used these lingual devices to breathe colour into their stories and songs. Elsewhere there were the stark realities and reflections of a South London they inherited, tales of youth violence and prison and war stories from the streets, as well as the confrontational, clashing elements embedded within Grime from the Sound System cultures the genre descended from. These traits and experiences were reflected in the MCs coming out of the deep South, who bottled these influences and were then recorded on the *Pixel TV* DVD.

G, better vanish when I pull out the shank
Shank dangling in your flesh like key chain.

R to the Zilla
Run up on a nigga for his skrilla
Four-fifth make you bounce back like tigga
And your wife's on my nuts like a white man's on his ciga.

My first sentence was my worse sentence
Missed my exams so I felt worthless
Locked up over Christmas
Banging out kgs quick
I was getting big
Three times I was getting fed.

Pixel TV was a relic of an era found and then lost, its videos timestamps of a generation of kids in the deepest waters of South London channelling their experiences into song and bringing the region into the city narrative alongside more renowned areas like Brixton and Peckham and Lewisham.

They filmed Cadet, too, outside South Norwood train station. He turned up in combat trousers and a green hoody with a woolly hat. Weazy was by his side. When he began to spit, the music seemed to move through his bones, his arms lifting and waving and flapping across the lens to act out his lyrics, eyes glancing around, body rocking and stammering back and forth, jaw chattering as words left his lips . . .

'Listen
Shot gun lift him
I have him back flipping . . . It's CADET
My niggas run up in your sedet'

Something stirring deep within him until every muscle and limb began to rattle and words seemed to pour out from his skin as if he couldn't hold what was coming through, his energy spiking, adrenalin boiling over until he lets out an elated scream. Then he rocks back on his feet and faces the lens, ready to go again, a teenager feeling out his early gift, hoping to piece these fragments of his mind and imagination into a long-term livelihood.

After the filming came the slow process of editing, long evenings after college sitting and letting hours of footage play as the raw files were ripped and then rendered onto a home PC, hours and weeks of using editing software like Adobe Premier and After Effects to comb in subtitles and sound effects and wheel-ups.

Then came the long road to release, getting the copies pressed at the record store Mixing Records in Croydon. While waiting for the DVD to be readied, Joey had kept in contact with Cadet. There was something different about him, he thought: the charisma, the energy. When the editing process began, Cadet would come and sit with them in Shamer's house during those long shifts after college, keen to study the process of putting a DVD together. They exchanged MSN details too, and would chat from time to time. Cadet would talk about his father a lot, about his upbringing and his relationships. Sometimes he would send through new music he was working on, or Def Jam poetry videos he was keen on, a distinct emotional maturity bleeding through that seemed rare for his age and the rest of the kids team Pixel had filmed.

Cadet began writing poetry alongside his raps, sometimes writing to his mum, and other times using the form to exercise thoughts about his dad, Paul, not being around, about his dad's addiction issues, and how these incidents had all hovered over his life as he began the journey from boy into teenager, teenager into young man. When Chandler handed the poem to Paul to read, he couldn't believe his son had written it.

Joey was not the only one to glimpse that side of him. The Brotherhood had seen it too, nicknaming Cadet 'the Sweetest Gangster', and teasing him for how he balanced the introspective poetry with the rawness, and at times violence, within his raps. At the end of every conversation, he would tell them that he loved them, odd for a boy his age, but he continued, so much so that everyone else adopted the sign-off too. Sometimes he would call Tech just to tell him he loved him, and if they ever hung up the phone without the affirmation being spoken, he would call back laughing, and say, 'Why didn't you say "I love you"? I love you innit.' Tech would respond with, 'I love you too,' and then they would hang up.

Maybe it was that streak of self-awareness that saw him avoid the blind alleys many of the kids from that era walked into. *Pixel TV* took almost two-and-a-half years to be filmed, edited, pressed and then released. By the time it came out, many of those featured were no longer around. Some were in jail; some were dead; some had moved on, swallowed by the long jaws of the city. Grime was changing too, the culture they had built, evolving and growing into something else, something darker, one sound ending where another begins. The boys from the deep South followed this movement.

———

In a time where many young people in South London had come of age watching Garage fold into Grime, there were breakaway casts of MCs who never followed that route to its end. These were the handfuls of artists who at first embraced darker Garage and Grime and Ragga, playing on radio sets and growing comfortable on 140 bpm, but who later gravitated towards the street and hustler Rap anthems and artists rumbling out of New York. They were often hustlers themselves, deeply entrenched in the roads with a vivid archive of experiences to pull on. Some of them stepped straight into Rap from their teens. For others, Grime beat a pace too frantic for their experiences to be clearly heard and vocalised, so they began to slow their style down, swapping out 140 bpm for the slower tempo of Rap, building an adjacent scene of their own.

They came out of estates around Lambeth and Southwark, Brixton and Peckham. Their sound began to be referred to as Road Rap. Crews like PDC from Brixton adopted the genre early, with artists like Jaja Soze and Tanna, who migrated from Handsworth, Birmingham, to South London. Many of this first wave rapped in American accents at a time when street Rap in South was still a scene underdeveloped.

But these early rappers set a benchmark, allowing those a few years younger to model the fledgling genre into something that closer resembled South London, a new breed taking the flow patterns and energy and techniques gained from years on Grime and Garage and Ragga into street Rap, evolving the art form to fit the outlooks of Black kids with British tongues.

Among young men and women, innovating by chance, there is always one whose efforts bring wider change, who meets the fertile conditions of time and place and character and experience to etch themselves and a wider moment into history. Giggs came out of the Gloucester Grove Estate in Peckham, Southwark, during the nineties, son to parents who were born here and a family line that stretched back to Jamaica, Guyana and Grenada. He was into Reggae when he was young. Back then the estate would gather outside, and he would DJ and mix songs from his flat window, the sounds of Bounty Killer and Bugle and Beenie Man carrying over out over the flats. By 2002 he was spitting over Garage riddims, like everyone else, and in 2003 he went to prison on gun charges. When inside, his friend Buck, who would eventually become his manager, would send Giggs Rap CDs. And so Giggs began to rap too, touching road the year after in 2004 and committing himself to music.

A 2004 DVD called *Block Patrol* captures the early climate in Peckham and Walworth Road, roaming the estates and studios and houses in the area. At the time, boys from the many estates of Peckham and nearby came together under the banner Peckham Boys, a notorious gang with subdivisions and smaller sets fitting under its larger umbrella.

The DVD captures this dynamic. Boys are fanned out across council block stairwells, coated in hoodies and caps, the designated rapper standing in the front. In one of these scenes, a rapper says:

'I'm on my UK tip, f the American Dream
I'm in a room, one scale and I'm bagging the green.'

In another scene, a Congolese kid, Bobby Kasanga, drops an impromptu freestyle over Ciara's 'Goodies' about trying to sell his S-reg Chrysler. Elsewhere, on Walworth Road, boys are chilling in the famed Bagel King restaurant, or are outside on the high road, double-decker buses steaming past in the foreground. They are in music studios or out late, parked up on a side road, lyrics grieving over Roc-A-Fella and G-Unit instrumentals, one saying:

'Yeah my mum's in the council flat, she works hard, she's grateful
But hearing her prayers at night got me picking up this weight too.'

When the focus of the video falls on Giggs, he is with his brother, Joe Grind, and a friend, Kyze, at a studio called Unit 10. Together they form part of the set SN1, short for Spare No One. He is free-styling to the camera, his early allure caught on record. There is a baritone, deep yet steady voice that rolls over the instrumental like a foghorn, and a stark, gritty strain of storytelling to match, a real-ism in his raps that sheds light on what life in the darkest corners of South London could mean.

In the years that followed, he built his buzz on a string of mix-tapes, capturing the attention of the surrounding regions with cult classics like *Hollow Grind* in 2006 with his brother, Joe, and *Hollow Man Meets Blade* with the former Grime MC, Blade, who had also made the transition to Road Rap, or UK Rap as it was also called. *Ard Bodied* with Dubz, a rapper from South-West London, was released in 2007 too, and encapsulated Giggs's pull. It carries a haunting sound-scape for the two to shed on the bleak and at times brutal nature of life in the capital. There is also a distinct vulnerability. On songs like 'Always on the Rebound', the instrumental mellows and Giggs opens his mind, his lyrics a space for confession and release, saying,

'I ain't living the worst, but I ain't rich
Low pees got me feeling like I ain't shit
I don't mean to be making cocaine trips
Forgive me God I'm sinning for my wages.'

'Pain Is the Essence' follows this trail of introspection, leading lis-teners into the mist behind their eyes. Over a wistful instrumental, originally used by New York rapper Prodigy, the two dial back, taking a moment of pause to reflect on the experiences that set them down a slippery road, as well as the trappings they have found themselves caught in on the way. Dubz brings an aura and a swagger. Giggs speaks on childhood memories in Peckham council estates, friends living in the surrounding flats; speaks on money that was hard to come by and the roads he walked down to obtain it. He speaks of suffering: of the streets, of wars and prison, of the pain his stumbles caused his mother, the grief of parents whose sons fell victim to the dark sides of South London. In the middle of the first verse, he leaves himself with a question. If he had the chance to do it all over again: 'Would I step through another door?'

But the frankness of 'Pain Is the Essence' was offset by UK Rap anthem 'Talkin the Hardest', a freestyle over the menace and thump of an old Dr. Dre production. Here, the heart-searching and self-observation is sealed off and instead he confronts life as it is: big fur jackets and lurking women. Cocaine, weed and heroin packaged and sold, friends on the grind and friends in prison, violence and revenge, action and reaction on the road, playing out over the near three-minute song.

The video saw Giggs in the fur jacket, surrounded by a large coalition of his boys from in and around Peckham, gun fingers waving, reciting the lyrics with him, giving face to an area and a crew that had rung bells in the city for over a decade. In the years to come the video would resemble a mural, with many of the faces glinting on the screen lost to jail or early burials. The song spread throughout South and then the wider city and country, swapped and exchanged on school buses, blazing out of car speakers and barbershops, at BBQs and birthdays, sung like a national anthem at house parties, the baritone voice swamping the roads, Giggs establishing himself as legend.

His debut album, *Walk in da Park*, followed in 2008, and like the mixtapes, put forward a young man unafraid to speak on the many shades of his life, of the pain, the greaze, the loss, the grief, and by doing so, captivating a generation, alarming authorities and entrenching UK Rap into communities across the country. A door was opened, and UK rappers began to walk through, musicians like

Youngsta and Page and Face Squeeze in the deepest parts of South London, the sets CFR and PIF from Brixton, Mashtown in Hackney, Nines and Skrapz in Harlesden, Stardom in Birmingham.

As their influence spread, Grime MCs in South were teased away from their birth genre. They started slowing down too and opting for the gritty beats ripped of YouTube, transitioning from 140 bpm over to Rap. Cadet and the brotherhood were among them. Their MP3 players were filled with Giggs and SN1, and rappers like Fix Dot'm from Walworth Road. The genre became their dominant form of expression, a line being drawn between what was and what was to follow.

That convergence between Grime and UK Rap marked a period of intense innovation in MC culture. Varied Black communities in South London had surfaced together, a meeting point eventually beginning to combine into one.

———

The Black community in South London had long been defined by sustained waves of immigration from the Caribbean, by those early settlers who wandered into foreign territory and began the slow process of moulding the land into a place that could feel like home. But migration patterns began to shift in the eighties, as young men and women from African countries like Nigeria and Ghana, Somalia and Congo began to arrive en masse.

In 1991, in the borough of Lambeth, which contains Brixton and parts of Clapham, there were 16,021 Black African people, and 30,789 Black Caribbean people. But by 2001, as African migration continued and immigration from the Caribbean waned, there were 32,139 Black Caribbean people in the borough and 30,836 Black Africans. These shifting dynamics were prevalent in Croydon too, the Black Caribbean population growing from 15,326 to 26,065, and the number of Black Africans rising from 4,984 to 14,627. In Southwark, where Peckham had become a hub for West Africans, even nicknamed Little Lagos, the Black African population jumped from 15,713 in 1991 to 39,349 in 2001, the Black Caribbean population standing at 19,555.[1]

A Black African presence was emerging in South London, a product of those who arrived in the eighties. Their sons and daughters, born and raised in Britain, walked similar roads as the second and third generation of Black Caribbean people before and among them: hybrids with birth certificates marked by London hospitals, homes that resembled Africa and daily realities that resembled Britain. This new generation of British-African kids inherited towns and boroughs where Jamaican and Trinidadian and wider Caribbean culture had been engraved on the land for decades. They mixed in at schools and in changing neighbourhoods, bought into Grime and descending Sound System culture, Black communities overlapping; second- and third-generation African and Caribbean people finding common ground on British soil.

This union was reflected in the music they produced, too. After a generation were teased onto Rap, they took things further than the predecessors who had settled on East Coast instrumentals. Their early education on Grime, their experimentation with Rap, and the looming presence of Bashment and Dancehall in South London, gave them a versatility. Many began rapping over Dancehall, their scattered influences allowing them to ride the jumpy instrumentals, weaving in and among the shifting pockets.

In and around Peckham, younger rappers from a set known as PYG & Y SI, with members of Nigerian, Bajan, Jamaican, English and wider African and West-Indian descent, laid UK Rap over Jamaican producer Notnice's 'England Town Riddim'. Elsewhere, in

Brixton, an area that has long been a stronghold for Britain's wider Caribbean community, Babatunde Odusina of Nigerian descent, who went by Sneakbo, covered legendary Jamaican Dancehall artist Vybz Kartel's 'Touch a Button', alongside fellow Brixton rappers Political Peak and JJ.

This merge seeped into the deep South, too. In 2011, Stormzy out of Norbury, and of Ghanaian descent, released 'Gunshot', with friends Deepee and Swift of a crew called Section Boyz, and another boy, Don D. The instrumental was Notnice's 'Boxing Day Riddim', popularised by a Vybz Kartel cover. Here, on the edges of South London it had found a new home, the Black Atlantic bringing sounds in, and Black British boys of African and Caribbean roots, adapting them into their own and pushing new sounds outwards.

But as the genres evolved in South, many of the old crews began to come apart as education lines ended, college and school casting them out into the next chapters of their lives. Most Rap groups were fleeting, breaking and reforming as early adulthood beckoned and then settled in. Gipset were no different. Some went to prison. Some got jobs and set out to find careers. Others became producers. Krept went down the university route, studying Accounting in Portsmouth. He and Konan kept with the rapping, rebranding as Krept and Konan, after everyone else went their separate ways. Cadet went to uni for a short time, then dropped out. He headed down the work route instead, among the hundreds of early MCs and rappers who put music aside when life's pressures pushed them away from big-sky dreaming. He got a job, a music flame dampened and subdued. His South London dream deferred.

8 **0121**

WEST MIDLANDS

Despa gets out by giving it all up, by committing to the straight road. He gets out by leaving Darlaston for good, moving to Leicester and then Birmingham. He becomes a youth worker and goes to the Prince's Trust, seeking a grant and some funding, then with the money develops a youth programme called the Fresh Outlook Project, aimed at engaging wayward kids through music. To get by, he hustles legally, starts a succession of quick boom-and-bust businesses that sustain him for a while, starts an internet business, then orders a haul of SIM cards for free and turns a nice profit by selling them to clamouring hands. He finds something within himself, a resilience, a hard centre at his core. Nothing will be given to him in this life. He will find his way.

In the era of crews forming and breaking again like waves on the water, he is there. By the mid-2000s he has founded the label and collective StayFresh, a coalition of MCs and producers predominantly out of Wolverhampton. They are among the third generation of crews and MCs. StayFresh was a label and a music group and a production company, a contingent of Midlands MCs and producers fanned out across the revolving roster. StayFresh was Despa, and his co-CEO Jamie Dred. It was MCs Macca, Mayhem NODB, Raider, MoveZ, J1, Deadly, Pressure, Don Menna, Saf.One and Casper. It was producers Moky, S-X and Preditah. It was a sprawling music collective and a haven for a growing Grime scene in the Midlands.

There were other groups too who formed part of that third generation. By this time Vader and the Midlands Mafia have disbanded and Vader has started a crew called Invasion. Elsewhere there is NODB and Grime Squad and Messy Organisation. Together they are the generation who stamp the region onto the frontiers of the sound.

They fought in order to thrive. They came out of a nervy time. North Birmingham split in two, a hangover from the early gang era, boys in neighbouring areas bound in disputes that sometimes turned fatal. Areas like Handsworth, Winson Green, Ladywood on one side of the line, areas like Lozells, Aston, Nechells and Newtown on the other. These frontiers handcuffed a growing Grime scene.

Brum's early Grime culture pulled heavily on the Sound System DNA of its forefathers. It was born in the dance. The live arena was its oxygen. Young MCs walked through the fire in under-eighteen raves, a handful emerging out on the other end, many more lost to the wayside. It was in these arenas where a genre unfurled into full spread, sons and daughters of the ends pulled into close communion, sweat steaming from foreheads, limbs woven on hardwood dance floors.

There was a distinct currency in the dance, a natural order sorting the teens-turned-musicians. The MC who drew reloads from DJs, who raised gun fingers from a gathered crowd, who tugged screw-faces from stern jaws, were king or queen. By these merits a man or woman was judged and a sound was built. But the violence of the day put a culture's sacred space under threat.

Some raves were off-limits to MCs with certain associations because who and where you grew up could be a marker. Some, like Vader, managed to toe a narrow line, a reputation for music and nothing more allowing him to roam free across borders. Some evenings passed without incident, some ended in violence. In the years when Garage and then Grime dominated dance floors, there were twilight shootings in and around North Birmingham and city-centre nightclubs. A pattern began to emerge. A new venue would open. Promoters would put MCs and musicians on the bill. Opening weekends would pass smoothly, and then something would happen.

At the club La Mystique out in Aston, handfuls of MCs were billed for Elimination, a live clash with six crews, the winners judged by crowd approval. The clash was shot up before a winner was announced.

'We'd have the odd dances,' an MC says, 'but then they'd give us a chance, and suttin's happening again.'

Some saw worse, saw bloodshed in raves and lives lost. There were incidents at Carnival and incidents in the city. Birmingham became a black spot. A music scene stuttering to a stop. Travelling Garage and Grime raves touring Britain's major-city circuit removed Brum from their programme. To rave you went to Nottingham or Derby or Sidewinder in Milton Keynes.

With the difficulties in performing and getting paid for your craft, some MCs stopped taking music seriously. Others found their way via different roads. Trilla, an MC who grew up in Winson Green to Jamaican and Trinidadian parents, was part of the city's leading clutch of Grime MCs. He started making noise in the third-generation crew Messy Organisation. When things with Grime became difficult in the city, he found himself wandering into a new genre, leaning into Bassline, which was dripping into Birmingham from the cities further north like Leeds, as well as the adjacent regions of Wolverhampton and Leicester, Nottingham and Derby.

Bassline was different from Grime. Bassline was about vibes and fun, partying and release, something he saw as a cross between Garage and Drum & Bass, the sound putting a strong emphasis on captivating the dance floor in a live venue. Bassline wasn't social commentary. It wasn't a vessel for political and social angst. It was for the few hours on a Friday or Saturday night where the many would gather into the nightclubs on local city strips to forget about what had passed, what was present and what lay ahead.

By the time Trilla was introduced to it in around 2007, the genre was ringing off in the clubs across the northern half of the UK. In raves, many DJs were playing entire Bassline sets. When the sound started to creep into Birmingham, Apostle, a DJ and producer from Wolverhampton, asked Trilla to vocal a dubplate. Over the instrumental, Trilla recorded his popular Grime bars, branding his vocals onto a different sound. With many of the Bassline ravers already familiar with his work from Grime, the dubplate immediately drew big reactions in the dance, and he was swept into the scene.

Weekends he was performing at places like Vibe Nation in Sheffield, Warehouse and Rio's in Leeds, clubs in Manchester, clubs in Derby, and clubs in Leicester, his songs like 'Nastee Boi', 'Wobbler Part 3' and 'Etap Riddim' clamoured for like gold dust in the dance, so much so that sometimes it would take him fifteen or twenty minutes to perform one song. Eventually he began to perform in Brum too, in clubs on the Broad Street strip, getting paid for a craft he loved in the city that he was raised. At a time, he was one of the biggest MCs in the Midlands, using Bassline to represent for the city in a way no other artist was. This was his way around the problems Grime ran into.

Others were not able to follow this road. Ultimately, the conditions proved difficult for a genre like Grime that was anchored around live music, the tense climate stealing a livelihood from the MCs and DJs who made wages at weekend raves. It was a scene unable to sustain itself. The early MCs and DJs were victims of a few violent nights in a hostile time, witnesses of a city turning in on itself and suffocating its own sound.

———

The young drift in and out of music, setting pure passions aside when teenage years bleed into adulthood. The days dragged out in studio sessions and radio sets, in raves and on the roadside, are shed for parenthood and new responsibilities. Boys become men, and men become fathers and partners with bills to pay and work hours to account for. A music dream stays a dream, the buried wonderings of *what if* nagging their waking hours.

In 2007, Despa got a job. Music was on the wane for him, and he joined Apple instead. It was a move set in progress years back when he left the roads and was steering his life into a new chapter with the Fresh Outlook Project. The grant agreement with the Prince's Trust stipulated that he buy a computer. He opted for a Mac, and as he waited for the funds to greenlight the purchase, he pored over the product's back history, making sure it was value for his money.

First, he learned about the computer and its possibilities, and intrigued by what he found, he began research on Apple, the company producing them. Then he went deeper, on to Steve Jobs, who had founded the company. He became obsessed with Steve, who had revolutionised the tech industry by starting Apple, the film industry by founding Pixar – the studio who produced *Toy Story*, *The Incredibles* and *Finding Nemo* – and the music industry by creating iPods and iTunes. Despa was inspired. He watched Steve's interviews on YouTube, studying a man whose life had started with adoptive parents, who had dropped out of college, who said he wanted the computer to be the 'bicycle of the mind'; his technology a tool for people to do amazing things seamlessly. He was a man who had founded Apple, a tech company, and then hardwired his love of creativity into its ethos. By 1985, when it had grown into a billion-dollar organisation, he was ousted by his own board members in a dispute over product prices he believed to be too high, only to return in 1997, the company failing without him, Steve correcting a drifting ship. Ten years later, Steve Jobs unveiled the first iPhone at a convention in San Francisco, ushering in a new age for mobile technology. By then, the company had a global footprint with hundreds of stores scattered across the continents.

In 2007, the same year the iPhone launched, Despa was sat in one of those far Apple outposts, encased in the caves of a Birmingham city-centre shopping mall, beginning work as a Creative. He had first applied for work with Apple as a Back of House Specialist, stacking shelves, but was rejected. After a little while, they called him back for the Creative role, and after a few interviews where he blagged qualifications he didn't have, he began work in the store part-time. In the daylight opening hours, his brief was simple: know everything about Mac hardware and software, then train and teach customers how to operate them. In those first few months he thrived, climbing the local branch ladder, went from part-time to full-time, then from an entry role into management, drifting out of music and into something concrete, something he could see and hold, a job that paid in a company he admired.

Music slipped away. After a year at Apple, he was out of StayFresh and was working full-time. In the same period he moved out to Leicester, helping open the new Apple store in the city centre. He was a company man. He was on the straight road, making straight money. He had balanced out, given himself and his life what he had lacked for so long, a steady job with a steady routine, climbing a company staircase that, if he continued to ascend, likely levelled out with a nice wage, an easy mortgage and the comforts of a stable middle-class life. A new life, so different to what he had been raised in, was in the near distance. All he needed to do was reach out and grab it.

The Leicester branch was another store entombed in the cages of a city-centre shopping mall. During shifts he would stand on the top floor, in the retail section that felt like a stainless-steel box, and help customers. In his downtime, he would stare through the glass windows, watching the world pass by, yearning for the sun sparkling out on the city, then watching it fade over the horizon. He held fantasies of being outside, of seizing the daylight. But when his shift was over and the working day finished, he would emerge into darkness.

On one of those long shifts, gazing out of glass panels, a man came into the shop asking to buy a Mac. Despa was three years into his career at Apple at this point, seasoned in dealing with the wide string of characters tumbling into the store. He watched on as the man looked around at the systems on display for a while, then left. The next time the man came back, he asked to buy some training sessions.

In those sessions, he and Despa became friendly. He found out that the man's name was John, that he was a roadshow DJ, that after enquiring about a MacBook in their first encounter, he went home and bought a cheap version on eBay instead, John revealing that he only needed the device to download songs, to send emails, to make his life easier, and so a cheaper, used version would pass. Despa had judged John at first, assumed he didn't have much going for himself, but as the sessions unravelled, he saw a man who had staked his claim in the world, who many wrote off on first appearances, but who was content. He worked just enough to live a life on his own terms, wasn't rich or wealthy or maybe even middle class, but made enough money and time to do as *he* pleased.

One afternoon when the sun was beaming through the glass, John came in for a session, and seeing Despa cloaked in the steel box, grinding away at another long shift, sarcastically asked how he was spending the day.

'Working,' Despa said. And then John told him something profound, said that your time is fleeting and you must own as much of it as possible, that you need to buy as much of it as you can, work only as long as you need, then spend the remaining days and hours as you please. Time was the only thing that was truly ours. Then he left. He was going to spend his afternoon in the park playing football.

The conversation gnawed at Despa. A mirage had been shattered. He had stability and a good job with good prospects, but somewhere deep within, things weren't right. And he knew it. The spark for music and creativity that had simmered within him for so long, that had carried him through Walsall and Wolverhampton, through start-up record labels and DIY Pirate Radio, was wasting away, a melodic impulse frittering into ash.

Then one day, while talking to his mum, she asked him, 'Are you happy?'

'No,' Despa said, but he was comfortable.

'That's nice.'

'It's not,' he said. He didn't want to be comfortable. At his most extreme he felt like he was dying.

Despa pushed his own stake in the turf. He went back to part-time work. He went back to music, eventually leaving Apple for good in 2013, never to work for someone else full-time again. Apple had been six years of his life, six years of his time. And now he was out, living back in Birmingham, the impulse for music resurrected, a childhood dream for his own record label revived.

To start he brought back StayFresh, the music collective he had started years ago. They emerged at a time when old crews of the early 2000s were falling away and new collectives, and a new generation were emerging, the young melding with the seasoned and established, one generation clearing the route for another to emerge. In the same period StayFresh reassembled, Vader left Midlands Mafia and started Invasion Alert, a turning roster of MCs who included Sox, D2, Yaseen

Rosay, Jaykae, Tempa, Hitman, Tazzle, Subzee, MK, Big Mikee, Lady Leshurr, Casp and DJ Free. Invasion depicted Birmingham and the West Midlands, a gathering of Black, Brown and white MCs from around the region. Alongside StayFresh, they ushered in a golden era for Grime, Rap and further Black music in Britain.

Further afield, down the M40 in London, the genre was changing. MCs were moving away from the roots of the sound, lured by major labels and the tease of mainstream recognition. Songs became prayers for chart success. Tinie Tempah's 'Pass Out' and Wiley's 'Rolex Sweep', Tinchy Stryder's 'Number 1' and Chip's 'Oopsy Daisy' defined the swing. Young men and women seemingly eager for music to pay, for a passion to bear out into profession, reached far from what they knew into easy, digestible melodies that had the ear of a nation.

When London MCs' forays far from home left worries about the slow death of a genre, it was Birmingham and the scene in the Midlands that kept Grime alive. Crews like StayFresh and Invasion were at the pulse of the sound in the years stretched between 2009 to 2013. They crystallised the moment with a string of singles and cult music videos, recorded radio sets and kerbside freestyles. There was StayFresh's song and accompanying music video '16 for 16', a lyrical round table that sees the roster parade over a stuttering S-X production, the crew assembling on a cold night, staring down the camera in StayFresh T-shirts and black tracksuits. The video ends with a fleeting glimpse of Despa as the visual fades into blackness.

'16 for 16' sat alongside a string of legendary StayFresh moments: sets on Rinse FM and Kiss 100, and the release of S-X's 'Woo Riddim', a production that, when released in 2010, became Grime folklore with MCs across the country freestyling to the brooding drums and echoing synths, establishing itself as one of the genre's greatest and most coveted releases.

The local scene was built on sets recorded at Oxygen Room studios in Digbeth, and then DC Studios in Wolverhampton, its premises hovering outside the city's train station. DC housed sets on Saturday, starting in the early afternoon and running through into the evening, hundreds of MCs from across the Midlands making the weekend pilgrimage to take part. It became a hub, with estimates of five hundred spectators arriving every session, mingling with and glimpsing their favourite MCs, the crowds eventually growing so large that the organisers had to cage the clashes off from the watching audience.

YouTube channels began to emerge too, documenting the growing scene. Among them JDZ and P110 covered the upper half of the United Kingdom, lending platform and outlet to the legions of MCs emerging from the Midlands up to Manchester. Invasion Alert were a regular presence on these channels, and on the channels like SBTV based down in London. Vader's crew had loose borders, members moving in and out, some more active than others, a group of forefather MCs melded with a new generation being bled in the ranks, young MCs like Jaykae and Lady Leshurr, Depzman and D2 building on what he had started.

They recorded freestyles like the classic SBTV cypher in a quiet street just outside the city centre, told tales of the road, of a Birmingham never seen. They were on radio, and they were at DC Studios. For those long years, a major milestone seemed to be uncovered and checked off every few months. Depzman recorded back-to-back legendary freestyles in Ibiza, standing on the beaches and in the villas of the summer destination. Lady Leshurr started a freestyle series titled 'Queen's Speech', hit a viral slipstream and gathered fans across Birmingham, then Britain and then continents across the world, allowing her to buy a house for both her and her mum.

She was raised in Kingshurst on the eastern edges of the city where Birmingham blurs into Solihull. Both her parents were from St Kitts, the same island as Vader. Like him, she shifted things in the city.

Growing up, she was raised on a spread of Black artists and sounds. One sister showed her R&B and Hip Hop, her brother was into Drum & Bass, and her mum played Reggae records like Sister Nancy's 'Bam Bam'. Elsewhere, some of her brothers rapped in underground Hip Hop group Fifth Element. MC culture had been with her, and in her, since knee high. She started off in poetry, writing lines as early as aged six, and then after discovering Eminem at twelve, decided she wanted to rap herself. At house parties she would spit over Drum & Bass, Garage and Grime. Other days she would head to the local youth club down the road from her house in Kingshurst, learning how to build her craft as an artist and a lyricist and a performer, spitting alongside the other second-generation Grime MCs, a rare female presence in a crowded scene of young men.

Big Mikee remembers her on the radio, and Vader remembers taking her to Oxygen Rooms, guiding her fledgling career. Birmingham was in her tone, in the multi-syllable style of MCing that some in the city say was pioneered by Vader, in the dry humour woven into her lyrics, and in the accent that elevates slightly in pitch at the end of every bar, bringing the last word into distinct clarity.

Eventually, she joined Invasion Alert alongside a crop of the city's most exciting MCs. By then, she was already threatening to be a breakout star in a growing scene. Birmingham was known for its grittiness. But Leshurr was playful in her songs, her punchlines a tool to humorously speak on the gentler realities of everyday life. The accessibility drew a wider, and then international, audience into her music, and by extension, the rest of the scene's. In many ways, Leshurr was the breaking of a seal. MCs in the city credit her as one of the first over the hill, an MC who led Birmingham's Grime scene onto an international stage.

These are the sounds and moments that coalesced into a golden hour in the West Midlands. These MCs and producers, DJs and managers persisted despite the doubt, leaned into Grime when London veered away. They followed through. They never succumbed. They held a genre at its seams, sons and daughters of the Windrush generation in the Midlands carrying their sound into a new day, setting the stage for Black music in Britain to bloom across the country and then the world. For Despa, it was maybe personal. He was making true on the private pledge he had made to himself and his grandad all those years ago. He was pushing to make the original Despa proud.

9 **CF10**

SOUTH WALES

Astroid Boys can be traced back to 2010. It began as a solo act, a one-piece, with Phil on the club and bar circuit in Cardiff's city centre, opening up for London boom-bap MCs. Back from Cyprus, he pushed forward into music, into what he had been called to do. The solo act became a duo when his friend DJ Comfort came on board at the small shows; and then a trio after one evening at the Urban Circle over in Newport.

There was a buzz in the Urban Circle whenever the boys from Cardiff came across to Newport. Sometimes, while visiting their neighbours, they would jump in on the radio set's broadcast on Urban Circle FM. On one of those evenings, Phil came down to shell on a set. That was the day he met Dell. The two were introduced and spoke for a while. Dell played some productions, and Phil, liking one of them, asked to vocal it. It was the first official Astroid Boys song, and they recorded it together at Jamie Winchester's studio. They titled it 'Jungle Buku' and shot a music video shortly after. It was a meeting of genres, a Grime MC over Dubstep; a meeting of cities, a Cardiff boy on a Newport production. It was music standing on community shoulders, songs pulled from the long threads of youth centres and youth workers. It was Astroid Boys taking hold. It was the next decade of their lives taking shape.

In those early days, Dell and Phil would gather in Dell's bedroom in St Julians and play around with sounds and ideas until something became concrete. In these informal band meetings they bonded over a shared love for alternate British genres: Grime and Rap and

Punk and Dubstep. From those early sessions came a sound that was not quite Metal and was not quite Grime, a sound somewhere in between, a mongrel fashioned from the DNA of these two, radical, seemingly warring genres. On the outskirts of both, they chiselled out new territory of their own.

'We were creating something you could play in *that* venue and kids would mosh to it,' Dell says, 'and you could play in *that* venue and get a wheel-up because of the bars. Thinking back, maybe it was a happy accident, but we made tunes where there was something for *that* crew and something for *that* crew.'

The group broadened with two more additions. There was the drummer and Metal fan Harry, and finally, another MC, Benji. Benji and Phil had met on the youth-club circuit when they were younger, clashing at a house party where over thirty kids crammed into a top-floor flat and watched them wade into a dogfight. War softened to peace when Phil, determined in his pursuit of music, became keen for Benji to join the band. He rung him relentlessly, and when there was no answer, would turn up at his doorstep, Benji watching him and thinking, *I've ignored your calls for three weeks, bro, why are you coming?*

'I just had Phil on my fucking back', Benji says, at him for months and months, 'talking about Astroid Boys, Astroid Boys, Astroid Boys.'

Benji was a Cardiff kid, a Welsh boy like everyone else. Half-Jamaican, quarter-Greek, quarter-Irish from Tremorfa's terraced housing out by the coastal roads and the old industrial estates. He moved around with his mum when he was little. First from his grand-parent's place in Tremorfa, to a hotel in the city centre, then out east to Rumney, a brief stay in Trowbridge. Then back south at four years old, back to Tremorfa, to a council house on a narrow road with a stepdad and a younger brother, the house he still lived in when Phil came calling.

Tremorfa and neighbouring Splott were once steel towns, industrial districts from a time when coal and iron were the lifeblood of South Wales. The looming East Moor Steelworks sat at the heart of its tight working-class communities, exporting half a million tonnes of steel per year at its peak, moulding imported iron ores into steel plates and ship parts, its blast furnaces and flaming chimneys dominating the city's skyline.

But when the need for coal dried up and steel became cheaper to import from Japan, factories began to close, and the area's iron heart faded and crumbled. Towns like Splott suffered in the aftermath, casualties in complex post-industrial legacies, victims of a region inching into a new time. By the eighties and nineties, regeneration had been promised to the aging Cardiff Bay and towns across South Cardiff. But as Cardiff established itself as an international city, Splott and others were left behind.

By the time Benji was growing up, the area was classified as economically deprived, with high levels of unemployment and struggling education standards. Many towns in south and east Cardiff were defined by this dynamic, a 'southern arc of unemployment'[1] as a city councillor once described it, inequality and loss ripening the soil for working-class sounds of defiance to take hold.

Benji remembers music in his family, in Tremorfa and Splott, remembers fiddling around with his uncle's decks in his grandparents' house when he was a kid, Hip Hop and Drum & Bass seeping into his early palette. He remembers one afternoon when he was nine years old and making his way to the shops, remembers cutting through an alley, and the smell of weed and the sound of Jungle hitting him, drifting over from his cousin's back garden.

He followed the scent of burning blunts and the sound of steaming decks, followed it through the side gate until he saw his cousin and friends smoking, and MCing into a headphone. He remembers watching for a while, remembers the smoke, remembers the pulse of the music, remembers eventually asking for a turn – his first freestyle, remembers the nerves and the rush, and remembers when it was over, the overwhelming feeling that the music he had just glimpsed was something he wanted to be a part of.

By thirteen he was entering local DJing and MCing competitions. A few years later he was freestyling in local clashes filmed at the riverfront in Newport. By secondary school he was freestyling in school music rooms and had started a small Rap group. But he struggled in school and was turfed out to a music and media training enterprise called Immtech for two days a week. Founded by Ian Gallivan and John Lenney in a huge warehouse in Butetown, Immtech allowed kids to craft songs in the recording studios and take training courses. Many local MCs passed through its doors, the centre a safety net for those who had lost their way. There, Benji kept gnawing away at music, shepherded by the guiding hands of community workers walking kids back from the edge.

Rap careers are birthed from quiet moments of reckoning. Benji's decision to finally pledge himself fully to music arrived in an epiphany similar to Phil's. Out in Salou, on holiday with a few of his boys one summer, he sat drunk in a boat tied to the bay, smoking a spliff and speaking with two random German guys. The sea was spread out beyond them. They spoke for a while, strangers in a lonely land, and then after some time, the Germans got up, and left. Benji was by himself. He was in his late teens, boy shifting into man, an old chapter closing out and early adulthood beckoning in the near distance. Sat, looking out to sea, he was thinking to himself, *What am I gonna do with my life?*

He looked over his years to date and decided that he was done with college and with suffering in education. He wanted to pursue music, he wanted to rap. He promised himself that when he got home, back to Wales, back to Tremorfa, he was going to commit himself to the art and give this Rap thing the full swing. That is the road that led Benji to Astroid Boys, the road that broadened out the band with a technical MC. He was a bridge to Dell's Dubstep and Drum & Bass influences, and to Harry's Metal drums.

Phil's vision was beginning to take shape. With five members, the band was fully formed, MC kids with a scattering of tastes and genre influences.

Musically, Phil sat somewhere in the middle, a kid who also played both sides, a child of Punk bands and MCs. There were the years he had spent MCing in the youth clubs and on radio, opening up at under-eighteen nights and freestyling under Cardiff streetlights. But he had also been attending Punk gigs since he was a younger, raised himself on Hardcore bands like Trash Talk and Ceremony, and rare Black Punk outfits like Bad Brains from the American north-east. They were bands who represented the most extreme iterations of a sound, hidden behind the commercial veil of popular outfits like the Sex Pistols and the Ramones. He pulled towards these seventies and eighties groups, who were from mixed communities and jumbled backgrounds, who played small-capacity venues and cult festivals, bands that were radicals in thought and in lifestyle: some being straight edge, refusing to drink and refusing to smoke and refusing to eat meat, tribal movements hooking audiences into trance away from the mainstream glare.

This ethos and attitude shaped Phil and the early years of Astroid Boys. That drive and pull towards the extreme is why Astroid Boys gathered steam early, in the same year they came out; it is why their arrival onto Cardiff's music scene was steeped in Punk-ish folklore, why their debut *Space Jam* EP allegedly sold 1,700 copies and then disappeared without trace from the internet; why they pressed on in hope.

Why Phil pushed through with music in an era where Rap had never paid for Welsh kids, when no MCs from Cardiff or Newport were making viable incomes from their lyrics. Why they played in empty venues up in the Valleys and then eventually, a local buzz building, promoters began to book them for local festivals in places like Swansea and Cardiff, then the Bigga Fish tour, and raves called Bedlam, which took them to Oxford and Bristol and Bournemouth. In 2011, only a year or so into band life, they played a late-night set at Glastonbury, billing themselves as 'The Dragons of the Grime scene', Phil's vision of a 100,000-strong crowd pulling slowly into reality.

This Hardcore and Punk philosophy is why they were stage diving at a time when Grime crowds were still frowning at mosh pits. It's why they caved ceilings and turned anarchy at early Astroid Boys shows, why they once roamed in a ten-car convoy and broke into an Iceland, then threw an impromptu show in the supermarket, installing a PA and a generator in the loading bay, and then raved like they were locked in a squat house. It's why Dell describes Phil as 'all gas no brakes' with 'a lot of heart'. It's why they shot a music video in a biker-gang hangout on City Road, paid the gang some money to shoot in the room on the top floor then rolled in speakers and equipment and blasted their new bastard genre through the Sound System till the ceiling began to wobble and the lights were torn from the sockets, till the snooker table was smashed and the hangout was reduced to ruins. The bikers pulled a gun in retaliation. But the band survived to play another day.

When Phil was asked in those early days to describe their embryonic sound and movement, he told an interviewer that Astroid Boys was a space to 'wig out to radical music', a base, 'for kids that ain't rich to stage dive and act wild'.[2]

And so, perhaps it's why in its early years, emerging from the working-class communities of South Wales, Astroid Boys became a haven for outsiders and misfits, a sanctuary for the excluded who never quite fit. For skaters who loved Grime. For MC heads who loved to mosh. For drug dealers and Valley kids. For working-class Welsh teenagers and the country's second-generation immigrants. For those who had grown in the gaps, seeking out space to call their own, Astroid Boys was for them. Every generation has its time. This was theirs.

————

The earlier stuff has that tone where it's just a bit unforgiving, it's raw, it's a bit silly. I didn't know what I was doing as a producer; I was just learning as you go, putting beats together. Phil and Benji weren't trying to be conscious rappers, weren't trying to spit a bar that would change the game. They were just saying their truth – being them. Maybe they're not our best bits of music, but they are products of a time.

DELL

Fleeting buzzes turn granite on the hard wax of albums and EPs. Among the live genres like Grime, which at first lived anonymously and uncatalogued in the fleeting hours of nightclubs and Pirate Radio sessions, the release of albums and mixtapes set solid ground for legacies to be sealed. They are the physical and digital artefacts that mark lines in the sand between the preserved and the unpreserved, the forever and the local folklore that burns to ash with the slow passing of every generation. Many a hood star has been forgotten. Many local champions of their time have faded without trace. South Wales will remember Astroid Boys, will remember Phil, will remember Dell, will remember Benji, will remember Comfort and

Harry. Their trio of official projects, *Bacon Dream*, *CF10* and *Broke*, remain etched on the land, visions of a Wales remembered and a community that once was.

Bacon Dream came first in 2013 on the fumes of hard graft and the cult following they were building in towns and cities across the UK. It was the tape that built the Astroid Boys' soundscape. There was Grime and there was Rock and there were mellowing Hip Hop instrumentals. There were Drum & Bass and Dubstep influences and slightly off-key productions sculpted to Phil and Benji's turning vocals. Both MCs were in their early twenties at the time of release and weaved in and among Dell's scampering instrumentals. There are many fragments to its whole: the aggression of youth-club radio sets lingers among tense introspection and social reckoning, an unchained righteousness of youth seeking out meaning and change in the world they have inherited.

'What's good about being broke?' Phil says on 'Tayluh Swift'. 'We don't have to rap about being rich.'

Other songs are adrenalin binges, rowdy instrumentals that dip and crash around Phil and Benji's shattering war cries.

'We don't need a reason,' Benji screams on 'Dusted'. 'Imma start this riot.'

Bacon Dream was poetry handcrafted for the mosh pits, a piece of work, that like the Grime and Punk from which it came, had to be experienced in the live arena, rolling among flocks of outcast teenagers for its offerings to be truly understood.

But bands don't play out like fairy tales. There is more here than dreamlike fantasy and smooth cruises into crimson sunsets. During the recording, Benji got into an altercation, was arrested and eventually found guilty of unlawful wounding. They recorded the project with a prison sentence swinging over his head.

A candid self-produced Astroid Boys documentary titled *Straight*

Outta CF10 captures the fallout. Six days out from a court case that would stretch for nine months, Phil, Benji and Dell sit on a bench, the early evening settling in, police sirens wailing in the distance. They are reckoning with the prospect of prison and a band dead in the starting blocks. Dell and Phil sit quietly as Benji, gaze fixed somewhere in the distance, reflects on the uncertain road ahead.

He felt like life was on track, he says, until this.

He says that he misbehaved a lot when growing up, until Astroid Boys came into his life at eighteen and he, Phil and Dell pushed hard for new realities.

Then he fixes his gaze into the lens as flashbacks of gigs and stage shows trail over the screen while he speaks.

In life all it takes is one mistake, he says, and you can lose everything: your friends, your partner, your career, everything you have worked for, gone, the consequence of a snap decision.

He continues, turning his attention to Phil and Dell, telling them that if the judge hands down a long sentence, when released, he'll start his life over. But if the boys push on with the band, he'll at least have something to come home to.

Before the scene fades, he freestyles to the camera. The boys listening in on his solemn last stand.

'I guess this might just be the end of the road,
They told me to slow down, but go go go,
Let them know, know that you won't go down without a show,
Blow smoke,
Don't gloat,
Try float,
'Cause we're all up in this boat together.'

In court he was found guilty on two counts of unlawful wounding and was sentenced to three years and three months. He would serve sixteen months in prison and then spend a further eighteen months on probation. Astroid Boys patched together the remaining fragments of *Bacon Dream* without him, punctured.

A few months on, Dell would describe the loss as a punch in the face.

Phil says it was scary, and confesses how Benji was always the strongest rapper in the group, and how with the sentence and other issues running in the background, the band almost ran aground.

They had been hit, he says, and then hit again while they were on their knees. Now, he was unsure how they were going to carry on.

But they finished the EP, and when *Bacon Dream* came out, Phil and Dell hit the road. Everyone stepped up in Benji's absence. Dell emerged from the behind the stage to stand in as second mic, performing Benji's lyrics to the crowds. He trembled with nerves at the first show, hood up, cap forward, 'shitting myself'.

'I'm a producer . . . I sit behind a fucking keyboard; I don't fucking go out on stage; I usually stand on the side of the stage and chill and people don't recognise me.'

But over time he relaxed into his role, began stagediving, and screaming Benji's lyrics with newfound confidence.

Bacon Dream set the tone for their run. They toured after its release, played Download Festival in Derby, Festivile in Sheffield, Red Rooms and Scala in Nottingham, holding open rebellion in grassy fields and dimly lit venues. When Dell's instrumentals crept to rollercoaster peaks, faces out in the audience got tense, supporters bracing for carnage as the bass rumbled in like a war drum and Phil bellowed a choral battle cry. At one venue, out in Coventry, during those hours of sweet chaos and release, the ceiling cracked, and the owner rushed upstairs to tell them that they would need to stop before the place caved. He then extended an olive branch, telling the boys, 'Look, if you can get all the equipment downstairs into the bigger room, then you can just carry on down there.' The crowd helped the boys ferry the equipment. Amid the delay, the audience began to swell, people drifting in from across the local area having heard about the chaos underway. The boys eventually restarted the set and baptised their cluster of new supporters, finishing the show with a bigger crowd, in a bigger venue than they had started with. And so, this is how they built themselves, roaming city to city, pulling in new supporters at every stop, *Bacon Dream* the soundtrack of a curious but rowdy sect unfurling from British Rap's sprawling family tree.

In a scene from the documentary shot shortly after Benji's incarceration, Phil speaks. Since Benji had been gone, he says, they had been on four tours or five tours. They had played numerous festivals, and 'it just keeps going, incline, incline, incline, just keeps climbing'.

Benji rang him from prison one day, dejected, worried that the music was over, that the early buzz had petered out, unaware that in venues across the country hundreds of kids were screaming his lyrics, unaware that the pendulum was swinging, that Astroid Boys and Grime were breaking out onto a national stage, unaware that their South Wales story was finally being heard.

On 11 November 2014 Benji became a free man. He walked out of lock-up and into studio sessions, came home to Cardiff, to Tremorfa, to a band that was blowing up and a new EP titled *CF10* that needed finishing with his verses.

The band's reunion was captured on camera, the boys turning up at his doorstep in Tremorfa, an animated exchange of hand slaps and extended hugs. He was held on electronic tag and curfew for six months, so in the afternoons he would toast freedom out in Cardiff, and then every evening at around 7 p.m., he would be back home, the boys turning turn up at his doorstep like the old days to record and write music.

'They started cracking the whip on me,' he says. 'It was nice to come out and have stuff to do, have purpose . . . it was like, "Right I know what I'm doing for the foreseeable future."'

In December 2014, to celebrate his release from incarceration, they headed out on the 'Benji's Back' UK tour, running through Southampton and Manchester and London and Cardiff. The restrictions of Benji's enforced curfew and electronic tag barred him from evening shows, so they improvised, playing headline slots at midday, held matinee mosh pits in crisp British daylight. They played to sold-out crowds at The Joiners in Southampton, and The Old Blue Last in East London, tore up Sound Control in Manchester, broke Benji into a new audience, and then skated home down the A48 to Cardiff for curfew.

'I felt really guilty,' Benji says of this period. 'I was making people have to come out at a stupid time because of me. I carried a lot of guilt about that because I was holding the tour back. But it made for a great story.'

A verse he wrote on the song 'Scrambled Eggs' from *CF10* captures the relief and respite of those who have been liberated from prison and climbed back out into the free world. It is a quiet meditation on the subtle qualities of freedom, the undervalued appreciations born out of a man who for more than a year had gone without it. He speaks of waking to the sounds of soulful birds singing in the trees, crooning a melody so sweet 'that I could've died'.

There is the choice to smoke weed and to fish for dates on Tinder, or to eat scrambled eggs for breakfast, and because 'there are no locks here' he says, his voice rising slightly, he's going to go outside. The instrumental distils as the song draws to its close. When the bass hollows out and the synths fade, his voice echoes back into focus. 'Somebody tell me that this is real?' he questions. 'I know how it feels. It feels like I'm free.'

*

At its essence, MC culture is an act of narration, a history of a city, a town, a country now documented and made permanent, cave paintings that linger in the ether reminding us that on this land, in this time, a community once stood. The soul of British Rap lies in these recorded accounts. And since MC culture took root on these soils decades ago, working-class kids, Black, white and Brown, from towns across the UK, have flocked to its tones, their lives glimpsed in song through this string of revolving genres.

In Grime and through UK Rap, through Garage and through Bassline and through Jungle and through UK Hip Hop, local realities have been filtered into songs, producing poignant social commentaries of people living in the shadows of towns never seen. The alternate history of Britain has been written in Rap, spokesmen and -women surfacing the lived experiences of their separate but connected localities.

CF10 was cleaved from this lineage. The EP, named after the Cardiff postcode, came in 2015, two years after *Bacon Dream*. It is a staking of territory, a claiming of turf, the boys attempting to bring Cardiff and South Wales as they had known it onto record. Built on the foundations and soundscapes ploughed deep into the earth by *Bacon Dream*, the record added new texture to the rising Astroid Boys movement. The old influences were still alive, Grime and Drum & Bass and Newport Metal, as were the youth-club aggression and lyrical fluttering of feathers. But all were now layered with something else, something deeper, encased in the smoother tones of Hip Hop and refined guitar placings, a unique sense of purpose and authority rumbling deep from the vocals.

Throughout, Phil and Benji lay rough sketchings of Cardiff over Dell's seamless harmonic productions. They take apart the dynamics and conditions of the southern arc of unemployment in the city they call home, holding them to the light of Rap's eternal flame:

'There ain't no love where I live,' Benji raps on 'Slammed 2 Razz', 'just too many kids that don't have shit.' On 'Justice', Phil screams, 'We're poor but it's lovely.'

In a BBC Radio documentary, Benji said, 'I walk through town, and I see boys that I went to school with and they are homeless and they are drug addicts. They have nothing. And when I know that the system did that to them, of course that reflects on my art and my music. My music and my lyricism is a social commentary.'[3]

By doing so, they gave voice to and made permanent the realities of a Cardiff many do not see: the towns and estates that exist beyond the idea of a green and peaceful Wales. The EP links with a string of Rap and Grime projects from this era that in union present an oral history of working-class South Wales. Then they took this message across the country.

In April and May 2015 Astroid Boys headed out on the CF10 tour. The Welsh flag, the Ddraig Goch, was draped behind a live band as they took their stories of home on the road. The cities and venues were familiar – Liverpool and Manchester, Glasgow and Bristol – but at their shows now supporters began emerging for something more than the bedlam and thrill of bodies colliding in the darkness of the dance.

The pull is explained outside a gig at The Key Club in Leeds by two friends standing in conversation. They were both university students from deprived backgrounds, one remarks, and both had gravitated into the Astroid Boys' orbit because in Phil and in Benji and in Dell they saw themselves, working-class kids refusing to play the hand they were dealt.

'The important message to grasp', from their shows and their movements, one of the girls says, 'is that no matter where you're from, no matter what your parents do, you can succeed, and you can do what you love.'

The other agrees:

'That's what Astroid Boys are about. I know that sounds stupid being a band, but a band has shown me that I can do whatever I want to do, whenever I want to do it. Because with [the] Conservative government right now I feel like your background defines you. If you can afford to pay for your school and colleges, that means you're going to get higher up in life.

'And I do feel like tonight, Astroid Boys, they do make me feel like I can get there. Like, Benji went to prison, he learned from his mistakes. You can make something of yourself no matter what you've done with your life.'[4]

There is another quiet message in *CF10*. Deep in the soul of the project there are indications of Phil changing. Somewhere along the way, on his path to pursue music, he had begun to outgrow his surroundings. There is a song on the project that perhaps best encapsulates this dynamic. 'A48 Blues', a forlorn reflection on home, sets pensive thoughts against a backdrop of the road that crosses the England–Wales border and crawls along the coastal roads, drifting from Newport into Cardiff, Cardiff down to Neath Port Talbot and the Valley towns. The song hints at sombre returns home after adrenalin-fuelled weeks chasing live crowds across the land, the intensity of touring fading and the pace of life slowing as Cardiff on the horizon welcomes him home and swallows him whole. Back where he started, in a place that never changes, a hometown that feels like it's shrinking.

'I'm from a place where man rely on spray tans, girls rely on waste-man,' Phil raps over a hazy instrumental, reflecting how 'back when I was on tour nobody could judge me to my face then'. They are the words of a man outgrowing his shell, who, by luck or by chance or by drive, had wandered out far from home and, in doing so, had begun to realise that maybe he never wanted to return.

PART III
THE BRITISH DREAM

10 **9 TO 5**

SOUTH LONDON

n Richmond, south-west of the city, out by the Thames where the water bends away from the capital in a deep-bowed blue S, young men and women gather in an office block for their first taste of the working world. They are marooned at The Listening Company, a customer-communications service that acts as an outsource for Sky TV. There they pitch cold calls, take requests from querying customers, and wait on the other end of a phone line for something that needs fixing or needs selling.

They come here from Tooting and Mitcham and Kingston, from Clapham and Norwood. Come fresh out of college and university, or seeking relief from the relentless grind of the roads. They come from everywhere, the company a stopping point and a mixing zone for the many kids of South hoping to start anew.

Here, out by the Thames, is where the lost tread water, where first-time workers begin to figure out new lives, where Cadet crash-lands in 2010 after college has ended and Gipset split and boys who once dreamt of music were scattered into the wind. He still writes poetry. He still loves Grime and Rap, wears a hoodie sometimes with *Cadet* printed on it, even releases songs from time to time. But he isn't taking it seriously any more, a pipe dream starved of action.

The Listening Company is filled with these kinds of boys, MCs with semi-retired stage names who grew up on Grime or UK Hip Hop or Garage, who once piled into studios with So Solid Crew dreams, and then turned to something else, like telesales, when reality failed to take hold of their South London longing.

Cadet is walking to his desk one day, when a boy wanders up to him and says, 'You're Cadet, right?'

Cadet points towards his hoodie, 'Yeah, man, it says it here.' The boy's name is Ashley. Some call him Bigz. He's from Mitcham. He has a younger cousin, Matt, from Tooting, who had told Ashley that Cadet works somewhere in the building. Both descend from Jamaica. They have a friend too, Adam, a Kingston boy of mixed heritage. Together they all work at The Listening Company, young men who once flirted with music, now out here in Richmond trying to find their next step.

After Cadet and Ashley's first meeting, a fondness begins to grow, starting with head nods and hellos whenever they pass, a casualness unfolding into fully bloomed friendship. Ashley, Matt and Adam meet Cadet in his wilderness years, when a music career has drifted far off downstream with Krept and Konan and some of the other boys from South who decided to stay the unsteady course. And even though he wasn't a part of things like he was a few years ago, music and Rap are still there, knitting together the quiet moments of his life.

He raps to himself while sitting at his desk. Lunchtimes, he and the boys stand outside the building and spit bars to one another. And when they grow really close and start heading out on long boys' weekends together, driving down south to Plymouth, they freestyle in the car, playing a game where they each rap one bar at a time, the next person rhyming a new lyric based on what was said previously. Other times, as they drove, they'd sit and listen to Cadet's songs.

He was levels still. All the boys could see it and hear it. Matt rolled to his music in his car. And the first time Adam saw Cadet spit, he thought, *There's something special about this guy.* Ashley too, deep down, thinking, *This guy will blow, he's just got to put the work in.*

But still, there seemed to be some internal fencing stopping him going full bat.

Maybe it was fear: there were mixtapes he made and never put out, entire catalogues that never saw the light of a proper release.

Maybe it was frustration. Sometimes in the office, people would ask Cadet why Krept, who was beginning to enjoy success in his own career, was not pulling Cadet up with him, why his cousin was seemingly beginning to prosper, and he was not. And though Cadet maybe fronted it off, Ashley could see that behind the mask, the comparisons were getting to him.

Maybe it was faith. He had converted to Islam at fifteen, like Krept and Konan and many kids in South London who grew up in that time, a shift allegedly starting in prisons and then spreading intensely among pockets of Brixton and Streatham and further afield. At The Listening Company, there were many Muslims, and Cadet would talk about religion with Adam, eventually encouraging his friend to take his Shahada, declaring a belief in the oneness of Allah.

Adam said he wasn't sure, that he was still sometimes smoking and drinking. That he was not yet ready.

'You're never going to be perfect,' Cadet told him, 'you might as well do it now.'

And so, one lunchtime soon after, they went outside the building and a colleague took Adam through the oath, officially bringing him into Islam. Ashley took his Shahada a few weeks later. Together, the boys would attend mosques in Clapham or Kingston, some days sacrificing their Friday lunchtimes to go and worship. They were committed to a new faith, staying on their deen, and because of that, Adam says, 'When you start going to the mosque and praying five times a day, the last thing you'll do is go to a studio and spit this and that.'

But Cadet still kept his MC skills sharp. He was hosting Funky House club raves put on by his childhood friend Aaron who went to

Clapham Manor primary with him, grew up into DJ Grievous and eventually started a group called 2Dark Entertainment. They hosted nights in bars scattered across Croydon, before finding a permanent home at a place called The Roxbury in the town centre. At their peak, they'd allegedly file hundreds of people into the venue every week by blasting promo over BlackBerry Messenger and flyering the city. Cadet hosted the Funky House sets, learning crowd control, tongue-rolling on the mic, experimenting with one genre while another got away from him.

UK Rap was moving forward without him. Krept and Konan were among its new pioneers. Krept was at university in Portsmouth, and so he and Cadet weren't seeing each other as much as they used to. Those Sundays at Nan's weren't routine any more, and the distance slowly drifted them apart. After everyone went their separate ways, Krept and Konan pushed on with music, becoming a duo in 2009 and continuing to build on the early school and local buzz Gipset had laid. They started with mixtapes, releasing *Red Rum* in 2009, and then *Tsunami* the year after. By this time, at the onset of their twenties, and slowly removing themselves from the madness and loss that engulfed parts of South throughout the 2000s, their music began to change. The punchlines were still present, and some of the crud too, but among it all was a heightened vulnerability, music a space for the two to reflect in as they gradually inched away from their teenage years, Rap a vessel to consider and make sense of who and what and where they came from.

Many of their releases in this time play like memoirs. 'My Hood', released on *Tsunami*, is a sombre reading of home, the two unburdening over a stripped-down instrumental. Konan speaks of single mums burying their sons and the looming threat of incarceration, Krept about encounters with police and the long list of boys from their generation who never made it to manhood, his verse a testament to the local legends whose names live on in memory and in song.

The monochrome music video cuts through the ends, capturing South London in bleak autumn, the leaves stripped from trees, puffer jackets wrapped around bodies, passing first through Gipsy Hill and the Grey Estate, home to Krept, and then nearby Thornton Heath, home to Konan. The video brings their manor to life: the high roads and the barbershops and the record stores, the estates and the friends who inhabit them, the strangers walking the street, the gravesides and the tributes to boys who rest there. This was Gipsy Hill and Thornton Heath and the wider ends as they had seen and experienced them.

An early 2011 freestyle for the *Behind Barz* series on UK Rap YouTube platform Link Up TV further captures their evolution. The two are stood in the studio, mics hovering in front of their faces, Krept with plaits and a white jumper and black shades, taller than Konan who has headphones over his head, a silver-capped tooth in his mouth and a buttoned-up shirt. An altered and refixed version of Adele's 'Hometown Glory' flows through the room. The singer-songwriter had been raised in South London for stages of her life, went to Chestnut Grove, the same school as Cadet, and wrote the song in tribute to her old neighbourhood of West Norwood. The same chords, the same keys that ran through her, were now running through them. On the freestyle, they too talk of how the deep South raised its men and women.

Krept goes first this time, opening up about his relationship with Islam and the pressures faced when trying to stay consistent with his faith, and then about the bleakness the ends exposed him to at a young age: flesh torn by blades or by bullets, elders telling youngers to wash away gunfire residue by bathing in petrol, walking out of his house one day as a kid and seeing a man dying having been shot, and how all of these things, over time, became normalised. Then there are the fallouts from his own early stumbles: the warnings from his mother he never heeded, the police raiding her house when he strayed into trouble, and the promise to one day make things right, to make her proud.

Konan's verse follows a similar path, speaking of the year he served in prison for robbery in 2007, and how he sat reckoning with life in his jail cell, thinking, *I don't wanna steal again.* There is the passing of his father, Delroy Wilson, an iconic Jamaican Reggae artist. And there is the drive that comes with not having, and how life can push a boy to the edge, can tempt kids to take dangerous risks because

'It's hard not to lose the plot
When your mum's telling you she's gonna lose her job.'

It is hometown glory and suffering, hunger and loss, a war between the internal and the external. When it was released, it touched the soul of a generation of people across Britain growing up listening to UK Rap, the boys' inward thoughts tethering them to their supporters, their songs an embrace for those in need.

Later that year, this bond grew deeper. On a late night in July 2011, Konan was approaching his family home after attending a party. As he walked towards the house, two gunmen began to pursue him, forcing their way through the front door. He ran up the stairs to his mother's room, who had been asleep with his stepdad. When inside he shut the door behind him and started shouting. His parents jolted up, and when they realised the danger, tried to hold the door closed while the gunmen kicked from the other side. But the hinges gave way. A gun was poked through the gap and then fired. The bullet struck Konan's mum, and when his stepdad chased the gunmen down the stairs, he was shot too. He passed away at the scene – Konan's mum survived. A man from South London was eventually found guilty and sentenced to thirty-five years in prison.

The harrows and traumas of that experience were purged into music. The following Mother's Day in 2012, Konan covered Drake's 'Look What You've Done'. Sitting next to a pianist he delicately unloads his grief. His usual energetic delivery has been replaced by a near whisper, his stress relieved over tearful piano keys that hold his cracking voice:

'When times have been the hardest
You're the light to my darkness
I lost two dads, you lost two partners
That would've made anyone heartless.'

Not long after the shooting, the boys freestyled over Jay-Z and Kanye's 'Otis', reverting to type with a volley of punchlines like they were in school days. They shot the video in Crystal Palace Park, a lightness and a playfulness present as the two pretend to battle with boxing gloves and a string of props. It felt like an off-the-cuff free-style, something they could enjoy while personal lives behind the scenes had been cast into turmoil. But it became their first break out, going viral on YouTube and climbing to five million views in a matter of days before a cease-and-desist letter allegedly came in from Jay-Z's legal team and the video had to be removed.

But with new eyes watching, they doubled down, and released another punchline-heavy track, 'Paranormal Activity', in September of the same year, their music spreading out of London, following the So Solid trail into homes across the country. Something was building.

Cadet was still spitting on and off too at this time. There was a bitterness simmering with his cousin, who he felt was not throwing spotlight on his music. Sometimes the sourness would seep into his songs, where he'd throw shots at his former best friend. Overall, he had fallen into a habit. He would release music, it would connect, and just when an opportunity to build presented itself, when it felt as if now was the time to capitalise on open ears, he would let it slip, not drop again for months, potential buzzes slipping away into regrets of what could have been.

After 'Paranormal Activity' came out, Cadet dropped his own remix, which climbed to 20,000 views in one week, and received a flow of accolades from treasured and respected rappers across the scene. He messaged the Brotherhood group chat, asking them to make sure he kept consistent this time. Ashley and others at work told him to turn the screw, that now was the time to up the work rate. He dropped a few more videos, and then lapsed, disappearing from the scene and back into the world of work.

Krept and Konan stayed on. The buzz had seen high-profile MC Skepta bring them on tour, and in July of 2012 they were booked for Wireless Festival, a rare Rap act among a sea of guitar-band music and Grime MCs who had gone pop. They played the Bandcamp stage, crowded on a line-up among bands and vocalists who had fleeting seasons as musicians in that summer before disappearing back into anonymity. It was a stage where little was expected. American Rap giant Wiz Khalifa had been billed at the same time, and pop star Labrinth was performing his set simultaneously too. Krept and Konan were supposed to be fodder, throwaway acts rounding out the festival.

But their set reeled in hundreds of screaming teenagers who knew every word to every song and freestyle. Some were wearing Krept and Konan's 'Play Dirty' merch. Other teenagers clambered over the metal gates to meet them backstage. And when they brought out Sneakbo and Political P from Brixton, and their friend Yungen from Herne Hill, who went to Chestnut Grove, the crowd knew all of their songs too. It was the start of something, an early showing to a distant music industry about what was coming down the line, that in working-class communities across the country there were young

MCs and rappers drawing legions of loyal listeners. They could only be overlooked for so much longer.

Krept and Konan were a part of this reckoning, among those whose music and whose following forced the issue. In 2013, their mixtape *Young Kingz* debuted in the Top 20 of the Official Albums Chart, landing them a Guinness World Record for the highest charting UK album by an unsigned act.

It included street anthem 'Don't Waste My Time', which, like 'Talkin the Hardest' by Peckham's Giggs, and 'Touch Ah Button' by Brixton's Sneakbo, etched itself into South London folklore, ringing out on the roads across the region. The video was shot on the ends. Everyone came out for it, young men who used to MC, witnessing their two friends, who were in many senses just like them, take steps into territory they never thought possible.

The equaliser to this was 'My Story', and its accompanying video. It was a recalling of the shooting in 2011, Konan giving a vulnerable account of that evening and the brutal weeks that followed. He plays himself in the video, retracing his own footsteps, acting out the dart into the house, the family holding the door on the hinges, and the gunshots. A stepfather lost, a mother wounded, lives changed. 'It should've been me but it's him lying there,' he raps.

Krept's verse takes in the aftermath of that night, the shock, the anger, the fear, and how among it all their rising music careers gave them an avenue to direct their focus towards. Through laying their traumas bare, the two had bonded themselves to the people growing up alongside them in South London, as well as their new listeners wading in across the city and the country, the boys' grief and darkest moments shared on the public stage, lifted to light by the close gathering of their growing, loyal supporters.

And with it, the first recognition from the industry landed. At the 2013 MOBO Awards they won the award for Best Newcomer, claiming the prize by public vote. They collected the award on stage with their friends, an audience cheering on loudly in the background. Back home, the boys and girls of South London were watching, ambitions broadening again with dreams and visions of what Krept and Konan had made possible.

Stormzy, the MC from Norbury who went to the same school as Krept, was working in an oil refinery in Southampton at the time. Watching his childhood friends win the award on the telly, he sat thinking to himself, *What? Why can't I spit and get a MOBO?* He quit his job a few months later, came back to London and started again seriously with music. The areas around Croydon and deep South are filled with stories like this, two local boys the torchbearers for the kids whose music dreams nagged at them in their daylight hours.

11 **BROKE**

SOUTH WALES

For seven years they fashioned songs about the young and the excluded in the margins of South Wales, and took their cross-bred sounds and empty pockets to stage shows across Britain. So they called their only album *Broke*.

It was 2017, a time when Grime and UK Rap burst inner-city valves and spilled over middle Britain like floodwater. A time of renaissance, when the kids from the youth clubs and Sound Systems and Pirate stations seeped their music into the fabric of contemporary British youth culture. A time when the MCs and rappers out of London abandoned the fatiguing pursuit of pop-music playlists, and instead joined arms with their distant brothers and sisters from the regions, together sitting on the frontlines of the sounds they had collectively built for decades. A time when British MCs and rappers began to first gain commercial success on their own terms, where they were forming their own record labels and the traditional music industry began scrambling for these Black British working-class genres.

Many artists were being signed in this period, scrawled ink signatures wetting paper, and champagne glass kissing champagne glass in the record label offices on High Street Kensington. East London's J Hus signed to Black Butter Records, a division of Sony Music UK. Lotto Boyzz of Birmingham signed with Columbia. Krept and Konan were with Virgin EMI. Yungen with RCA. Astroid Boys signed to Music For Nations in November 2016, a Rock and Metal imprint of Sony Music UK who had shuttered in 2004 after a period of sustained success throughout the eighties and nineties.

They relaunched in 2015. Astroid Boys were their flagship signing.

Phil and Benji announced the deal in a short video uploaded to Facebook. It was nightfall and they were stood outside a kebab shop in Cathays. Phil looked into the camera, smiling, while Benji floated in and out of shot. A few boys hovered in the foreground, one with a thick gold chain glinting in the darkness. Phil said: 'Basically we signed a deal with Music for Nations at Sony and we've got an album coming out next year. We've been working hard, and we're about to drop some new music. So, there you go, that's like an announcement innit. Tell your family and friends.'

It was the season when I deepened my work as a journalist, covering Grime and UK Rap, seeing British MC culture flower in the regions. I went across the UK stalking its trail, seeing the music unfurl across the country. There were the afternoons I spent in Birmingham with Despa and Jaykae and Dapz, the evenings at stage shows in London when supporters turned up in their hundreds and their thousands to venues in Camden and Kentish Town. The nights in small basement clubs glimpsing the musicians who, in a few years, would evolve into the defining artists of their day.

From that time, an afternoon in the North of England sticks in the memory. I was in Manchester with Bugzy Malone, an MC who had broken out of the city and altered perceptions of what a rapper from outside of London could become. By the end of 2018, Bugzy had four projects, all released on his own label, all debuting in the Top 10 of the Official Albums Chart. Three are now certified Silver with over 60,000 sales each. He had sold out his own tour. He had YouTube views in the millions. He had partnered with JD Sports on a clothing line, and when they unveiled the collection with an instore meet-and-greet at the Manchester Arndale – the eighth biggest shopping centre in the UK, which sits at the heart of the city – the queue stretched from the store through the shopping mall of 155,200 square feet and out into the street. He was on the road to becoming one of Grime's first self-made millionaires. He was among the most successful artists of his time. He was an ex-career criminal, who, during the British Rap renaissance of the last decade, had become among the most popular contemporary artists in Northern England.

That afternoon in Manchester we drove the timeline of his life while he filmed a vlog for his YouTube channel. We stopped in his old boxing gym where the walls were peeling, the trophy cabinets were coated in dust, and where legend has it that the famous Fury boxing family once honed their skills. After leaving the gym, we drove out to his old estate in Cheetham Hill, where in the decades before Bugzy lived among the low-rise flats and terraced red-brick homes. I hovered around while he filmed with childhood friends Lyndon Arthur and Zelfa Barrett, boxers who would go on to have successful careers in the sport, and listened in as they reminisced on their childhood years wandering around the walkways and rambling grass patches that outlined their early kingdom.

It was late afternoon, and the estate was quiet, and yet every so often a stranger would notice Bugzy standing at the kerb and wander over in disbelief. They quivered in his presence, called their young sons and daughters from their homes, and then drifted to his side like pilgrims.

One said, 'I think I drove past you the other day in town . . . But I wasn't sure if it was you, I was looking in the window, thinking, "It can't be!"'

Another man came to his side and said, 'I just want to shake your hand, man. You're representing Manchester, bro.'

School kids waved. Some widened their eyes in disbelief, shocked that the King of the North, as he was called, an emblem of this changing country, was standing in an old housing estate on the outskirts of the city. But he was like them, the brick council flats of Manchester in his veins.

A few minutes later, the second man returned with his mother. She seemed to be in her sixties, and frail. She gracefully shook Bugzy's hand. The three posed for a picture, and after, the boy turned to her and said, pride swelling in his lungs, 'He's putting Manchester on the map, Mum.'

And it was like that all across the United Kingdom. Artists and MCs emerging out of anonymous towns and housing estates, bonded together by sound, and detailing the routines of their lives, the frictions of their days, offering hope to those who listened. I met rappers from Harlesden and music managers from Northampton. Brothers who MCed from estates in Ipswich, a boy named Shogun on the outskirts of Glasgow. There was Aystar in Liverpool. Ransom in Aberdeen. Astroid Boys in South Wales.

And so, in many ways, *Broke* is a relic of that time, a product of a scene's loud emergence from the shadows, British Rap's entrance into a space alongside traditions such as boxing and football as tools for the country's marginalised young people to work day-dreams into golden realities. They were kids in a changing world, and as they moved with it, pulled by the momentum of the time, pushed by the bravery of the past, they captured the climate of the moment in sound and in song. It was the British Dream made manifest. *Broke* is one of many testaments to that historic homecoming.

Astroid Boys recorded elements of *Broke* in the Freedom Church, rooted in a large warehouse on the quiet no man's land of an indus-trial estate that sits between the docks and the city centre, between Cardiff central and the water. The warehouse had steel frames and iron rutters fanning the roof, and in the evening dusk it stood lonely like a large army barracks silhouetted against an ashen sky. On a given weekday back then you could drift in through its glass doors, past the empty main hall the size of a small auditorium where the pastor practises his sermons to the ghosts of next Sunday's congregation. Up the staircases, on grey breeze blocks, is a collection of small national flags, a world map dotted with the homelands of their multinational Cardiff congregation and a sign that reads 'Anyone, Anywhere'. On the first floor in a side room, you may once have found the boys, huddled together, saving on their label budget by recording songs of South Wales longing in a holy house.

They wrote and recorded songs while prayer meetings wafted through the thin ceilings, even shot a never-released music video in another side room. The connection to the Freedom Church was through Phil. God first came to him in the ocean all those years ago. But even epiphany takes time; no profound change is sudden. Faith flowers gently, like oak seed into forest.

When he was young, before Cyprus and the band, his mother was declared disabled. She recovered into full health. The family determined it a miracle. God found her way in through this divine reconciliation, and in its aftermath, a family waded into the church. As the years in the band progressed, from *Bacon Dream* to *CF10*, *CF10* to *Broke*, Phil's faith began to deepen. He began reading up on Scriptures, learning the Bible for himself, was baptised at twenty-five while his boys watched on in the congregation shouting 'Brapp! Brapp!' as the pastor dunked his head into holy water. Eventually he began frequenting local churches. This Freedom Church on the outlands of an industrial estate was among that handful.

You can chart this shift in his music, the anarchic notes of old softening into subtle preaching as faith took hold. On *Broke* he still clambered over Dell's misfit instrumentals but with a religious refinement, his changing outside world feeling its way in, his words treading a righteous path on a first and final Astroid Boys album.

Before *Broke* was released, Astroid Boys unveiled a string of singles. Among them was 'Foreigners'. It was written at a time when the UK was wrestling with the wreckage of Brexit and the growing Black Lives Matter movement, which had begun to stir in 2016 after the killing of two Black men by police in America resulted in summer protests across the UK, led by minority communities speaking out en masse against racial inequality. In Cardiff, protestors marched through the city centre on a summer Saturday afternoon.

'Foreigners', Dell says, was written in response to this tension, a statement of solidarity from a mostly white band who felt that as participants in Black music they needed to use their voice and platform to speak out. On the song, Phil and Benji and featured rapper Sonny Double 1 from Cardiff by way of Libya step onto their erected podium, shedding new light on the time-worn frictions between ethnic minorities and the Welsh state, between the 'foreigners' and the Establishment.

In the music video they stand on the city steps, foreigners in their home city. There are maybe forty young men and women in the video, siblings from the extended Astroid Boys family. Together, they are all dressed in black tracksuits and thick hoods covering Afro hair. They have dreads falling softly by earlobes, gold-hooped earrings dangling by brown jaws. They are bobbing to a tense, brooding melody, and are howling lyrics of defiance and unity into the Cardiff night. They are from Wales. They are from Cyprus and Greece and Jamaica and Libya. They are from Cardiff and Newport, from Grangetown and Tremorfa, from St Mellons and St Julians, their song a reminder that, in a piece of land that has for a century been dominated and shaped by the steady waves of migration, beneath the markers of skin colour, they are all wanderers in a foreign place. Everybody comes from somewhere. Black and minority communities in Wales have long taken a stand for their people.

———

I once took a journey to the old heart of Black Wales. The way to Butetown Community Centre is to head south from the Cardiff Central train station and follow the roads down to the water like a turtle beckoned towards sea. You walk under the railway bridge and across the industrial flats of the A470 roundabout where steel skeletons of new-build apartments and offices staircase the skyline. You walk, as the sun shimmers in a dull sky and the wind wraps around the city like a wet blanket, into an alleyway that leads to a narrow path with a muddy canal running parallel. And as you leave the centre of the city behind, glass-panelled buildings crumble to industrial lots tagged in graffiti, dusty cars are parked, or abandoned, on cracking back roads.

Follow the lonely path south, until you see hints of community distilling into view. At the end of the path, you hit a mosque and some low-rise, yellow-brick flats, and then Canal Park where Tiger Bay FC, the local football team erected by first- and second-generation Somali immigrants, play their home games on Saturday afternoons. Their football field marks Butetown pulling in from the near distance. I had reached ground zero, a stronghold, a quiet enclave moored somewhere between the city and the water, historic territory where one of Britain's oldest Black communities claims its home.

The path opens out onto Loudon Square, a large estate where looming tower blocks cut against bruising sky in the heart of an area that for so long had been the settling ground for immigrants who came in from the seas. For more than a century, immigrants had waded into Cardiff from the bay, settled among these roads and remade the land in their image, carving a Black presence on Welsh soil. The old neighbourhood at one stage stretched another kilometre south until pebble beaches met the sea, but now, in this new era, these estates and flats were all that remained, a close community in refuge, Somalis and old Caribbean families, Yemenis and Sudanese living quietly in the shadows of the new, regenerated Cardiff Bay.

It was a weekday afternoon. The estate was dormant. Seagulls circled overhead, drifting in from the water, raiding down on the paving, where a man in an ankle-length robe and a white kufi scattered the road with bread scraps and seeds. On a corner of the square was Butetown Community Centre, where elderly Black Welsh community members sometimes gather on these weekdays for coffee and conversation. An exhibition about the history in Tiger Bay and Butetown and the Cardiff docks was being held in the space, the community banding together to gather their presence on the tip of South Wales into concrete archive.

It was hosted in the main room, a space the size of a school assembly hall with stations pulled out across the floor, each decorated in the specific details of their rooted history. The exhibition detailed the different communities' origin stories, and was translated in English and Welsh, breathing life into the early West African and Caribbean, Yemeni and Somali and Greek and Malaysian settlers who arrived in a foreign land and began to build a home. There were wedding photos more than a hundred years old, showing nomadic seamen of many continents pledging their love and their lives and their future to this small town by the docks.

At the exhibition's far end was a sprawling mural made in tribute to the victims of the Windrush scandal, the Black British residents mainly of Caribbean descent who were wrongly detained, deported and denied legal rights by the Home Office. Flags of the Caribbean and Africa dotted the wall canvas, and young women were painted in protest along the bottom, gripping signs that read:

WE FOREIGN WHEN DEM DECIDE IT'S TIME FOR WE TO GO.

NO JUSTICE, NO PEACE.

POWER TO US, WE ALWAYS FIND A WAY.

A family bruised but not broken, siblings scattered across a hostile country, loosely tied by faint memories of home, our shared stories blending into one.

After the exhibition, I walked through the estate, stopped at a small Yemeni restaurant on the corner of Loudon Square where locals broke bread over white tables, and after the restaurant I walked down Bute Street and on towards the bay and the old docks to meet Keith Murrell, a pioneer and longstanding resident, an activist in the city, a descendant of those early seamen.

He was a light-skinned man in his sixties, born and bred in Tiger Bay. By the time his generation came of age in the seventies and eighties, coal had waned in global influence and prosperity had long left the docks. The area had been renamed Butetown and a close community endured a difficult period. The economic heart had been torn from Cardiff's chest. The old docks were rotting after decades of disuse and disrepair; now just mudflats and wastelands growing weeds where ships had once docked. By the nineties, unemployment was high among the working-class areas across the southern sections of the city, and Butetown was isolated from the rest of the city in location, and in character.

And so, their community was often ridiculed by media as a dangerous no-go zone for the rest of Cardiff. This dynamic meant that in 1990, it endured one of Britain's greatest miscarriages of justice when a local sex worker, Lynette White, was stabbed to death in the area and five Black and mixed-race men of Butetown were wrongfully accused of her murder. They were known as the Cardiff Five.

During the trial, the prosecuting QC David Elfer mocked Butetown and the docks 'as a place where knives are worn as part of the clothing, as a place where the arm of the police and criminal law don't run very far . . . an upside-down world. When we go home from work, they get up and go to clubs, then when we get up to go to work, they return home to sleep.'[1]

They were Welsh. They were foreigners. They were outsiders.

Three of the five were sentenced to life imprisonment, their convictions eventually quashed on appeal two years later after waves of protests and a retrial exposed the corruption of the South Wales police force.

A resident remarked at the time that, 'It weren't just them that was on trial, it was the whole community . . . They don't know who killed Lynette White. [So] *anybody* will do, and they thought we were just *anybodies*. But they made a big mistake down here because we're *somebodies*, we're not *anybodies*.'[2]

Keith and I sat at the steps of the Welsh Assembly, a mass structure, home to the chambers of the Welsh parliament and built in a five-year span during the aftermath of the country's political devolution from Westminster in 1997. It has a glass-panelled frame exposing its interior and a sprawling steel roof that extends over the steps like the brim of a flat cap.

The building rests on the edges of Cardiff Bay and looks out into the water and across the mouth of the Severn Estuary. As we sat, the rain coming in, the streets quieted by its downpour, our clothes shielded by the unfurled steel roof, we could stare out over this small stretch of land and water, where the waves quietly broke on the shore and see a place that had, for over a century, been Wales's meeting point with the world.

'The thing connects right down to the waterfront and actually into the water architecturally,' Keith told me about the building. 'The notion is that this is Wales looking outward, a new modern Wales looking outward.'

He had been born a few hundred feet from where we sat, and was a product of the Tiger Bay melting pot. His grandfather had come from Barbados in the early twentieth century, a sea worker in ship engine rooms who settled with an English woman running a local boarding house. Keith had Barbados and England and Norway and the Philippines and Wales in his blood. He had half-siblings of Taiwanese descent, in-laws from Ireland and Somalia, Egypt and Jamaica. He remembers when Sound Systems rattled Reggae on the street corners, and Jazz and Bluebeat, Calypso and Soul wafted out from the houses.

He remembers how, back then, the nightclubs in the bay, like the Casablanca Club, playing Soul and R&B and Reggae and Blues, were the only hosts of Black music in a time when the term was a dirty word. He remembers how there were small-scale riots in 1981 when police raided a venue and smashed up their Sound Systems, and remembers how the council tore the community to pieces in the final slum clearances of the nineties. He is a docks boy at heart, a man relocated who now lives a few towns along. His is a true Tiger Bay story.

In our conversation by the Assembly steps, the water stretching beyond us, a blue mass melting into the pink of a setting sun out on the horizon, he told me how music arrived in waves from Black settlers moving in from across the Atlantic: the Black American GIs who moored at the ports during the Second World War, bringing Jazz and Blues, Reggae coming in from Jamaica, steel pans and Soca from Trinidadian immigrants who arrived as part of the Windrush generation.

These sounds from across the Black diaspora, and the docks they found home in, would supply building blocks for music in Tiger Bay and Butetown. They had Reggae clubs and Blues Parties. Shirley Bassey was born in the neighbourhood in the 1930s, and legendary Welsh singer Patti Flynn came shortly after. Keith assisted in establishing Butetown Carnival, which still runs today.

He wanted to tell me the story of its origin.

When they were young, during the 1970s, the Butetown Youth Club entered Caribbean-themed floats into the Lord Mayor's Parade in Cardiff alongside institutions like the Boy Scouts and trooping bands. One year, as the docks boys and girls passed through the parade, a racist comment was thrown out from the crowd. They reacted by confronting their aggressors and were subsequently banned for the following year. So, they began a carnival of their own in Butetown, inspired by the wave of similar Caribbean carnivals that were being hosted in cities across Britain, such as Leeds and Manchester and London's Notting Hill throughout the seventies.

Butetown Carnival became a permanent fixture on the calendar in 1977, and every August Bank Holiday weekend the roads would ring with Sound Systems and New Orleans-style brass bands, processions and parades along Bute Street. As the decades passed, its popularity grew, peaking with a rumoured attendance of 25,000 people per day in an area that housed only 4,000.

Black bands and performers would come from across the country to play the carnival, infusing golden memories in generations of kids who grew up in its wake. In Cardiff, people from wider ethnic minorities would participate. Phil's Greek mum played drums on the floats while he wandered around the fields and the parades as a young boy. Butetown Carnival, like so many carnivals across Britain, planted seeds for the music and genres of today, a link in a chain of Black music on these shores, combing in sounds of the diaspora and tinting their tones in a Black Welsh dye.

'When other music came from the Islands or West Africa,' Keith said, 'we would be like, "That's ours." And it may not be my grandfather's, it might be my friends' grandfathers' [but] it would be embedded into the community.

'There's something about us being open always to the influences but also being settled enough to do something with it and make it our own . . . It's the movement that brings it, it's the settlement that does something with it . . . This is the docks, this is what we fucking do. It's all we've ever done, that's how this fucking place works.'

After a while, when the rain had stopped and the streets started to reanimate, Keith turned and asked me a question. He wanted to tell me a story, wanted me to understand the distinctive dynamics of the docks and Black Wales.

'What's your background?' he said.

I replied, 'My mum's from Cameroon and my dad's from Nigeria.'

'I don't know about the history of Cameroon so much,' he said, 'but Nigerians were *here* before *Nigeria* was here.'

And then I listened as he told me his story.

In a photograph dated 1917 from his grandfather's wedding at St Mary's Church in Butetown there are Black groomsmen and white bridesmaids. A while back, Keith posted the photo to Facebook and a lady living out in America got in touch. She was eighty-five years old and a GI bride, a Welsh woman of mixed heritage who had married a Black American soldier stationed in Tiger Bay during the war. She recognised her father as one of the groomsmen in the photograph.

He was born in Calabar, she said, a port city in Southern Nigeria, not far from my own father's homeland and village.

He was born in a place and time when they had no birth certificates and was estimated to be a hundred years old now.

His existence pre-dates Nigeria, a country still only around sixty years old, a mass region where over 250 ethnic groups were crowbarred into one nation state during the aftershocks of the British Empire.

At thirteen or fourteen years of age, he fled his grandmother's farm in Calabar and bolted for the sea, stowing away on a ship and finding himself in Newport, before moving along the coastal roads into Cardiff, appearing as a groomsman in the photograph along-side Keith's grandfather, West Africans and Caribbean people in early union.

The homeland he had left was still half a century away from inde-pendence and the forming of a new nation. He was a Calabar man before he was anything else, Welsh before he was ever Nigerian.

The man, unnamed, spent his working life in South Wales as a seaman, toiled in the merchant navy through the World Wars and received medals for his service. After retiring at seventy-five, a coun-tryman arrived from Nigeria, seeking to bring him back home, back to a country he had never known.

'I'm at home,' came the reply. 'Apart from the weather,' he report-edly added, 'this is my home.'

We sat for a moment, quietly, Keith in his sixties, Bajan in descent, alongside myself, the coastal regions of Nigeria in my blood, both staring out at the sea like his grandfather and his groomsman likely did a century ago. The waves broke on the shore. The wind echoed off the roof, the daylight receded quietly into dusk. Eventually, Keith spoke again.

'The story', he said, about his opinion on the Black presence in Wales, 'is a success story.'

———

Astroid Boys was a breakthrough for Rap in South Wales. *Broke* was their message. In those golden years when Grime and UK Rap con-tinued to surface on the shores of mainstream Britain, MCs would arrive on the scene from working-class regions across the coun-try, curling their way around ragged instrumentals as they drifted into focus. Yorkshire, South Wales, South London, Glasgow, West Midlands. Their conditions the same. Their pain shared. Black and working-class stories moving through the spirits of poets we have come to call MCs, their songs a vessel for the unheard, a choral voice refining in silence for generations until a moment like this one laid their stories bare to the world.

'We were young kids listening to a sound that kind of reflected how we were feeling,' said Benji at the time in a BBC documentary. 'Suffocated.'[3]

Broke, released on 29 September 2017, carries South Wales in its soul. It is biographical in places, sees Phil reflect on the life he had left behind, the violence in his teenage days, the friendships of MCD, the dangers he had seen of the roadside. It sees Benji touch on the prison stint, on the days when he would tag the city in graffiti, give perspective on the communal mentalities that have taken root in a scatter of their marginalised CF postcodes. In theme, it is Cardiff at its core, a coming-of-age novel about the moulding of a generation. Songs like 'Raz' are named after South Wales slang words. Mace, an MC from Splott, and Sonny Double 1 from Grangetown are two of the three features. The boys slip in references to Cardiff dress code and Cardiff war stories.

The production wanders through the influences that dominated their upbringings. Over the twelve songs, Dell's instrumentals weave their Cardiff stories into cohesion, pulling their scattered genre palette into one. Grime feeling its way into Metal. Metal feeling its way into Rap. Electronic Music and Rock and stoner Hip Hop pushing and pulling together in this unruly dance. On the pulsing guitars and drum clashes of 'Dirt', a Metal and Rock blend hand-crafted for stage shows, Phil slips into the rhyme patterns of Grime pioneers Flirta D and D Double E, paying homage over guitar riffs and dark drums. This album, these songs, is where isolated genres meet.

Its release marked a shift. With *Broke* and the work that had come before it – the stage shows across the country, the three projects, the major label signings and the music videos dotted with sons and daughters of the ends – a new image of South Wales was presented to the country. It was a South Wales that resembled South London and South Liverpool, Moss Side and Handsworth. Working-class areas, home to boys of all ethnicities. The soft satire and stigma of comedy bands like Goldie Lookin Chain that, for almost two decades, had set a cast-iron image of Rap in Wales, began to give way.

Whenever Phil and Benji headed east across the Severn Bridge into studio sessions and radio broadcasts in London, Cardiff boys in the English capital, they would hear remarks about a Wales they did not recognise; were told that the country was rural and unassuming – as if its sum total was the green farms and fields and herded livestock of the North. They were judged and written off by those who did not know the country as they did.

But in *Broke*, South Wales was estate kids. *Broke* was brown and black and Greek faces and the tail-ends of immigrant family trees. It was their country as it was. It was home told by those who had lived it. It was a signal of Black music in Wales forcing itself into the national conversation.

They took these stories across Europe. In January 2018 they played their music to the Dutch at a festival in Groningen. In February, supporting Rock band Hollywood Undead, they trailed through the continent, rolling into Munich and Warsaw, Budapest and Bologna and Zurich. With legendary Punk band Trash Talk, they did the same, touring across Europe.

Elsewhere, they had unravelled the album's meanings in magazine and radio interviews, had shot and released videos; had worked brand campaigns and editorial shoots, worked intensely on promoting their debut album. Their South Wales story would be heard.

Then, six months after *Broke* had been released, they went back home, back to the city that had served as their oral canvas, back to the city from which they had pulled their stories and identities like flowers from the earth, back to the Welsh capital to attend the 2018 edition of the annual Cardiff Music Awards.

On the night the boys crowded into TramShed, a music and arts venue that sits by the banks of the River Taff in town. Cardiff's tight-knit music industry and a sea of paying punters were crammed into the audience. The award show, erected to celebrate the sprawl of talent emerging from the city, had received over 3,000 nominations. The organisers had carved the harvest into a shortlist of twenty categories, and the boys had rolled onto the stage to collect the awards for Best Album and Best Group.

They were leaning over a makeshift podium. Benji was in a black sweater and a woolly hat, clutching their trophy in his fingers, animated. Dell stands on stage too. Phil, in a bomber jacket and a skin fade, held the microphone close in his palm. Among the yelps and whistles of the gathered audience he began speaking to the room:

'It's sick that there's an awards thing going on in Cardiff,' he said, looking out over the crowd, riding the cheers drifting in over the arena floor. 'But I have to say, I think there's a whole scene that's being neglected, a whole urban music sector of this city which is absolutely massive.'

He continued:

'Massive shout-out to Cardiff Music Awards for putting this whole thing on. We're grateful for the award and everything, but there's a whole scene that needs to be recognised, so next year let's see that scene in here, involved.' He paused. 'There are so many people out there, that need to be in here.'

———

Astroid Boys and their extended family shot the 'Foreigners' video on the city steps.

Before the visual fades to black, the video trails over a series of cutaways. Standing outside family homes and by wrought-iron gates, in darkened rooms and on front porches flanking residential streets, they gather on South Wales soil with their loved ones. Hanging in the foreground are pinned home flags of their motherlands. There is Dell with his old man, the sky-blue and white of the Greek flag looming over Brussalis father and son. Benji and his younger brother stand in union, Jamaica's black, green and gold cross, and the whites, reds and blues of the Union flag spread out behind them. Sonny Double 1 is shrouded by Libya's tricolour. Harry and Comfort sit beside the Ddraig Goch.

They are from Britain. They are from Wales. They are from Greece and Jamaica and Libya. They are from Cardiff and Newport, from Grangetown and Tremorfa, from St Mellons and St Julians. As they've always known, everybody comes from somewhere.

Phil stands with his mother. They are outside a house on a residential road. His arm is curled over her shoulder, the white, gold and green of Cyprus hanging over their front door. The two stare down the lens while the music fades.

12 **THE 7**

SOUTH LONDON

The Listening Company laid everyone off at the Richmond office. The boys went separate ways after that. But they remained tight. Ashley and Matt went into security. Adam's partner had a baby on the way, and he was about to be a dad. He found a job in Croydon. Cadet went through a few jobs. He worked as an estate agent at one time, and as a will-writer at another. He tried to start a business with Matt, buying and selling cars, but that went left when the first car they bought at auction turned out to be stolen and they had to get their money back. So he moved on and tried something else, another job, while still dabbling in music every now and then.

For a long time, Cadet worked at the betting shop William Hill. He had gritted through many jobs but this one was the worst. 'A legal crackhouse',[1] is how he described it. There was a sad sense of a full circle about it too. Years ago, when he was still a boy, still in school, still a big dreamer, he had walked down Clapham High Street with Tech, past a Ladbrokes, and spoke passionately on the big dreams he had for his life.

He had wanted to be someone back then, to push his efforts into something that meant more. But here he was, threatening to become the thing he feared. Something started to gnaw at him. He was working for nothing else but the month ahead, cheque to cheque, and shift to shift. He was working for a faceless business owner he would never meet. He was paid what the company decided, not what he wanted or valued himself at. And one time, when he called in sick, he was asked to prove that he was ill.

Yes, he was faking it. But it was the principle, he thought. They breathed the same air he breathed, walked the same earth he walked, fell in love how he fell in love, got sick how he got sick. They were no better than him, and yet he still had to prove his state of health. Through it all, he realised that he had no control over his life, realised that in his current position, even if he stepped up his work rate, or yearned for more money, what he could earn was capped at the number of hours he could get.

The music he was putting out in this period reflected this flux. On freestyles he was rapping like the old Cadet, like the Gipset Cadet, about beef and violence and causing terror on the roads. But in truth, his life had not been like that for a while. He had grown up and out of the streets. He hadn't been involved in beef for years. Like he said in one line on a freestyle in January 2015, when the occasional truth about how he was living found its way onto riddims, 'I work in William Hill nigga, yes.'

He was twenty-four and seemed a man caught between worlds, his music leaning heavily on who he once was, and his dreams trying to scurry away from where he was actually at. Something had to give.

There were two incidents that changed things.

Jamal Edwards had been running his YouTube channel SBTV for almost ten years. Since 2006, the West London boy had recorded a generation of MCs and musicians across the country. The early Grime and Rap scenes were diarised on his videos, the channel a platform for the emerging and hungry to make a name for themselves.

By 2015, he had amassed views in the millions and a subscriber base in the hundreds of thousands. He had branched out from just Rap, too. He had filmed an anonymous kid from Suffolk called Ed Sheeran, helping Ed walk the road to become one of the world's highest-selling musicians. And then he helped break platinum-selling vocalists Jessie J and Emeli Sandé too, becoming a celebrity himself during the process, accepting an MBE, starring in Google adverts, developing links with Richard Branson, starting a record label with Sony Music, and releasing a self-help book with Virgin Books. In 2015, the *Sunday Times* Rich List estimated his worth to be £8 million.

Despite all of this, the core of him remained Grime and UK Rap. And the focal point of SBTV was its freestyle formats F64 and Warm Up Sessions. The set-up was simple: an instrumental played and an MC freestyled over it. Cadet, who like many in the scene had known Jamal for a while, met him to film a Warm Up Session. At the shoot, Cadet spat a few minutes of crud, his lyrics still looking backwards and pulling on the threads of who he used to be. When they finished up, Jamal said the video would be out in two weeks.

But a fortnight passed, and there was no video. Then another a week, and still nothing. Text messages with no reply. Then a month went by, no response. When two months had passed, Cadet sent Jamal a long, angry text message, saying that Jamal shouldn't take him for a clown, that those bars could've been used for another video, that it's been months now with no movement. Jamal replied and said that he liked the freestyle, but felt like it wasn't truthful, that he didn't feel the words mirrored who Cadet really was or how he was living today.

In response Cadet said he would rewrite the session and bring in his truth. They shot the retake near the SBTV offices in Regent Street. Cadet is wearing a pink polo top. He has a beard stretching from his earlobes to his chin, and slits in a fresh fade. When the instrumental kicks in, he looks inward, starting with the conversation with Jamal and how the man holding the camera had told him:

'Your last freestyle was all rage
But now I want to know the cause for the flame
I don't want to hear about gold like first place
I wanna know how it feels when you're in your worst place
Don't wanna hear about a weapon and a burst face
Wanna know why you wanna burst it in the first place.'

And then he told his story, about his dad, about pain and rage, about the allergies and eczema he suffered as a kid, about the metal plate he had inserted in his arm, about Clapham and Gipsy Hill and paranoia from the roads, about old-school days freestyling with Krept, and the subtle tension that had wedged them apart in recent years. The freestyle was Cadet at his most honest. For him it felt like a release. When the session was uploaded and posted online, it blew up, listeners gravitating to his openness. It changed the way he would approach music as well as writing, and was one of two moments that year that changed his life. The other was Wireless Festival.

Krept and Konan's success set off a trigger in the ends. From there, younger rappers from Croydon and the deep South began to emerge, following the prints the boys had left in the earth, moving from the edges of the scene and the city to centre stage. Throughout 2015, they defined UK Rap.

Stormzy, who had watched them claim the award that night from his temporary home in Southampton, was back in London now. In the two years that had passed, he had risen in the slipstream of a resurgent Grime scene. His songs, like 'Not That Deep' and 'Know Me From', and his mixtape *Dreamers Disease* had captured the moment. In 2014, a year after Krept and Konan, he claimed his own MOBO Award for Best Grime Act. What followed was an abnormal rise, Stormzy cresting a crowded UK Rap and Grime scene, becoming a star of South London, then taking things further, his sound streaming into white working- and middle-class communities across the country. He had tipped the scales, a Black British MC who had crossed over without warping himself or his music. By 2015, he was carving away at an awakening industry, landing third on the BBC Sound List of 2015 and walking out Anthony Joshua at the O2 Arena for the boxer's fight vs Brixton's Dillian Whyte. His journey was only beginning.

Elsewhere his cousin Nadia Rose, half-Ghanaian and half-Jamaican, broke to a national Rap audience via SBTV. She grew up on the Whitehorse Road Estate in Croydon, juggling university while working in betting shops on Croydon High Street, writing her lyrics on the betting slips. Then her song 'Station' caught a wave, and she rode it into a record deal and hundreds of thousands of views. 'Skwod', her first single proper, was shot on a high street in the borough, home never far off.

There was the rapper Loyle Carner from South Croydon. And there was Section Boyz too, a collective from around the deep South. They were kids and products of the ends. They were kids descended from the Caribbean, raised in Britain and South London. Some of the members had schooled in Stanley Tech in South Norwood like Krept and Stormzy. Some started their music journeys in Grime. Some were raised on the UK Rap movement spearheaded by Giggs and others from the late 2000s onwards. Together, they had united these sounds of the city into a blend of Trap and Rap with lingering influences of Grime, local kids standing on a national vanguard, as UK MC culture once again showed signs of evolving into something new and uncharted. UK Drill would eventually follow in the mid- to late 2010s.

Many members of Section Boyz were close friends with Stormzy, and like him grew up in their school days listening to Krept and Konan and Cadet. Together, Section Boyz appear in the visual for

Stormzy's 'Not That Deep', barrelling through Croydon town centre on pedal bikes and on foot, marching through the high street and the Whitgift shopping centre, where years ago teenagers used to break out in random freestyles across the strip. A tide was rising and washing overland, the overlooked and the unheeded careering through the doors So Solid had first cracked open.

I saw the revolution first hand. At the music venue KOKO in North London, I was among carnage at Stormzy's headline show, hundreds stampeding in a chain of mosh pits, the floor appearing briefly at the onset of songs like 'Not That Deep' and 'Know Me From' before disappearing again at the drop, lost to the hooves of the possessed. He brought out both Krept and Konan and Section Boyz as special guests.

Months later, in the west of the city, I watched Krept and Konan at Shepherd's Bush Empire. The account was similar, the scent of anarchy and rage and South London ringing through the speakers. Cadet was the opening act that evening.

A month after that, I went to the ends, to deep South, and sat in a house somewhere in Thornton Heath speaking with Section Boyz as weed smoke fogged up a dim front room. Music had changed things for them. Some had never left the country before, and then Rap came, and the ends blew up, and they were performing to crowds out in Germany. All of that from them recording each other on old phones, from Grime days in secondary school, from listening to Krept and Konan and Roadside Gs and watching *Streetz Incarcerated* and seeing Heartless Crew on the MOBOs.

Collectively, everyone from the ends referred to their neighbouring areas as The 7, after Thornton Heath's CR7 postcode. They were all pushing, and there was a buzz in the area during those golden years. Parties were being thrown across the region to celebrate their collective victories. Some even feel the success helped lower the crime rate in the area, that when everyone realised a bigger cause was at stake, they cut out the dramas and the bullshit and cracked on with music.

Among it all, Krept and Konan were still leading the charge. When Wireless 2015 came about on the first weekend of July, they were a few days on from releasing their debut album *The Long Way Home*. It was among the first full-length records that arrived in this renaissance period, and was led by their first top-ten single 'Freak of the Week', which flipped a Beenie Man sample into a playful, contemporary club hit. It would go on to be certified platinum. The album would land at number 2. A performance at Wireless was the midweek push to get it there.

At Wireless, the boys had come from scattered tours and album release schedules and studio sessions across the country to converge upon the erected stages and pulpits of Finsbury Park. Video footage captures the fallout: at Stormzy's set, hundreds of teenage boys and girls of many skins collide in mosh pits under the summer sun. For Section Boyz, it was their first time at Wireless. They had never been, not even as visitors, and if you had told them in college days that this is what lay in their near futures, Sleeks, a member of the group, would've called you crazy. During their slot, with hundreds gathered, the members stalk the stage, playing their blended songs to a growing crowd.

Backstage, during a lull in the afternoon, Krept and Konan sat down for an interview with American Hip Hop DJ Peter Rosenberg. They sat on a bench in the holding area; Stormzy sat in between them too, all speaking about how far things had come.

Konan said, 'We're knocking down all the doors that they had closed on us for a minute,' before speaking about Stormzy and saying: 'He's a problem, man, he's hungry. He's from our place where we all grew up and we've just got a different energy there. Like ambitious and hungry.'

'Where exactly is that?' Rosenberg asks.

'We're from South London, but we're placed like Thornton Heath, like Norbury, that's our little area. We call it "The 7" because that's the postcode. That's our bit . . . and right now we're kind of winning. Our area's winning right now. Anyone that's making noise is from our bit.'

Then Konan passed the microphone along to Stormzy. He had a cigarette balanced behind his ear, and when he spoke, a silver tooth glinted in his mouth. Rosenberg asked him about Krept and Konan, and he said, 'I generally see these man as the door openers.' And then he spoke about how they were always the first to breach a barrier, how he had followed their trail, winning a MOBO Award the year after they did, winning a BET Award the year after they did, walking a path they had helped set out.

'Man's been listening to you man for ten years,' he said. 'From when I was in Year 7, Bluetooth days, which is like 2004, 2005 I was listening to Krept and Konan, now it's 2015. I've been listening to man for ten [years].'

A short while after, Krept and Konan played the Pepsi Max Arena tent, with thousands packed tight under the tarpaulin. The sound system rumbled heavy bass into a sinister darkness. During the set Section Boyz and Stormzy came out as special guests, all wearing black T-shirts with *The Long Way Home* printed on the front.

Then Krept and Konan dived back into their own catalogue, the crowd reacting as if they had caught the Holy Ghost, shaking and screaming to every song performed. Some scaled the railings. The tent ripped, and when the build came to a head, the darkness and the shuddering bass and the thousands pounding the earth made it feel as if Finsbury Park was about to cave in on itself. The show had to go on emergency pause, the organisers worried about what could unfold if the rapture were to continue. That afternoon is carved in folklore, a moment for the boys, a moment for everyone who came out, a moment for the ends.

Cadet was standing side of stage for that set. Distance had brought friction between the two: Krept winning a MOBO and a BET and not hearing from his cousin, as well as watching Cadet take shots at him in songs and wondering, *Why does he keep doing that?* And Cadet feeling Krept should've helped boost his career, still holding a deep love for his cousin but quietly agitated, thinking to himself, *You're my cousin, you're meant to buss me innit.*

But Krept had messaged him out the blue, asking if he wanted to roll with them to the festival, hoping that the scenes would inspire his cousin. The set shook Cadet; he was watching in near disbelief. For him, music had always been YouTube: you upload a video, and then move on to the next one. He never knew that it could be this, that it could be thousands of people chanting your lyrics as you roved across a stage, never knew that it could take you this far.

When everyone began to filter from the stage to the back, Cadet stayed, watching in awe. He didn't want to leave, because up there among the lights and the supporters and the sound systems, he felt at home. Eventually, when it was only him left, Krept had to grab him, and help move him on. As they left, Krept told Cadet that someday this could be him too.

The 7 finished 2015 in celebration. At the MOBO Awards up in Leeds, they all sat together on a string of extended tables: Krept and Konan next to Section Boyz, Section Boyz next to Stormzy, a mass of other friends from the area on the surrounding seats. They brought five awards back home that evening. Section Boyz claimed Best Newcomer, Stormzy Best Grime Act and Best Male. Krept and Konan Best Hip Hop.

For every acceptance speech they all flooded the stage, gathering around the winner, tracksuits and black-tie suits glinting in the lights.

Krept and Konan won Best Album too, the one they really wanted. On stage, Konan gripped the trophy in one palm, with a microphone in another. There must have been around twenty of them up there, beating gun fingers into the air, clapping and rousing the crowd into ovation. The cheers rose as the arena and the watching nation took in the moment: sons of South London, of African and West Indian family lines, forming a new, distinct identity of their own, the boys pushing the limits of what a British rapper could be.

Raising the microphone to his face, Konan signed off:

'Big up all my brothers on the stage, man.
Big up my mum.
Big up MOBOs 2015.
Play Dirty.
Thornton Heath.
7 Side.'

13 A BRITISH DREAM

WEST MIDLANDS

When Grime entered its second bloom, in around 2014, inspired by the works and actions of a few men and women out in the West Midlands, the scene found itself ready for renewal. The crews like StayFresh and Invasion and Livewire, which had carried a sound to shore, faded. Ensemble casts fell apart, tugged in different directions by the strong tides of parenthood and work and solo-career pipe dreams. Those who remained, eyes fixed on the goal, determined to stay the course, followed the genre into its new day.

Change for Despa was becoming a dad to a little girl, Ayaana, and realising there can be no excuses when you're living for your seed. Change was StayFresh growing apart and then breaking up. Some went solo. Some stopped music for a while. Some ended up in prison. One of the members, Raider, would say a few years after the end that, 'You can have a group of friends in school that you roll with every day and then when you hit a certain age you've got other things to do.'

Despa was proud of what they achieved. They left their mark, never forgotten by those who witnessed the climb. In a documentary he said, 'The legacy of StayFresh was we can be from the Midlands and actually make noise, not just nationally, internationally as well.'[1]

The crossing of one era into another was archived on his YouTube Channel BE83. In October 2013 he began a long-form interview series titled *Meet the Artists*. The series was born on the Apple store shop floor in the days when he still had one foot in full-time work. He had moved into a world and an environment far from Walsall and Darlaston, working his shifts with colleagues from a certain class and background, who never knew him before he was Despa. From some of them he began to sense a judgement and stereotyping of those who were like him, those who had come from where he had come from and had lived through what he had lived through.

'These are my friends,' he would say, 'and I know them to be intelligent, caring, loving people that have dreams and aspirations.'

Meet the Artists became a vessel for his friends and wider acquaintances from the scene to share their stories at length. Here they found space to speak about the conditions that had shaped them and their music. Who they were and how they lived was immortalised over a through-line of more than fifty long episodes running between October 2013 and April 2017. There were stories of hope and loss, love and music, MCs who rebuilt their lives after homelessness, mothers grieving for lost sons, ex-gang members who found the straight road. There were painters and clothing-brand owners, DJs and producers. Big Mikee featured in an episode in 2015 that lasted nearly two hours. When the crews began to disband, former members of StayFresh and Invasion were welcomed onto the channel too, the intimate conversation format a vehicle for these MCs moving into new chapters of their lives, casting a key era in permanent stone.

The series was a signal of what was to come and what was needed. For years the scene had drifted on without professional outlets and infrastructure. There were no major labels in the West Midlands catering to Grime and UK Rap. No licensed radio stations regularly playing their music. No magazines cataloguing the era. There were few A&Rs and PRs and radio pluggers to assist with the back end. Artists on the scene were cast asea in the heart of the country, fumbling to turn lyric books and melodies into legitimate careers. *Meet the Artists* was a breaking of this trend, a place for misunderstood musicians to unpeel layers for their listeners, a signal of what could be.

If the scene was to capitalise on the fruits of its work and rise with the tide of a genre going global, talented MCs and great songs were not enough. They needed infrastructure and their own industry built around their music. They needed a clear road for Grime and Rap to make its way out of the region and into waiting ears across the country and continents beyond.

Despa was to be a part of this laying of foundations. When the StayFresh era closed and the triumphs of the period were time-capsuled on *Meet the Artists*, he entered the grey area of the industry he had sworn to avoid. He became a music manager, starting his own management company and record label under the BE83 Music Group banner.

He began working with MCs and individuals like him – a stock of artists who came out of the West Midlands dreaming, and who had led the charge in the era just gone. They grew up in Pirate Radio stations and in local youth clubs, clashed in Oxygen Rooms and in DC Studios out in Wolverhampton. They huddled together in the crews that defined an era, told their life stories on *Meet the Artists* and stood on the frontlines when the sound had been abandoned in London. Together they had pushed Grime into its new tomorrow. Now they looked out ahead, seeing the tease of a new day breaking in, battling the fears of uncertain livelihoods, choosing to stay the course.

Among the handful of artists who assembled with Despa to preserve the legacy of a region, to push a sound to the masses, were Jaykae and Dapz. I met them all in the region's golden hour.

———

It was summer 2014. While on holiday in Orlando, Daniel, known by his stage name Dapz on the Map, or just Dapz, and the mother of his daughter were sitting with a palm reader. He believed in a god, was pulled into the Church and Christianity by his mother, was taught about Islam by Jaykae and his friends. He believed in astrology, believed in energies, had seen light moments and the dark.

'There's been times when I didn't want to be Daddy. There's been times where I didn't want to be Dapz on the Map . . . I felt like packing this in, bruv . . . There's even a time where I felt like packing Daniel in, through the pain of Dapz on the Map.'

The palm reader gripped his hand, claiming to stare into his past, his present and his future:

'It's something creative,' she said.

She told him that he was right to quit his job, that he was right to believe in himself, that the universe had been testing his resolve, attempting to figure out whether deep in the crevices of his soul, he really wanted the life and music career he so desperately seemed to crave on the surface.

'Oh, you're really good at this,' she said. 'You do know you could go all the way? You can do it . . . Congratulations, you've passed the test.'

Dapz turned to his daughter's mother. Earlier in the session, the reader had told her about her recently passed grandfather, said that he was watching over everything, that she should keep looking after Nan. And when Dapz looked at her now, the palm reader picking apart their lives, he could see tears in her eyes.

Then the lady read him a final prophecy:

'You're going to elevate; you're going to go to the next level. But you can't stop there, you can't stop there.'

Two years later, on 28 July 2016, he walked out to perform his own sold-out headline show at the O2 Academy in Birmingham. Two hundred and fifty tickets sold, among the first from the city and the scene to do so, the buzz hardening into a more concrete career. A prophecy fulfilled.

He played his part in those long boom years after 2015. They all did, a coalition of musicians reimagining what it meant to rap and call the West Midlands home. Some like Despa set about building management companies and infrastructure. But for Dapz, it was the music. He was among a few main leads in a generation of romantics, guiding their music out of radio sets and club bookings, and into landmark touring venues and their own stage shows, shattering the illusion of what a West Midlands MC could, and couldn't, become.

Backstage at the O2, he was scared. He could hear the crowd wailing and could hear the instrumental of the first song on his set. So he called out to God, asking him to walk with him on stage. Eventually, when he stepped out and saw the crowd gathered before him, saw 250 people who had in some way connected with his music, it was like he could feel their energy.

'I've never felt like that before,' he says. 'Never felt like that.'

The first day I met Dapz on the Map was a spring afternoon in Brum a few years after this O2 gig. We were out in Aston, sitting in Ace Barbers, his go-to guy gently stroking clippers through his scalp and down by his sideburns and earlobes, readying his face for a cover shoot in a magazine that never got off the ground. Aston is in North Brum, the barber's on a busy high road where from glass windows we could see the red-brick shops of a buzzing local high street, and in the near distance, the metal frames of Aston Villa's football stadium emerging above the crimson concrete canopy.

He had been in and out of the area since birth, sat in that same chair, hearing the same drone of afternoon traffic, car horns and revving engines drifting through the doors, blending with the buzz of steel clippers scraping across skin, the fused murmur underscoring slow days in the bits like these.

'How long have I been coming here, fam?' he said to his barber. '2010, 2012?'

Their first dance was a few years back. Dapz needed a trim for an evening show in town. And because he was dissatisfied with his regular guy out in West Brom, his younger brother brought him here. He has been coming back ever since.

'I'm like that, you get me? Loyal in that sense. Once I find somewhere that I like, whether that's studio or a barbershop, car wash, chip shop, it don't matter, you get me fam? Once I know where I'm at, it's family. I don't even think I've got a haircut from another guy.'

The path he has walked towards a livelihood and a career in music runs through these roads. For around seventeen years he grew up in the veins of Aston, with his mum's side of the family, who came from Montserrat, sinking roots into the earth across Aston and Newtown, Erdington and Lozells. They handed new Birmingham tradition down the family line: his mum played PCRL in the house, his aunt blared it from her blue Peugeot while he rode with her.

By thirteen he was listening to the founding fathers like Vader, Brasco and Midlands Mafia, tempo setters whose radio sets and songs poured into his ears through the pirate dials of Passion, Silk, Heat and Smooth FM. Elsewhere, there was his uncle who managed the youth club at Newtown Community Centre, a stronghold for Dapz and his cousins in the hours after school. And there was his big cousin, Liam, a regular at the community centre too, who pulled Dapz and some friends into a crew called L Dons. It was where he first exposed himself to MCing and Grime.

Dapz was among the second generation of Grime MCs to emerge from the city, a bold set who pushed for career-musician dreams in a time where nobody who came from where they were from, who made the music they made, had anything worthwhile to show for their endeavours. They staked their futures on a wish, pushed on into the lonely darkness, unsure and uncertain if the music careers they hoped for would be waiting at the other end. He was a kid out of Aston, wanting what he could not see.

'As long as I can remember . . . I wanted to be a musician, I wanted to do music. It's like an obsessive passion.'

When his trim was finished and the barber had snipped loose hairs, bringing his face into symmetry, we drove out across North Brum, scouting the outer city for cover-photo backdrops. We settled on a twin set of tower blocks, their exterior bricks washed light blue, their roofs folding into the ocean skies over Birmingham. Dapz stood upright in the estate car park, eyes melting into the lens, confidence in his gaze, post-war tower blocks in the background, navy skies above, his indigo tracksuit blurring the two. An anchor between ground and the heavens.

It was a snapshot of a special time, decades and generations coalescing in a frame. Dapz was a product of all of this, a child of a city rebuilt by Caribbean communities after the war, of generations of Black music scenes formed on the roofs of North Brum skyscrapers. PCRL the forefathers, playing Reggae and Roots, then Grime blooming out of Garage and Jungle, Dancehall and Rap, playing on Silk City FM and Passion FM and Heat FM. A baton passed down the line, now resting in the palms of Dapz, Despa and their friends.

But there is more to Dapz than North Brum, a side of him that sits just outside the city. Aston is only half his story. There are roots in West Brom too, a town in Sandwell brushing the edges of Handsworth and Smethwick. His career was forged on its rock, the headline show and the songs and the introspective tilt in his music never possible without it. And now he wanted to drive us out there, into West Brom, to show us why.

The Soho Road in Handsworth eventually bleeds out into West Bromwich, a teeming high road giving way to an intermission of industrial lots and a Halfords as Birmingham seals its borders and the metropolitan borough of Sandwell begins. We pull along the tarmac, driving this small stretch of no man's land, one home ending and another moving into view, the white steel frames of West Bromwich Albion's football stadium marking the change, rising from the roadside like a gateway into the ends.

The Black community in West Brom is made up of a handful of families, he says. Surnames like Francis and Walker, Ebanks, Miller and Louis deep set in the town since the Windrush era. Dapz is a Francis, the tail end of a family line stretching back to Brandon Hill, Jamaica – the same piece of land from which Cecil Morris rose. Dapz's grandparents were the first of the family to arrive in West Brom. They had a handful of children, who eventually grew up, had children of their own, and fanned the family out across the town.

He remembers how, when he was a young boy, his dad would bring him to West Brom for special occasions, how he would walk into Burger King or the cinema and see himself in the faces passing by, not realising he had wider family: cousins and aunts and uncles imprinted on the town's skeleton. At around seventeen, after those early years in Aston, he moved out here permanently, following a girl and a relationship at first, then never leaving.

West Brom and the Jamaican side of his family were the half that made him whole. They gave him a baptism in Roots Reggae, washed him in the songs of artists like Garnett Silk and bands like Morgan Heritage. Music that spoke for people, that struck at soul and spirituality. This is what he was raised around. These elements are now woven into his own songs.

The high street in West Brom is like any other strip in Britain. There are banks and local pizza places and Desi pubs and a Caribbean food shop. There are local nightclubs and a string of curry houses. There are betting shops and retail chains and Black hair shops and market stalls unfolded out over the pavement, traders hawking fruit and veg to the passers-by. There are mixed grills and local gyms on a road that runs through the heart of the town. This is where his story takes root. This is the strip that became home. This is where the climb began.

Around the time he moved to West Brom, when school and college had finished, Dapz wanted two things: to make music and to make money. He was doing both. He had established himself as a leading figure in the emergence of a new generation, clashing in youth clubs and in Oxygen Rooms, in freestyles and in radio sets. He charged his way into the scene, fearless, thinking, *I'm coming in the game, bruv, and people have to accept me. I don't give a shit, bruv, and if man don't accept me I'll clash man on the spot.*

To get by he was working day jobs. First, he helped out in Newtown Community Centre, picking kids up from school, and ferrying them over to the centre. He'd take them to the park, play football and kill hours until their parents arrived to collect them. After that he got his first job proper, working the phones at Direct Line in town. When somebody crashed their car, and needed to claim on their insurance, they would ring the office. Dapz would answer, patch them through to a local garage and book the car in for repairs. He would liaise to have it picked up and then delivered again when fixed. He'd charge the excess and the call would be over. Then the phone would ring, another car crash, another claim, and he'd start the process over.

At twenty, he moved on from car insurance over to HomeServe, a home and emergency repairs business. He took calls about burst pipes, about electricity faults, then sent a repairman over to tackle the issue.

'I'm a wordsmith, I can talk to people, so I'm getting all these sales, smashing it.'

HomeServe dangled incentives for successful salesmen. Company gifts sat on the other end of sales targets. Dapz won everything. A Nintendo, a TV, a holiday, reaching out and grabbing whatever they had to offer.

But there was something missing, something eating away at him in those office hours. Music gave him a feeling that regular work never could. The income was steady and the hours fine, and he was a good salesman who earned well, but no call with homeowners asking to pave patios and fix electrical faults could match the buzz that came with music. Could not match that feeling of recording a love song like 'Okay', made in 2013, where he was crooning on the record like the Roots Reggae souls he was raised on. Recording is so pure, so still for him, a knowing that in that precise moment he can be 100 per cent honest with how he feels, not caring who hears it. Then there is the lead-up to the release of a song, the rush, the nerves, as if he were teetering at the peak of a rollercoaster, staring down into the abyss, feeling that churn run through his stomach, knowing that soon his cousins, his brothers, his mum, his dad are going to hear him bare his soul.

Two incidents sealed his fate.

He was set to clash an MC called Bomma B from Smethwick. In a clash, no areas are off-limits. An MC says what he wants about another and feels no way about it. Humiliation was a fatal wound. Any personal information was wielded like a dagger. Bomma knew a guy called Peter who worked at HomeServe too, and so while at work in the weeks leading up to the clash, Dapz would sit at his desk, paranoid that Peter would reveal what he did at his job, and tell Bomma, 'He's not who he says he is.'

Though he never claimed to be on the roads in his music, in songs he implied that he was, as he says, 'around the badmen . . . around the gangsters'. His secret life at HomeServe would not correlate with the idea of who Dapz was as an MC and a man.

The other incident was new life.

On 23 October 2009, two and a half months before his twenty-first birthday, Dapz became a dad.

'I was a spring chicken. I don't know about mortgages or life and I've got this little princess in my hands.'

Leah changed him. Leah forced him to grow up, to reckon with himself and his future. Music careers don't combust from the ether like spontaneous flame; he had to take it seriously now, to pull and drag it into reality. Some days he would be at his desk, writing bars, leaving waiting customers on mute, their voices calling out into his headset for help, their drone passing him by, too lost in his own world of lyrics to notice.

He began putting the squeeze on work, telling his boss that he wanted to go part-time, that he was there too much, that music needed more of his energy. She told him not everyone makes it in music, told him to think of his daughter, that he was doing well, that what he wanted was like a fish in the ocean. 'What makes you think you're going to make it?' she said.

He told her again that he needed to work part-time, that he needed to give the music more. And when she said that she couldn't let him go, that he was her top seller, he cast his line in the sand.

'I'm not coming here tomorrow,' he told her. 'I'm not coming in.'

She threatened to put a disciplinary on his record.

He said, 'What you on about? I'm not coming back ever again, what the fuck you on about? I'm not going to have another job. I'm not having another job.'

The next morning, 17 December 2009, she phoned him three times. Dapz never answered. And that was it, out into the lonely world of self-employment and music. He never worked another job.

————

It has been almost eight years since he walked out of full-time employment. We are sitting in a shawarma spot on the high street in West Brom, cars drifting by into the afternoon quiet. Since then, he has built a buzz within the region, and with Despa on his management team, it was vibrating out across the country. In 2015, after MCing through Brum's Grime revival and into the genre's second peak, things began to pick up. He released a string of singles and visuals on his own YouTube channel, gaining momentum with every drop; an MC coming to the boil.

The songs 'Murdah', 'I Swear', 'Shinobi Part I', 'Oh My Days' and 'CHAMPION CHAMPION' were released in a prolific nine-month stretch between October 2015 and July 2016. There is soul in the sound, songs that take a deep gaze at his life, etching those self-reflections over pensive productions by Walsall producer Thomas Mellor. The soundscape grumbles like an approaching night storm, sacred tones roaming the lonely land in the West Midlands twilight.

Among them, 'Murdah' brings the many parts of Dapz into a whole. It is a love letter and a testament to faith, a defining passage from that second generation of Brumtown dreamers. Eerie synths whine and shriek like fireworks, rolling over a groaning bass, as Dapz details the long grind and the road that still lies ahead:

'Looking back, I always knew it was going to be like this,' he raps, 'only a few who were doing it then are doing it now.'

The accompanying music video is a subtle reflection on the places and people who defined his life. It straddles Birmingham and West Brom, shows him being trimmed in Ace Barbers out in Aston, then outside St Andrew's football stadium with Jaykae, and then in town gazing over the central Birmingham skyline, staring out at the skyscrapers floating like clouds in the distance.

'I need to remind myself who I am sometimes,' he half-raps, half-sings, the influences from the Roots Reggae of his youth disguised now in Grime.

The video takes us into West Brom, captures Dapz standing

outside a council block, the road sign reading Francis Street. Then it is nightfall, and he is on the local high street, the walkway empty, him and a gathering of his boys crowded under, outside and atop the market-stall tents.

The camera scans the landmarks of Black West Brom. There are clips of his friends. There are moments in the Jamaican food shop and moments outside the West Brom African and Caribbean Resource Centre. There are clips of his daughter on his shoulders, the two playing in a toy store. She talks on the song's hook, her stretched-out chants of 'Murdaahhh, hey Daddy murdah every day' bending into a soft warble. She is the reason he seized music, why he left his job and emptied his soul into his songs, and in October 2015, the month 'Murdah' was uploaded to YouTube, the world was listening to them, father and daughter in union. One generation carving out space for the next.

———

The first time Jaykae appeared on *Meet the Artists* in November 2013, one of his best friends had just passed. In September, Depzman, an MC in Invasion Alert with Jaykae and Vader, was stabbed at a memorial event for another friend. He died the next day. The family and Jaykae and the city's scene mourned his loss; another Birmingham boy taken too soon.

Weeks after the passing, after Jaykae had carried Depz's coffin on his shoulder at the funeral, he seemed on edge. The day before the interview with Despa, he had been in London recording a Fire in the Booth freestyle with Charlie Sloth at the BBC building in Westminster. On the way to London from Brum to record the freestyle, he had felt himself overcome with emotion, frustrated that Depz wasn't making the journey to a holy grail of British MC culture with him.

In the BBC studio, large black headphones are wrapped around his ears, his 6 foot 2 frame towering over a dangling microphone. Charlie, usually animated, is quiet as Jaykae vents, music unravelling the tension in his head. The eight-minute freestyle captures a young man in the clutches of grief, reeling from the loss of a friend he considered a brother. Throughout he speaks on 'going through hell'. He speaks on the struggle to move through the suffering. How he hadn't been sober for a month, drinking and smoking to numb the heartache; how he was starting trouble on the roadside 'so I can have a fight'. He claws at the past, raps about how he was missing his departed friend and their years in music together and their time away in Amsterdam and Magaluf. And there were flashbacks to the fatal night, wonderings and anger at why the doctors couldn't save him. 'I'm lost without you,' he said, staring into the microphone.

Amongst the grief, he contemplates his future in music. He wants to leave it behind he says but owes it to Depz to continue. A young man at a crossroads.

In the studio, the day after the freestyle, Jaykae and Despa, who had known each other for four years, sit on two ends of a long red leather chair, orange brickwork in the background. The two shake hands. On the back of Jaykae's right palm he has tattoos reading 'RIP Depzman', and '2 Real', the name of Depz's last project. Then Despa opens the floor for Jaykae to share his story.

He is from Small Heath, working-class South-East Birmingham. In the years after the Second World War, South Asian families migrated into the city and settled in the area. By 2011, 74.8 per cent of those in Small Heath were Asian. The core nationalities were Pakistani (53 per cent), Bangladeshi (13.8 per cent) and Indian (2.5 per cent, including a major Punjabi community too). Jaykae, born Janum Khan, was a result of this movement into Britain: Afghanistan, Egypt, Ireland and Pakistan all knitted into his heritage. He grew up in a part of Brum where Bengal communities lead into Somali communities,

Somali communities into Arabic communities, an enclave reflective of a city that is among Britain's most diverse.

As a kid he watched Channel U and listened to Midlands Mafia, Grime inscribing itself on his spirit. Then an older MC from the ends called Subzee, and the passing of a friend, inspired him to start MCing. By his teens, Jaykae was spraying bars and clashing in the park. Every area would bring their best local MC, and then they'd go at it. He never lost.

Eventually Vader, who he had grown up listening to, got wind of his skill and reached out on Facebook, inviting him to a set. Jaykae was seventeen. At the set, he met Dapz for the first time, and not long after, he joined Invasion, becoming part of a crew that truly reflected the city: Arabs, Jamaicans, Pakistanis, Indians, white kids, Afghanis and Kittians all among their ranks.

In that post-2010 era, as part of the younger generation of Invasion alongside MCs like Depz and Sox, Jaykae rose to national prominence. By the first *Meet the Artists* interview with Despa he was among the most popular MCs in the local scene, revered and feared for his blend of aggression and introspection.

'I'm the hype guy with content,' he told Despa. That marriage had carried his career to this crossroads, had underscored his Fire in the Booth, and now, sat next to Despa on the red leather couch, he teetered on the brink, pushed forward by his lost friend.

'I'm lost, bruv, lost, bruv,' he said. 'From the day it happened I've been drunk every night and that's not good for someone like me . . . people grieve in different ways innit so that's my way of grieving . . . I just, I feel lost without him.'

But among the pain, there were cracks of optimism, hopes for a sound gathering momentum and a scene starting to mature.

'People are thinking, "Now I can actually do this and I can make money from this,"' he said, '"either a full-time hustle or a side hustle."'

And so, in spite of what's happened, he'll keep moving forward, he says, with an enduring mission to squeeze what he can from music, using his skill to take care of both his mum and Depz's mum.

As the half-hour interview draws to a close, the two shake hands again, and Despa says he hopes to see new music in the future.

Then Jaykae signs out.

'Rest in peace, Depzman,' he says. 'That's it.'

A few seconds later, the camera cuts to black.

The second time Jaykae appeared on *Meet the Artists* in December 2014, he had just come out of prison. Some time after that first appearance, he'd ended up in a fight in the early hours. He spent a few months in jail as a result.

'What happened?' Despa asked.

'Just a fight, bro. It was about five in the morning, and it just happened.'

When he came out, Jaykae was put on electronic tag and given a curfew. For at least another month, he would need to be home every evening by 7.15 p.m. Almost free.

The dark clouds from Depz's passing were still there. There were certain songs he still struggled to listen to, certain songs that still made him upset. He was missing his best friend.

But his momentum in music was beginning to pick up. In the summer of that year, him and Dapz on the Map had released a joint EP, *Froggy*. The tape was a fusion dance, merging their spirits into one, Jaykae the introspective hooligan, Dapz an inward-looking crooner and MC. A candidness underlay their words, a shedding of heavy weight on six songs woven into union by Thomas Mellor. On 'Almost But Not Quite' Jaykae says, 'Sick of talking about "this time next year".' Dapz follows his verse, saying, 'Thank God Jaykae found the spirit to put down spirits.'

The EP's first song dropped at half-time of England's World Cup Quarter Final vs Italy, and despite the football holding the nation's attention, *Froggy* managed to cut through the noise. It was a symptom of a changing time. Music was an option.

When he was eighteen, and decided to give music a go, Jaykae told himself, 'If I get to twenty-one and I'm not happy with where I'm at I'm going to lock it off.' By the time *Froggy* was released, he was twenty-three, and had set himself a new target: by age twenty-five he aimed to make £100,000 from words and verses.

The arc of his career was tilting towards that goal. The West Midlands had an established Grime scene and he could see his words vibrating across Britain. He had been performing out of town. In London he clashed East London MC Discarda on Lord of the Mics. In Peterborough at a Sidewinder rave he had one of the best nights of his life as an MC. Then, after a show in Cardiff, a crowd of what felt like seventy-odd people followed him down the road and into a local chicken shop, packing out the storefront, trying to spit bars and gain his attention. After that, both Cardiff and Newport became two of his favourite places to visit. Elsewhere, he had performed on the Bigga Fish tour, on two dates with Skepta, and had received reloads in Magaluf with Depz. A door was opening. To walk through he needed to stay on the steady path.

'What does the future hold?' Despa asked him, the two sitting on a brown corner couch.

'No more going back to jail.'

As the hour interview winds to a close, the two shake hands: 7.15 p.m. is drawing close, and Jaykae has to leave.

He hurries off the screen, and Despa signs out.

'He's got to go now,' Despa says, 'and get back in before the tag man catches him.'

*

The third and last time Jaykae appeared on *Meet the Artists* in February 2016, he had just become a father.

'Music?' he says. 'Yeah, I've been slacking but it's coming, fam.'

The two sit in opposite chairs in a new, plush studio, grinning, seemingly closer than they were before, recognising that this conversation completes their trilogy. Like Dapz and Despa, Jaykae was a man newly changed by entering fatherhood.

'How has being a new dad affected you?' Despa asked.

'I've always got him to think about first, whereas I didn't have no responsibility in my life at all. I didn't have nothing. Nothing to tie me down, nothing. Now I've got a son. He has to come first. Financially, I've always got to be able to look after him.'

The past few years had been dark. Depz had died, and the drinking and the smoking and the pain in his Fire in the Booth freestyle had waded into his life. Then he went to prison. Three days before his release, his nan died. When he got out, he was overcome by a numbness that took a while to shake. The milestones that marked his life, that defined his passage into adulthood, had been scarring.

Sitting opposite Despa he said, 'A lot of things have been negative in my life for a few years now . . . I ain't got nothing good to think . . . But, fam, I believe that I will get my break.'

He was emerging out of heartache, entering a new season. In the stayover between the last interview and this final conversation, he had left Invasion too. In 2010, Vader had had a brain haemorrhage. Doctors implanted coils into his head to keep his blood vessels together. After, Vader began to move away from music, followed by some of the older members who had bills and jobs and life to contend with. Some of the younger members left too, like D2 who quit music for marriage and religion. The crew began to pull apart. Then, after a few internal issues and Depz passing, Jaykae's passion for the crew began to loosen. He went solo, a twenty-four-year-old man with a new son and new energy, casting out on his own.

After his son was born, and after he left Invasion, Jaykae had slowed down with music, his new responsibilities more important for him to tend to. Grime and UK Rap had blossomed during his time away, the genres creeping from local to national, national to international recognition. Artists began taking consistent bookings overseas, performing at summer boat festivals in Croatia and winter skiing festivals in Austria, touring Europe and North America, Japan and Australia.

They were on prime-time television and in the broadsheets and the newspapers and on the radio. The first time he had ever heard his song played was years ago, in twilight hours when most of the country was asleep. But the other day he woke up and heard a remix of his old song 'Certain Man' blaring from the radio at noon. The seasons were turning, and Jaykae had been watching on, readying his return.

There was a project in the works titled *Where Have You Been?* It was an open letter, tracking the past few years of his life: the birth, the death, the prison, the freedom, the lost crews and the new beginnings.

'When can we expect?' Despa asked.

Jaykae told him to pull his phone out, to look in the calendar and pick a Sunday in May. Despa looked down at his phone, eventually settling on the third Sunday of the month.

'*Where Have You Been?*' Jaykae said. 'Out 15th of May 2016.'

As the forty-five-minute conversation winds to a close, they speak about the benchmark he had set for age twenty-five: one hundred grand earned from a microphone and some lyrics. Jaykae was excited, noting how in this shifted landscape, the goal he had set years back was, if he played things right, only a few bookings away.

'There's no limit in this thing. I don't think there's any limit, fam.'

Despa smiles as he listens, seemingly excited by Jaykae's enthusiasm, a bond formed in three long conversations readying to grow into something deeper, their lives about to interlock. The two smile into the camera and shake hands as it fades into black. Then the video cuts. A trilogy finished. A new friendship about to begin.

The first time I met Jaykae was in Prime Studio out by Digbeth, in a renewed part of the city where metalworks and production factories once powered Birmingham's industrial age. We were shooting an editorial for a website that is now shuttered. Digbeth was a creative quarter, razed and rebuilt, home to creative entrepreneurs, the O2 Institute, quirky restaurants and floral murals painted across brick walls. Jaykae was recording a song for a compilation album being put out by YouTube channel P110.

In Prime, there were no windows and the place felt like a war bunker, the neon lights dousing the room in a soft sapphire glow, the shadows leaning and cutting on Jaykae's 6-foot-plus frame, on his Stone Island hat, on the tattoos inked to his skin. The space was quiet. There were a few friends spread across the sofas at the back of the room. Despa was sat over a centre table. He was Jaykae's manager now, their interviews fruiting into friendship and a business relationship, the two arm-in-arm, leading the city and the region into a new dawn.

Every so often a song emerges out of the noise and catches a wave. On 15 May 2016, Jaykae released 'Toothache'. It wasn't the EP as promised in the third and final interview, but a single instead. It was a song that changed everything, armed with the original aggression and introspection that won him a listener base. Back in union with Thomas Mellor, Jaykae bares his teeth over low synths and the steady troop of a throbbing bass. A haunting melody moaning like a midnight ghost choir heralds his return.

The lyrics are an acute account of how, who and where he has been through this defining period of his life. The opening line, 'I was the best man when D2 got married, the pallbearer when Depz got carried', has been immortalised as one of the most powerful introductions in Grime's recent history, on one hand throwing reference to D2 from Invasion, who quit music for the joys of marriage and faith, and on the other, the eternal presence of the late Depz. New life and old wounds simmering under the skin of the boy from Small Heath.

Throughout he exercises his angst, speaks of loved ones lost and the reckless shotting days he has survived. He speaks on the time wasted in prison, and then how, three days before his release, he cried when the news of his grandma's passing filtered through.

The song is a freestyle, his bars and his mind racing on for almost three minutes, stress and ambition and jagged pieces of anger falling out over the instrumental. The monochrome music video captures him in a tunnel where Depz filmed a famed 'Mountain Dew' music video, flashes over his 'RIP Depzman' and '2 REAL' tattoos, and hovers over the bridge that signals the entrance into Small Heath.

Further footage captures him cruising the city in darkness, speaking on the break-up of Invasion, the arrival of his son changing him at his core, and how he sometimes phones the boys in jail, a place he has long left behind, and can hear his songs playing in the background on the radio.

'Toothache' quickly gathered pace, propelling him onto festival line-ups across Europe, and support tours with Skepta and The Streets. The track was featured on cult American TV show *Power*, and was among the most seminal pieces of British music released in a decade.

A year on from its unveiling, he stood in the neon-lit Prime studio, mumbling a new verse under his breath and fiddling with the production dials, carving out grooves in the mud for his river of words to flow along. In a few weeks he would headline his own

tour, walking a path Dapz had set. He had plotted out the opening evening in his head, the song he would walk out to, seeing the
crowd gathered in the O2, and the legions of loyal fans who would
coalesce on the night, like an extended family. When the dates were
announced, he began receiving messages from across the world, supporters in Hong Kong and Amsterdam, Australia and London who
said they would be making a West Midlands pilgrimage to see him
perform. Four years on from that first *Meet the Artists* interview and
his life had changed.

After the studio session was finished, we strolled out under the
fading sunlight, capturing some images. During the walk, a supporter
stopped him on the roadside, in near disbelief that one of the city's
leading musicians had appeared in front of him. Ever since Jaykae
was seventeen, he said, his life here in Birmingham, in one capacity
or another, had been documented on the internet. He would sometimes bump into supporters like this on the street, who on meeting
him would let fly on his personal business. And for a moment, he
would be stunned, not remembering that these events and memories
had been captured and crystalised in his lyrics through the years.

As we walked, he took a few phone calls, wandered deeper into
the industrial estate, past the spot where Invasion filmed a legendary
SBTV cypher years back, and entered a large car park penned in by
railway arches and some old factory buildings. He lit a cigarette and
began to climb the steel fire-escape steps attached to the side of one
of the buildings. 'The sickest raves in Birmingham here, fam,' he
said, once he reached the top, resting gently on the steel railings. 'I
remember performing to six, seven thousand people here, the biggest
crowd I've performed to. It was mad.'

The photos captured him at a city peak. Birmingham was spread
out ahead of him, council blocks and high-rises at attention in the
distance. When finished, we headed to a quiet dessert lounge just

outside of Digbeth. It was empty with high ceilings and varnished wooden tables and a dozen or so staff gathered behind the counter. Jaykae was eating a custard crumble. He had recently turned twenty-five, the benchmark age he had set himself all those years ago.

'I wanted to have £100,000 in the bank,' he says.

Things were different now, though. The deepest desires to set foundations for his mum and his sister and his sister's kids and his loved ones were still aflame. But there was more than just money on his mind, his mental state expanding as his songs moved across the world and success began to find its way to him.

'I don't get gassed over money as I would have back when I was younger,' he said, between mouthfuls of custard. 'I see a bigger picture than just that now. I want to have businesses and shit like that, have a fucking place like this . . . it's not just "I need a hundred grand and I need six figures in my account", it needs to be bigger than that, bruv.'

A waiter walked over and offered him a drink. He declined.

'This is my twenty-fifth year and I think I'm on track,' he said. 'I've been on it for fucking years, man, and now I'm starting to see rewards.'

———

Through this period, the breakthrough of Rap and Grime in Britain was not defined only by award wins and high-selling albums and ranging tours across the continent. It was a shift that was felt closer to home, a movement and an hour reshaping the casual, everyday lives of its most loyal contributors. This change moved quietly through the soul of a nation, impacted how people made sense of themselves in the quiet pockets of Britain, music filling their days with new meanings, drawing them away from traumas past and opening them up to possibilities previously veiled.

Across the country, lives were being recast, and handfuls of people, guided by their involvement with these sounds, were writing quiet but radical futures for themselves and their loved ones. This is what the revolution looked like away from the mainstream, and pop-culture glare. This is how Grime and Rap remapped the day-to-day lives of some working-class people who had devoted themselves to building this music. Despa, from the outskirts of Walsall, was one of these people.

In the Rock Up Adventure Centre, out by Ladywood, just east of Birmingham city centre, kids scrambled up climbing walls like squirrels in the trees. From the café area, with the rest of the parents, Despa watched his daughter Ayaana, in the fray, among a mass of children hanging from wedged boulders, hanging from zip-wires and splashing in ball pits, joyous screams of primary school kids cut loose, their wails and thrill giving the place the buzz of an indoor funfair. Ayaana was on the climbing walls, with her cousin Kamari, both testing fears and gravity as they ascended towards the netted ceiling.

It was an early August afternoon in Birmingham. The stretch of six weeks' holiday in summer, where the shackles come free and the schools close their doors, and the kids are entrusted back into the care of their mothers and fathers: parents bending into the kids, kids bending into parents as they bond across the summer season.

Despa's eyes flitted between the two on the climbing walls and a pram at his side, where his partner tended to their baby son Coen, six months old, who sat nibbling toast and blinking out at his new surroundings. Then Despa's phone buzzed. Another work email or message shooting down his line.

BE83 Records and Management was up and running. Jaykae and Dapz, Grim Sickers from Swindon and Remtrex from Highgate were all weaved into the fold. Together, they had become a hub and focal point for the region, defining Grime and UK Rap's arrival into mainstream consciousness as the genres continued to bathe wider Britain in their tones. After twenty years of work and dreaming he was here, his own label and business pushed into reality by decades of sacrifice, by the odd jobs he took to ward off the breadline, by the flee from Darlaston, by StayFresh and by turning his back on the security of Apple and a steady job. A twenty-year vision of what could be was now paying off, was now suddenly real, was washing over him with rushes of anxiety and nerves and excitement.

Music managers and entrepreneurs don't work nine to five. They work long days without end. They work late-night recording sessions and red-eye meetings down at the labels' and streaming services' offices in London. They are the first point of call, the emergency firefighters when something goes wrong, the middleman between artists and everyone else. The day before this, Despa was out the house for 8 a.m., down in London for a meeting, back into the city for 8 p.m., then with an artist till around three in the morning, burning it at both ends, stretching himself beyond limits. It is a 24/7 job that few outside it can ever truly understand. Wherever Despa finds himself, even if the occasion is the family day out, a part of him remains on alert, one ear pressed into phone calls, eyes scanning emails and text messages, desperate to leave something tangible, a business that his kids can profit from and work in, something solid for his seeds who will inherit the earth.

He always wanted a son first. But then Ayaana came along, almost seven years ago, and softened him, thawed a cold temperament. His life and experiences to that point had left him detached, with a hardness he never wanted her to know or feel. So he learned to become more loving, more open and caring, growing alongside her. And now there was Coen too, meaning Despa's character was again adapting itself to a child's needs.

Their arrival lit a flame within him, instilled a seriousness about music and his craft and career, just as it had done with Dapz. Before kids, when he answered to nobody else, he could lie and cheat himself, find excuses to never return phone calls, drift off the radar without consequence, and when the depression came, he could disappear for two months, no questions asked, and just sit inside himself. Then he had his daughter and realised, *Bruv, I don't have the capacity for this any more. I can't be in myself. For starters I've got to be with her half the week, so I can't be a depressed dad.*

'I learned the word responsibility,' he said, sitting at the table, because 'as soon as you have somebody else to live for, everything changes. I knew I couldn't fail before, but I definitely can't fail now. They are never ever ever going to live the life I've lived.'

This is the tightrope he walks. He wants time with his son and daughter, space to fertilise their early years with the love and care needed, and he wants time to pour into music and business, pounding the daily grind to build them an inheritance. He is determined to provide, to make something for himself and his kids, knowing at the same time that neither money nor success stack up to a present father. They needed Despa. They needed all of him. To cater for both he sacrificed sleep and hopes of a regular life. He sacrificed himself.

So these are what his days looked like for the next few weeks until school started again: a family afternoon out while still checking in at the office. Late nights and early mornings, a hundred miles down to London for a meeting then back again, draining the twilight hours in studio sessions, and then ready the next day for bonding time with his family.

The phone buzzed again. Music bubbled back to the surface. He opened it, pressed a few keys and then pushed the phone to the side. Then he pulled the pram closer to his side, broke a piece of toast from a plate and gently fed Coen with his fingers.

After the session at Rock Up, the family piled into the car. Despa drove out from Ladywood towards the city centre, moving across a busy A-road, electronic billboards and office blocks flashing in his windscreen. The radio was on and he sang under his breath as he drove. In his rear-view mirror he could see the kids chattering on the back seat, their adrenalin still up from the climbing. Coen was balancing on Despa's partner's lap. When the music broke for a news bulletin, Despa's singing stopped, and he said aloud, 'I've got to go by the Jubilee Centre for three. I've got to go and look at a place quickly. By Hurst Street. I've got to run in, it's not long, like ten minutes.'

He was searching for business premises, a studio and an office space for BE83 and the artists on the roster. The hunt was part of a wider drive to build infrastructure in the city for the MCs emerging now, and in the decades to come.

An industry isn't an industry without the back end, without the managers and engineers and studio spaces and media outlets to support a sound, to make music a viable career path for young dreamers in the West Midlands. For years they had stumbled on without these foundations. The scenes of Grime and UK Rap, which had taken root in communities across the country, were still, to a degree, reliant on London. To sign with a label you went to the capital. To record a Fire in the Booth with Charlie Sloth or a Daily Duppy with GRM Daily, you went to the capital. To meet executives at Spotify or Apple Music you went to the capital. And though artists like Jaykae and Lady Leshurr out of Brum, and Bugzy Malone out of Manchester were now stars in their own right, the infrastructure and platforms in London still loomed large over the scene. Despa finding a studio space and a label headquarters was another small step in eroding that gap, in overriding the belief that for an MC to make it from these sides, he or she must leave first.

There were a few studios in the city. Some MCs in Brum used

Oxygen Rooms by Digbeth. Dapz recorded at DJ Apostle's facility in Wolverhampton. Most of the other MCs recorded at a studio owned by Major. Major was Winston Mendez, a producer, father figure and confidant for generations of musicians out of Birmingham. The studio is in Hockley, North Brum, and for decades aspiring MCs have flocked to its grounds.

A studio is more than four walls, it is the gravel over which artists pour their cement, a meeting ground, a communal space for a sound and its musicians to evolve into something new. Major's studio has witnessed and prompted this cycle in Black Birmingham's music history. A process of loss and renewal as one sound and generation give way to the next. He has recorded Reggae and Drum & Bass artists, early UK Hip Hop pioneers, Grime and Baseline MCs, rappers and Drill artists in a time spanning decades. Major's brother is Pato Banton, the legendary Birmingham Reggae artist who topped the UK Singles Charts with UB40 in the 1990s. Black music flows through his family line. His son RM is a rapper of this era, as is his nephew Remtrex, who was being managed by Despa.

In Major, the Grime and Rap generation found a seasoned music man who would record their vocals, make them re-record for refinement, mix and master the records, probe them on layering, on chorus and verse, readying their songs for listeners and radio and streaming services; his knowledge and passion for teasing potential from the youth, turning aspiring MCs into fully fledged musicians. Artists from across all areas congregate in the building, his studio knitting together an entire music scene. It was hallowed ground, a sacred space, even in the years when the city was divided. If you ran into an enemy at Major's there would be no trouble, you would both walk on. Here was about creating something bigger than themselves. It is this legacy that Despa's studio space would form part of.

An hour later and he was driving still. The studio visit at the Jubilee

Centre had gone well. The owners ran decent prices, were set up in a good location, but still, he wasn't sure if it was the place to call home. The search would have to continue another day. For now, the family had plans for a pub lunch, were driving down through Edgbaston, a town once voted Britain's best place to live, where big houses with gates and gravelled patios fell past the windshield, the black smoke of exhausts choking the oak trees shading the streets. The car hummed as it skated through the city, another Jeep wading through afternoon traffic. The kids were now quiet in the back, Coen again resting in his mum's arms. Despa was on and off the phone, taking care of BE83 business and artists, even while he drove.

Things were busy. Remtrex was readying a project for release. He was among the most popular rappers in the city, his music a raw depiction of life on the roads of inner-city Birmingham. He was among the artists driving the music during the region's defining hour at the turn of the past decade. A string of freestyles from 2010 till now chart his life. There are passages about the streets, about buying and selling, about beef and drama in the city. Bars about how getting robbed at fourteen changed him, about illegal money running through his fingers, about run-ins with police and armed response units, and the sorrow for what he had put his mum through. But there was stark reflection too, a heart in his hymns, a recognition that his lifestyle was not one he wanted, for now or for his future.

The freestyles are scattered through the years, his inconsistency a consequence of coming in and out of jail.

'Fucking hell, I can't take this, I guess I got caught up in the Matrix,' he says in a freestyle.

And now in 2018, after another stretch in prison, he was back out, treading the thin ice between music and road, being managed by Despa and attempting to turn his life straight for good as he prepared his project. ('No money coming out my ears like before, it's fucking hard, this music shit needs to pay off.') The role BE83 was taking in the city was about more than just music.

Sitting now, the amber sun streaking through the big pub windows, the typical British carvery, with long oak tables, hard wooden chairs and tattered leather booths. It was almost empty inside. A few families fanned across the humdrum interior. There was nothing remarkable about the place, nothing more British than a chain pub and its thick paper menus. Despa sat at the corner of the table, watched Ayaana and Kamari crash through the pub doors, their legs bouncing, their arms flailing, heard one of them yell, 'We're playing hide and seek!' and then disappear into adjacent bathrooms. The kids owned the summer.

'They're not related at all,' he said, smiling, 'and they've only known each other like a year, but they move like brother and sister.'

The food trickled to the table in scraps, a waitress in a wrinkled shirt placing down cutlery and hard ceramics, then fish finger sandwiches and chicken skewers. It was late afternoon.

'I'm tired all the time and I really think I'm burning it at both ends at the moment. It's not easy trying to balance it all. But it's fucking paying off. I can see it, man, everything that I want, and I've been working for, it's paying off . . . I've always been a hard worker,' he said. 'I don't know why . . . I'm not a quitter, I'm not a quitter at all, you will have to kill me. I think it's because when you've been through stuff, and it hasn't broken you – and it nearly broke me – nothing else can.'

Sometimes it was hard being self-employed, he said. There was never any consistency. 'I make money on and off . . . I make money . . . life happens, you need to pay . . . you wait for the next invoices . . . Woah, bad times, I've run out of money . . . I could use a salary where every month money is coming, it's a nice comfort blanket. But if I'm doing that and I'm not building my own thing, I'm not being myself and I'm not providing the kind of role model I want to be for my kids . . . nothing is more important than what I'm going to leave for them.'

After Despa had declined dessert and settled the bill. After they had packed Coen's stroller into the trunk, and after Ayaana and Kamari had climbed into the back and blew tongues at one another. After the Jeep hit the road and smooth Drake burst out the radio; after the kids squabbled and shoved in the back seats and Despa's partner asked, 'Are you two bickering?' And after their quick cry of, 'No!' was followed by a brief pause, and Ayaana, confused, then asked . . . 'Wait, what does bickering mean?' After the Jeep continued to crawl through rich-district Birmingham, and after they had crossed over from Edgbaston into King's Heath and from King's Heath into Mosely, and Despa had told them that 'we're going to Grandad's'. After late-afternoon sun rained light down through summer-blue skies, and his phone had buzzed with good business news and he smiled to himself saying, 'It's the perfect day,' they pulled up to a brownstone terraced house and everyone except Despa filtered out. He promised to return shortly and collect Ayaana for her karate lesson, and then he drove a little further through the tree-sheltered streets, parking the Jeep on a side road and sat himself down on a peeling wooden bench shaded by a mothering oak tree whose branches fanned out like a sunshade.

For the first time that afternoon, Despa was without his family cast. So, he sat quietly on the bench in suburban South Birmingham, let his mind drift away from family and work and everything else, watched cars cruise down the hill and disappear over his shoulder, saw joggers canter past pretty red-brick houses, and pigeons flap among crumbling chimney tiles.

A few moments later, a car cruised past, a hatchback hurtling towards the foot of the hill, the driver peering out of the window, and upon seeing Despa sat on the bench, screeched to a stop. The driver, who was known locally as J Force, swung the door open, as did his friend, TB, in the passenger seat, both smiling, both friends of Remtrex, both thrilled to see Despa. Then J Force, who had a slim build with a fade, said, 'Wagwan, what you saying? Everything good, Desp?'

They stood to greet each other, the sun dappling the concrete, the tree shading their frames.

'I was just talking to Rem,' Despa said. 'Everything feels good man, just got to keep it pushing.'

J Force smiled, slapped Despa's palm, and as he turned to leave, said, 'Keep Rem on it, man!'

Then as quickly as the two had arrived, they were gone, speeding down towards central Birmingham, the entire encounter lasting no more than a minute. Despa sprawled on the bench, his hands at his side.

He had been managing Remtrex for four or five weeks now he said, 'and in being there for him and helping him get to where he gets to, he comes with his people innit. You take on them in a sense and they have to embrace you. It's not just business.'

It was the same with Jaykae, he said, whose friends have slowly welcomed him into the circle. When he was with them last night, Jaykae's best friend, Bradders, said to him, 'You're like a big bro now, Desp.'

'That actually meant the world to me. It's not just work; you're changing people's lives, man. Jaykae is from nothing, Remtrex is from nothing, I'm from nothing. We're all from nothing, man, and you're helping facilitate somebody's life changing, their friends' lives changing. It's a very serious thing and I don't take it for granted at all.'

In Grime and in Rap, in Jaykae and in Dapz, in Remtrex and in BE83, he had inherited a different kind of family. They were bands of boys-turned-men, emerging from difficult working-class pockets across the region, united in their love for music, and in their joining, seemed to have found a deep sense of brotherhood. BE83 and the music scene they held close were a version of family, something Despa had lost almost two decades ago back in Walsall.

He never spoke much about Walsall. But today, sitting outside in the summer, he did. That place would always be tied with grief and pain and would always remind him of his family fading away and tearing at the seams, his hometown a black hole, the great void from which he nearly didn't emerge. And on this afternoon, the tree shading him from sun, he speaks on what happened to him all those years ago.

'My actual family structure broke down,' he said. 'My nan, my grandad, my mum, that kind of just fell apart when my uncle died. In my second year of college my two-year-old little brother was kidnapped by my dad who left him in a house. He died of malnutrition and hypothermia because nobody knew he was there.'

There was guilt Despa felt about what happened with his little brother, Aiden. Shortly before Aiden passed, Despa had seen him with his dad. But he never knew that Aiden was deemed missing, and so didn't raise the alarm. By the time Aiden was found, in the living room of an unheated house, the young child had lost a third of his body weight, passing from lack of food, dehydration and hypothermia. His dad had abandoned him there on and off for weeks. Aiden was only two years old.

'After that, my big brother killed himself in prison because he wasn't getting the medication he needed,' Despa said. 'Then my dad came out of prison after two years and breached his bail conditions. Police went looking for him. He supposedly tried to climb between two apartments and fell to his death from the thirteenth floor. Then my grandad died that year. So it was like bam, bam, bam.'

'That shit nearly took me out, bruv,' he said. 'It was too much at one time and I just didn't know how to process it all, man. I'd talk to my friends but they're not with you in your room when you're on your own. You go in your house, close your door and it's just you. It was a particularly fucked-up period of time, that's why I say I'm unbreakable. I've been to the bottom, like the *bottom*, where I don't have anything left. I've been there, I've fought it, fought the demon, like, *Okay, kill yourself.* Like, *Nah you should just do it.*'

Home had taken everything from him, had pushed him to the brink, and now at thirty-four he was finally re-piecing the jigsaw. Ayaana and Coen would not inherit those scars. They visit Walsall sometimes, and when they do, it is for a get-together with their grandma and their aunt. They would never know Walsall and Darlaston like he knew it, would never know how a home could pull you to pieces.

'I was depressed for ages, I lost my smile for years, I got really serious. But then when I looked to my son earlier on and he was giggling, I smiled inside and out. When my kids are together . . . seeing the way Ayaana's taken to him . . . she loves him . . . and the way he looks at her, seeing that . . . that is home, and I've never really had a home. I've never felt at home.'

Then he remembered an incident from yesterday. He had emptied the loose change from his wallet into the money box, a piggy bank he bought to teach both kids the value of saving.

The change totalled only a pound or so. He gave it to Coen. Then Ayaana told him, 'That's good. Sometimes you give me money and I put it in Coen's money box, too.'

And now, slightly tearful he said, 'I haven't taught her that. I had to give her a hug and say, "I'm so proud of you." She's sharing with her brother. Even thinking about it now . . . the way she is and the way she's embraced her bro and the happiness and love she's got for him, that there is . . . that is showing me the power of family.'

He was quiet, rubbed a tear from his eye.

'Seeing them . . . seeing that . . . that thing that they're building is a bit mad, because that's like, that's family, innit? That's making me happy. When I talk about home and them, it's completely unconditional love. You're my kids. People will say their kids are amazing, but you know what, bruv? My daughter is a fucking angel, man, she's so good.'

A little while later and they were driving now, Despa and his daughter out on the open road, out towards karate. Local news grumbled from the radio and the Jeep ate the tarmac into the city centre. They had left behind the big green trees and quiet streets of suburban South Birmingham. Despa hummed at the wheel and Ayaana doodled on an iPad in the backseat. The sun was dimming. A charming Birmingham evening was setting in, and the summer holidays were still young for father and daughter.

'What did you draw?' he said, calling out to her in the back, eyes still narrowed on the road.

Ayaana looked down at the iPad, saw the green crayoned grass, the shaggy square windows and the crooked walls of her sketch and, without lifting her eyes from the screen, told her dad, 'I drew a house!'

Then there was a brief pause, just the murmur of the radio and the rumble of the engine.

'Okay,' he said, and they kept on driving.

14 HIS LIGHT
SOUTH LONDON

Wireless and the conversation with Jamal both changed Cadet. He was still working but had arrived at a point where he had realised that he wasn't happy, that music was the only thing he loved, the only thing he could really work hard at without it ever feeling like *work*. He had seen how songs could move a crowd, bringing listeners closer to who he really was, how it built a bridge only frankness and sincerity could cross.

There was something to chase now, too. Everyone from the ends was trying to make a success of themselves. So if you were ready for a change like he was, you jump. If you were him, you think to yourself, *If I'm not going to have a happy life there's no point living.*

And so, working at the William Hill in Streatham was the last proper job he had, the last time he would push hours into something that ate at his soul, clocking in for a wage and nothing else. He reverted to type, became who he once was, a kid writing music before money and security and need for the survival muddied the waters. This move from certainty into the music industry, from stability into self-employment was Cadet following instinct. This second run in music was not a chase, but a calling, a man led by a rhythm that beat deep within.

The second run in music was different from the first. After leaving his job, at around twenty-five, he saw this as his only option, music the only thing he had going for him. Greatness is moulded by these forces, elements of push and pull guiding a person who has something, some burning expression waiting to leak out, and who in leaping towards a dream, feels it too late and too risky to turn back.

There was pressure. For Cadet, music and Rap was a vessel, a journey to find and fulfil purpose, to take care of his family, and to provide for any future loved ones that may spring into his world, like a partner and some children. It's why he took it more seriously than before, why in interviews he would say, 'This is my only option in life . . . This is all I have going for me, bro, this has to work, fam.'

And why, when his manager Reuben took him to a DJ Target show headlined by East London rapper Potter Payper, he stood in the middle of the hundred or so crowd, looked around and then left. Reuben found him outside. Cadet said that he was happy for Potter, but the show made him realise that he needed to work harder, that it needed to be him on a stage too, putting his life on a song, hearing the crowd sing his memories back.

Rappers never make the walk alone. There are friends and producers and managers who help steer their path, those who push and are pushed when many hands braid together to offer music up on an altar. Cadet had Reuben, his manager, who he met at a video shoot in Oxford Circus. There was his DJ, Skaps, who he met at a string of club nights and comedy shows. There was the photographer E Man, a videographer Raz, and Yung Filly, an online comedian and personality who would host his shows. Then there was Wonda his producer. Together, they called themselves the Underrated Legends.

In all of this, the relationship between producer and MC is sacred, two halves of a wider whole whose existence depends on the other, vocals sculpted to instrumentals, instrumentals sculpted to vocals, a give and take and give again until a song rises from the white space.

Wonda's story followed a well-worn pattern. He was from the deep South too, growing up to Ghanaian and Nigerian parents in Gipsy Hill and nearby Pollards Hill. In primary school days, at Kingswood in Norwood, he was listening to Krept and Konan and Weazy and Cadet, the olders in the ends. In those days it was Gipset and

Roadside Gs, it was the Pixel TV DVD and Sly Merkage mixtapes; it was his older sisters listening to So Solid and him being gassed whenever he spotted Megaman cutting through the manor.

Wonda MCed at first, like everyone did. Then in college he began producing. The call that changed things came while he was enrolled at university in Canterbury, and taking his final exams. Cadet needed an instrumental, explaining to Wonda that he had just been in contact with Jamal Edwards about bringing honesty and truth into his SBTV Warm Up Session, and that a specific kind of sound was needed to match the direction he was about to take his music in.

Wonda sent something back over, and when Cadet heard the soft, soulful synths and instruments laid over the tender knock of velvet drums, he felt it was the first time he could be brutally honest on a song, felt that if he had not been totally frank on the record, he would've done Wonda's work an injustice.

The music brought out a vulnerability in Cadet. Shortly after the SBTV session came a new freestyle titled 'Slut', which was released in July 2015. Whereas the Warm Up Session was a wide-ranging look at his life to date, 'Slut' zeroed in on his romantic and sexual relationships. In the video he sits on a chair, microphone in front of his face. A white T-shirt clothes his hulking frame. He has a pebble earring dotted on his earlobe and a fade with his distinguished slit rivering through the left side of his hair. Two girls stand out of focus in the background as they listen in on him unloading over another soulful Wonda instrumental.

'Slut' is a story about the heartbreak he had held in, about how teenage traumas and volatile relationships stripped him of innocence and muffled any craving for true intimacy. This is his fall from grace, childlike naivety and openness fracturing as he grew into a young man. Throughout he speaks candidly on the many moments that defined his history.

There was losing his virginity. There was his college sweetheart, and the fallout from infidelity on both sides. There was the Moroccan ex who fell pregnant, and her parents who rejected their union: 'They said culture should go with culture, you know? And that's just how shit be.'

There was the abortion that followed, a decision seemingly made without his input. It sat heavy on his heart. And there was the outing of his own hungering for sex in the aftermath. A dog is how he describes himself, scampering from woman to woman, seeking out sex wherever he could find it, selling dreams to some partners, others attracted to him because of his name. His behaviour was the consequence of a long line of unrecognised and unprocessed hurt from prior relationships.

At no point does he make excuses for his actions. The freestyle, nearly four minutes long, is a brutal piece of self-reflection and analysis, with a nod for those listening in judgement that 'just because you might call me a slut, don't mean there ain't shit I ain't been through'.

In the background, the two girls gasp in shock or nod in understanding as he goes. They smile at punchlines caught and stare intently as he purges himself. It was a sign of something, Cadet speaking with a rawness about heavy wounds, shedding on topics rarely broached in UK Rap or Black and immigrant households in Britain. His daring to show a side of himself many men conceal endeared him to the audience. They began to watch him process his life in real time.

To go inwards and pull on the threads of painful memories, Cadet would sit and write in his car. He would drive, roaming across South, music coming through his speakers, an instrumental on loop, something stirring within him. When it felt as if whole sentences were ready to come out, he would park up, turn the speakers loud and fall into a zone. Then song lyrics would form. Sometimes, he would sit in there, writing for hours until he dozed off, then wake up with the car battery gone dead, and would have to phone his sister

Chandler or a friend to come and give him a jump start.

Music was moving through him in rhythm. Once, Tech and a friend stumbled across him parked up in Brixton Hill, writing. His door was unlocked, and they pranked him by opening it and pretending to be strangers. After that, they told him, 'Be careful where you're pulling up.'

On other occasions, people would see him posting on Snapchat at three or four in the morning, turning over his thoughts during the quiet hours of the night. If he couldn't sleep, he would get into his car and write, or he would go on longer drives to clear his head, sometimes ending up as far out as Surrey.

In those early days of the second stretch, he struggled to find consistent studio space, and so sometimes Wonda would join him in the car, get his laptop out, connect a Bluetooth speaker and begin producing. Cadet would rap as they drove around, vocals sculpting to instrumental, instrumental sculpting to vocal.

This is how he went to the well, digging into himself to bring the truest version of Cadet to a record. Therapy helped tap into this side of himself, too. He first started going with his dad, Paul. Their relationship had broken down after Paul had gone away while struggling with addiction issues. And so when he was young Cadet would say things like, 'I don't need my dad,' and, 'I couldn't really care much, forget it,' and, 'I'm my own man, I can do things for myself.'

During his teenage years, when his dad came back on the scene, they struggled to reconnect. Living together was a struggle at first. At other times, Cadet would refuse to laugh at his jokes, and would tell him, 'Because you haven't been around in my life you have to put in 70 per cent to build this relationship, and I've only got to put in 30 per cent.'

He was hurting. He felt there had been so much disappointment that he no longer held any expectations. A part of him had gone cold, and it was one of the few situations he didn't like to speak about.

But when their relationship hit a brick wall, Paul suggested they see a counsellor. Cadet was hesitant at first, thinking why would he tell a counsellor the same things he could sit down and tell his friends? Why would this individual make all of the difference?

But he was wrong. Counselling taught him about accountability, taught him that if he was ever to rebuild this relationship, effort would have to be equal. He had a responsibility too. If he knew his dad wouldn't say 'I love you' first but would only say it in return, then it was on Cadet to make that first step.

Their relationship began to heal through the process. But there were still some things he couldn't bring himself to say in the sessions. Then Wonda sent him a beat. It was a tender soundscape, and when it hits your ears, sounds like clear sunlight on a quiet Sunday morning. Cadet wrote to it in his car, and began to loosen the locks on his soul.

He shared this part of him on a Link Up TV Behind Barz freestyle, the same platform on which Krept and Konan had shed their stories of South London years back. This freestyle came a month after 'Slut'. This time he is standing in the booth, a Link Up TV-branded microphone in front of him. There are headphones coiled over his ears and he is wearing a blue tracksuit with a matching blue cap. A gold tooth sparkles in his mouth.

When the instrumental begins to play, holy light flowing through the booth, he shouts out his supporters, thankful for their backing, then closes his eyes tight and dials back . . .

The moment that broke him was a birthday at around six or seven years old. His mum was throwing him a party, and his dad was supposed to pass through, even telling Cadet that he was bringing him a Sega Mega Drive as a gift.

But by eight in the evening, his dad still hadn't showed. Cadet ran into his room and put his face to the window, peering down the road, hoping to see his dad appearing in the distance.

After some time, with still no sign of Paul, his mum told him to come away from the glass, to return to the party and at least blow out his candles. But he refused, falling asleep at the window, till the side of his face went numb.

The hurt and the memory burned him. By the time he was in the booth, eyes closed, sweat seeping from under his cap, grimacing as he dug up the past, he was twenty-five and hadn't really celebrated a birthday ever since.

When he linked up with his dad years later, he was able to hear what had really happened all those years ago, how he was addicted to crack, how he had the Mega Drive but sold it when he was on the high street, minutes away from the house.

And so, after the pain in the first half of the freestyle comes the slow road to redemption. There is the father he knows now, the dad who recovered from addiction and turned his life around, the dad who would take him to buy a new suit when he had job interviews, the dad who downloaded Twitter so he could retweet Cadet's music.

It took a lot out of him to put these stories into a song. He was parked up in his car writing, almost breaking down into tears as the traumas not even counselling could wedge free began to come loose. He spoke to his dad about it, asking if he was okay with his stumble and rise being put onto song for the world to see.

He was okay with it, he told Cadet.

'Are you sure?'

'Yes,' he said. 'That's not me any more. I used to be an addict but that's not who I am any more.'

When the freestyle came out, Cadet felt lighter, as if something had been lifted off him. He began to receive messages too, personal notes from far corners as the freestyle spread, eventually climbing to more than a million views. Grown people of all walks of life reached out, some saying it helped with their own relationships; one whose dad came looking for him after hearing Cadet speak, others crying because the freestyle meant more than words could express. Another person told him that the freestyle spurred them to check in on their own dad. The father passed away a month later.

By sharing himself in these freestyles scattered throughout 2015, Cadet began to build steam, his second run in music drawing in the expanding audience of UK Rap. He began to make a reputation as one of the most skilled and most honest storytellers active within the genres. His contribution to the scene was unique, and to consolidate the mounting buzz, he dropped his debut EP, *The Commitment*. Released in February 2016, it was seven tracks long, largely produced by Wonda. The title was about his devotion to music. It was a signpost of his transition. What was once a hobby had become a job and now a career.

As he readied to release the project, he sat for a video interview with a YouTube platform called Amaru Don TV, run by a man named Amaru. In their series of conversations, Cadet laid himself bare, each video acting as a time stamp and a reference point for where his mind was at as he navigated the music industry. Their first conversation was on the eve of *The Commitment* being released, when his walk out into the unknown was just beginning. They filmed it at the YouTube space in Tottenham Court Road. Cadet is dressed in black, sat in front of a camera. Amaru is out of shot, listening to Cadet speak about his journey and the intro song from the EP.

The truth was that financially he wasn't doing well. He had quit his job, closing off the safer road to making money, and with music being a slow, long-yielding grind for artists of that era, he was putting his faith in Rap, and the hope that eventually he would make ends meet. This was the sobering reality of self-employment and dream chasing.

He had been broke, flat on his face at times, he says. But, he added,

'It's better to be broke for the right reasons, than rich for the wrong reasons.'

What bleeds through in their conversation is an extreme drive, a determination to turn his words into something of personal, communal and material value.

'I am *going* to be here. I am *going* to be a name. I am *going* to be a force,' he says. 'My whole point is to be a legend. I'm going to be something that you would definitely remember. This is my commitment, it's like marriage, I'm going to be here for the rest of my life.'

Amaru left the interview feeling an honesty in the aura that emanated from Cadet, an emotional vulnerability and understanding that was rare. Cadet felt like a man you wanted to help, he said, a man who would eventually figure it all out. His prediction proved to be right.

———

I met Cadet in this period too. I was working at SBTV at the time, the YouTube platform owned by Jamal Edwards, where Cadet had first debuted his introspective freestyles. By the time I was there, early 2016, a few weeks before *The Commitment* came out, he was entrenched in the core of the scene, his freestyles shuddering the landscape, just as he had wanted. And now, he had another long piece written called 'Stereotype'. He wanted to share it with us and Jamal.

He arrived at the offices on a winter weekday evening. London had gone dark and cold. Throughout the afternoon he had been going round performing the freestyle to different people. Before us, he had recited the piece to Posty, owner of GRM Daily, and a few weeks before that, he had spat it to Krept and Konan and Section Boyz and the rest of the boys from The 7 when they gathered at a video shoot for Krept.

In the SBTV office, we sat in a large meeting room in the back. There were about five, six or seven of us: Jamal and Cadet, a boy who rolled with him and a few of us employees. The lights were beamed on. Chairs were huddled in a semicircle and Cadet was in the middle. After casual small talk, the room went silent, and with the floor his, Cadet began.

He had come to tell us about his relationship with his mum, and as we sat there, listening for around five minutes, ceiling lights charging down, London's wandering darkness out beyond the windows, a tearful portrait of a sorry son began to emerge. I was hearing about a Cadet who doesn't call her as much as he should, who when he got his car, told her that she would never have to lay a foot on the ground again, but whose heart sinks when he rings her and hears the bus groaning in the background.

A Cadet who would spend his last money on clothes, who would pay taxes but was too embarrassed to sign on, who felt he was slacking as a brother and a grandson, and who was here on the first floor of an office complex in central London, baring his flaws and mistakes and regrets to a handful of strangers.

The full song surfaced online a few weeks later. As the months went by, he again began to receive messages from people who had listened. Some said that 'Stereotype' compelled them to go and visit their mum the next day. Others told him that he gave them strength to get through their own difficult situations. One message came from somebody who went to check in on their nan. She passed the week after. Because of 'Stereotype' and Cadet, they had been able to share an extra day together.

These freestyles were a cleansing. They were Cadet owning his shortcomings and poor decisions, and not feeling afraid or ashamed to speak of them. Being comfortable in his skin was the only way he could move forward. He was using music to heal himself and his relationships. And, by fronting up, and broadcasting his process of personal and family healing, he gave a space and a crutch for others to do the same.

That healing became a fixture of South London Rap. He released another open song titled 'Letter to Krept', which patched things up with his cousin. Krept responded with his own candid 'Letter to Cadet', rebuilding and restrengthening their early childhood bond.

Through his freestyles Cadet was embedding a radical openness into the DNA of the sound, offering a new template for the next generation of rappers from the region to filter their stories and experiences through. This process of addition and refinement is how Rap and wider MC culture distinguishes itself in a region, local musicians incrementally carving at an imported genre until it resembles something distinctly its own. South London Rap, descended from a steady lineage of MC culture, born of Grime and UK Rap, influenced by Dancehall and US Hip Hop, and hand-shaped by the second- and third-generation British-Caribbean and British-African kids, had become a sound mirroring the gradual emergence and arrival of a distinct Black identity, specific to Britain and South London.

Beating through the blood of generations of Black people raised in the region were the forces of sustained migration and the unique conditions of working-class communities here. This continual melding had seen Black Britain extend out into its own singular branch of the Black diaspora's global family tree. South London Rap, and Cadet's work, were a soundtrack to this evolution.

In December 2016 he threw a headline show at the O2 Academy Islington where a sold-out crowd of 800 people crammed in under the lights to hear him speak. When the tickets were announced and then started flying, Cadet couldn't believe what was happening; was confused that people were actually coming out to see him. When the evening arrived, and he saw a long queue snaking from the venue, out of the event complex and almost onto the high street, he thought, *Why are you travelling to see me?* Watching the supporters in the flesh was overwhelming.

On stage, he performs the memoirs Wonda's productions pulled out of him, sharing his story with these loyal listeners. A chorus of camera lights dot the darkness. When he looks out, he can see the crowd squeezed up against the barriers as if they are desperate to reach out and grab every word and lyric leaving his mouth. It felt like a close family gathered in communal prayer. They recite 'Slut' with him, and for some of his more hype songs, he jumps into the crowd, performing among the mosh pit.

The relationships healed and mended because of his music will be celebrated tonight. For 'Behind Barz', he cradles over the standing microphone, shoulders hulking as usual, a black tracksuit fed down from his head to his toe. The crowd rap with him, and when the song is finished, his dad Paul walks onto stage and embraces him, a deep hug shared between father and son, the crowd rejoicing loud in the background.

He performs 'Letter to Krept', and as the song closes, the instrumental for 'Letter to Cadet' begins to play and his cousin walks out to surprised screams, two halves of a foundation-setting family sharing their renewed love for one another.

The stage begins to crowd as the evening goes on. When his centre-piece 'Stereotype' is performed, Cadet extends the microphone out towards the crowd and they cry out every word. His mum is on stage. She is with his sister, Chandler, and his little brother Dillen. She sways gently to the instrumental. When Cadet delivers the lyrics written in testimony to her, he bends down on his knees before her, rapping, 'Mum, I ain't been the best son,' shedding the loads he had carried around with him. As the music plays, she steps forward and lowers down, then kisses him on the forehead. He rises, microphone in hand, and steps out, ready to face the watching crowd.

———

Music gradually began to pay off. In July 2017, he was booked to play Wireless Festival. It was a full-circle moment, two years after he had stood side of stage and soaked it all in. Back then, Krept had told him that this could all be his, and that afternoon it was.

For so long, Cadet had felt like he was on the bench, watching the scene from the sidelines – now he was in the game. For that he was grateful, but also hungry for more. After his set, he wandered around the bigger stages holding visions of himself up there one day.

A part of him, no matter what he had achieved, or the road map his career was on, still felt unsatisfied, overlooked, underrated. He had a tattoo scribed 'Underrated' on his left arm. On his wall, there was a quote that read, 'You should be ashamed to die until you become somebody worth learning about.' Sometimes his status on WhatsApp said: 'Living as a failure is just as good as being in a grave.'

Wireless didn't book him for the following year, and that irked him. And at Leeds Festival, where he and the Underrated Legends tore up the set, a steward stopped him afterwards, congratulated him, and then let slip that beforehand, the organisers had tagged Cadet's set as one that would likely not be busy. He had proven them all wrong.

Others noticed this streak in Cadet too. His counsellor saw in him a young man who felt like he needed to reach a certain point before he could term himself successful, even though, in many ways, he already was. When their sessions would finish, Cadet would always head to the studio, eager to eke out every bit of potential resting in his bones. Purpose and a restless drive had brought him to this point in his career, and as music began to pay, they still sat in him, simmering in uneasy suspension.

By 2018, UK Rap had moved into a space where big singles were bringing in money, providing gateways to the kind of platform and success that could be life-changing. Songs by artists like J Hus, Swarmz and Not3s from London, Young T and Bugsey from Nottingham, and Lotto Boyzz from Birmingham saw artists bringing Afrobeat and Dancehall influences into UK Rap, with bouncy hooks and half-sung, half-rapped cadences cruising over melodic instrumentals. The subgenre was termed Afroswing or Afrobashment. These were the kind of songs that lived on loop in house parties and nightclubs, that played in the barbers and on daytime, mainstream radio, that sat with both the mandem and Middle England.

In 2018, this was the climate Cadet existed in. He wanted to make an anthem of his own. Around this time, in an interview with Amaru, he said his life had become so simple, so focused:

'My life is every day thinking how am I going to get a banger.'[1]

Nothing else mattered, he said, not relationships, not his family, not his health. He knew it wasn't healthy. But he had been teased by a glimpse at mass success, had seen sold-out crowds at his own headline shows, had caused carnage at festivals, he had quit his job for this, and now he was close. He wanted to see it through. He was searching, looking for the songs that would fulfil his dreams, that would provide for him and his family and his friends, and show tangible proof that the risks had been worth it.

The single that changed his life came by chance. Cadet had been cast in a short film, *Shiro's Story*, by the UK rapper-turned-director Rapman, also from South London. It was a musical of sorts, combining rapping with extended scenes of acting to tell a story about loss, youth violence and fatherhood in the city. When Part 1 was uploaded to Link Up TV, it quickly went viral, riding in the slipstream of the UK Rap boom, scaling views in the millions. A Part 2 was put into the works, and Cadet and other high-profile individuals from the scene like Konan and Ashley Walters were brought into the fold.

Cadet was on set one afternoon when Rapman dismissed everyone for an hour so a scene could be filmed in secret. Everyone went their separate ways, and standing alone was Deno, a young sixteen-year-old rapper from Brixton by way of Eritrea, who had blown up on social media with a few Afroswing songs of his own. When Cadet saw Deno standing alone, he said, 'Come roll with me, we got an hour.'

They drove around together, stopped for some food. Cadet brough Deno to his house, gave him a tracksuit, and when he realised they were the same shoe size, gave him some trainers too. After they got back into the car, Cadet even began to teach Deno how to drive, as well as giving him counsel about music. He told him that even though they were on a break from work, it was no excuse to ease off. So, they began freestyling over a hybrid Rap and Afroswing instrumental.

In their bars, they were bantering each other, not thinking too hard about the lyrics, just throwing lines back and forth as they sat side by side in the front, Cadet taking the role of the big brother by attempting to school his younger.

They filmed it, and after, he uploaded the freestyle to Instagram. It quickly began to spread virally. Konan rang him up and told him that the freestyle needed to be a full song, that he should capitalise on the moment.

The official track, 'Advice', came out in late summer, and continued to spread, playing in the house parties and on the radio, in clubs and eventually bleeding over into Middle England. By December, Cadet and Deno had been in the Official Singles Charts for weeks, rising from the Top 40 to the Top 30, and then hovering on the edges of the Top 20. They had cleared 10 million streams on Spotify, had surpassed that figure on YouTube, and through it all, they were independent, the song being released on Cadet's label Underrated Legends.

This was his crossover moment. When Krept and Konan played a sold-out Alexandra Palace, the 10,000-capacity arena in North London, Cadet and Deno came out as special guests. The crowd knew every word. Online, videos surfaced of white toddlers in far-flung counties nodding their heads to the melody and singing along to the lyrics.

From the outside, friends could see that his life was changing. Ashley, from the old days at The Listening Company, would be driving around in the daytime when his friend's voice and songs would suddenly boom out of the radio. When he, Cadet and Matt would go for their usual shisha catch-ups at a spot in Croydon, strangers would be staring in at Cadet through the windows.

Elsewhere, when Cadet and Matt tried to roll to Westfields, Cadet would constantly get stopped by supporters, so much so that Matt had to play security, telling the flocking listeners that there could be no more pictures. After that they only went post-9 p.m. His once normal life was slipping away.

His mum, Janice, could see the change too. His face was plastered on a billboard in Norwood Junction, and he took her one day to go and see it. On another occasion, she was out shopping for CDs in Tooting Market when a customer went to the counter and asked if they had any Cadet in stock. She was stunned.

New fame can be isolating for British rappers. They enter rare air, moving into a space far removed from the people they grew up with, staring down difficulties and time pressures and alien conditions neither they, nor their friends or family, have likely faced before. They are isolating shoes to walk in, a lonely road that sometimes grows a distance between an artist and the tribe they grew with.

Cadet walked this road, music eating away at his time, parts of himself unavailable in the way they once were. But at his core he never changed. He told Matt to think of a business idea, and that he would front him the money until the project was profitable. On another day he arrived at Amaru's house and randomly gifted him an iPad. He encouraged Tech to keep rapping, telling his friend that all of this was possible for him too. The pair remained close. After one of Cadet's sold-out London shows, they drove back to Clapham High Street and sat in a kebab house, chatting for hours.

At a food shop in Norwood, local to his dad, Paul, Cadet put money behind the till, meaning Paul wouldn't have to pay when he next visited. Paul was happy for his son and the progress he had made, was proud when Cadet moved into a new dream flat with a concierge and a gym. The only change he saw in him was that he worked even harder now, the joys of a music career running bone-deep.

One day, when the two were on the phone, Paul asked, 'Are you happy?'

'Huh?' came the response.

'Are you happy, son?' he repeated.

'Yeah, Dad,' Cadet eventually said, 'I'm happy.'

15 **BROKEN**
SOUTH WALES

'Maybe this isn't what I'm supposed to be doing? . . .
I remember being sat in an Addison Lee, going to my five-
star hotel in Kensington and I've got two grand of Adidas
clothes in the taxi with me, my phone's blowing off, I've
got a sold-out show; I'm feeling like the man . . . and then
it was like . . . I've still got a void in me . . . and . . . I'm
not happy . . . I achieved what I wanted to achieve to a
degree, and it's not it. I need to pull out and find myself.'

PHIL DAVIES, ASTROID BOYS

They were out on the continent for weeks, for months, for years,
forever on some motorway linking regions. Maybe somewhere
between Copenhagen and Hamburg, or Prague and Vienna,
peering out from a tour bus, the borders and backwaters of mainland
Europe drifting by on the windshield. Days out in Warsaw. Days in
Groningen and Novara. A new city. A new stage. A new crowd pulling in on the horizon.

Another show.

Another encore.

Another batch of merch sold.

And then the open motorway again. Fourteen hours till the next
destination. Just wheels and tarmac and a tour bus. Strap in.

'The touring life,' Phil says, 'I hit it hard for too long. I think I toured consistently for like six years . . . and we never took a break, we were just constantly on it.'

Your first tours are a baptism in the fire. The boys were on a mad one, South Wales kids cutting loose on the continent. But after a while, when the buzz waned and the thrill faded, and the tour bus stiffened to a silence, they fell into their phone screens, gazed at their distant, once-regular realities moving by on the other side of an Instagram feed.

Although you are with your friends for days on end, for eight-week tours and six-week tours back-to-back, out there, on the road, is isolation.

'It's just brain-numbing, man, driving for hours and hours,' Phil says. 'Your home is in your phone. Contact with the outside world is through this thing.'

The road can be a lonely place for a new Christian convert. He began to grow apart from the boys on those last few outings. He was new to faith, had been baptised, had found a church, had met a girlfriend who would become his wife. They had bonded deeply over their shared religion. He was realigning his moral compass, and, he says, 'that creates a little bit of division . . . because naturally it puts you on two different paths.'

Towards the end of their time on the road, Phil remembers how it began to feel as if 'I'm doing my own thing, you're doing your own thing.'

He would sit backstage at a show, reading his Bible and drinking ginger tea, praying and hitting pads. And then when the curtain dropped and the music kicked in, he would become Traxx: Rowdy. Unruly. Ready for a riot.

Another show.

Another encore.

Another batch of merch sold.

Then once the set closed and they were on the road again, he was back to Phil, back to his Bible and his God. It was a stagger between the old paths and new realities, a dance between his present and past selves.

There were conflicts as these two worlds converged. Once they went out on tour with a band whose frontman seemed to be a Satanist, carrying out rituals on stage as well as in his dressing room, while sitting with candles and other tools.

Phil watched from afar, standing backstage feeling uneasy, quietly praying to himself before he entered every arena:

Who God blesses, no man can curse.

'I felt I was in a war every day.'

Eventually, while out in the wilderness, he began to think to himself, *I need a break from this.*

Then the road eventually brought him home to Cyprus. He was in Ayia Napa. It was summer season in town, a time of year when the streets flood with young ravers from across the continent, and the annual spike in tourism breathes life into the steaming nightclubs and street bars on the local strip. Phil was in town for a show.

Some mornings, before sunbreak, with the island and its new residents finally at rest, he would ride his quad bike out to the bay by the border with Turkey, park up and leap from the cliffs into the water, just like he had done all those years ago. The place was still the same, the sand still a teasing white gold, the water still nibbling the coast, and the ridges still scratching at the heavens.

It was 5 a.m. now on one of those early mornings, and the bay was pitch black. He leapt from the cliff, and then floated in the shallows alone, wondering to himself quietly: *What am I doing with my life now?*

And then he remembered what had happened out here in the ocean, remembered where his life had been six years ago.

'Yo God, you're real!'

Still floating. Still crying.

'You're with me.'

Still breathing. Still here.

'I'm with you!'

Still alive.

And then there was what had come after. He had started Astroid Boys. He had worked his childhood visions into a band on the vanguard of a movement. They had shifted what was possible for kids coming out of working-class Wales with music inside them.

He had been reborn in faith. He was a man of God. He was growing distant from who he was once.

Then he heard that soft voice in his head again, the same whisper, the same intuition that guided him home six years ago.

And so, in those early hours out in the sea, the crest of an old yellow sun breaking over the water, promising a new day, he was realising that his time with Astroid Boys was coming to a close.

For the next chapter of his life to begin, what they had built would have to end.

He sat there alone, thinking:

But I don't even want to. This is what I do.

He was uneasy. He was anxious. He was afraid.

What am I gonna do next?

I've got nothing else; I've got no qualifications, I've got no other things.

I'm done for.

And so, Phil left Cyprus, conflicted.

Back to South Wales. Back to Cardiff.

Within a year, he was out.

———

In the late summer of 2017, the boys played Boomtown festival in the South Downs. It was a standard Astroid Boys affair: MCs stalking the stage, a crowded tangle of limbs at their feet. It was a prelude to the coming spring, when they were set to take *Broke* across the country on their first ever album tour, the beginning of a new chapter.

But when the show finished, Phil came to Dell and broke his news, told him that he no longer wanted to continue, that he would see out their remaining shows and then after that, he was done, he was out.

'I was, "Like, fair play, I'm not going to tell you what to do,"' Dell remembers. '"As much as it's my wellbeing as well, whatever, man, it's cool."'

They would split after the tour.

A band can be a lonely place for a producer. Dell made *Bacon Dream* and *CF10* in his bedroom back in Newport with a Mac and some speakers and a keyboard, pulling the Astroid Boys' soundscape out of cracked software and the fragments of polar genres. He was still in school at the time, studying for his GCSEs, playing around with beats, trying to make something work.

But things changed when they signed to Sony, who needed an album. For *Broke* he moved out of his bedroom set-up and into a studio in Newport: a garage he converted behind the leisure centre in town. For *Broke* he was forced to step up. For *Broke* he switched production software from Reason to Ableton and was able to record vocals and guitars in his new place, felt like his limitations were lifting, felt like his horizons were broadening, felt 'like a new fucking man, a new producer'.

He remembers how things started to turn. The label needed demo recordings, so he wrote them himself. And he remembers hauling his 27-inch Mac to Phil's house, or to a church across town to record the studio sessions. Then when he was finished recording and engineering the session, he would set aside time to treat and mix the vocals, blending Phil's slightly more nasal tones and Benji's more rounded and low-end voice into a simmering union, a process that took him months to eventually perfect.

He remembers crafting the instrumentals, mixing the instrumentals, pulling in ad-libs and shouts and then mixing these elements into a completed song. Twenty demos in total. Eighteen tracks finished. Dell sat by his Mac from 10 a.m. to 2 a.m. every day and every night, working and recording until the album was done, feeling overworked, feeling like he needed assistance, and knowing that the only resolution to these issues was to pay someone to step in and shoulder some of the burden; a resolution he knew would never happen. So he firmed it.

Years later, when he had space to look back on those years, he would say, 'I wish I didn't do that. I wish I didn't have that all on my shoulders.

'It made me quite fucking depressed to be honest. Everyone's chilling, living life, getting their money, and I wasn't vocal enough about how hard it was because I knew that nobody else could do it.

'Maybe I was precious over it. Maybe I knew offloading it to other people, you don't get the desired result. I just felt like I knew what I had to be. I knew what sound we were going with having done *CF10*, having done *Bacon Dream*, having played the shows, having been on stage doing the microphone. I just felt like I knew what I had to be, man, and sadly I had to go through that, get it done, to be like, "I ain't doing that again." But at least it exists.'

For those years in the band, Dell lived with two worlds in him, fraying lines separated by the thin boundaries of music and home, of Astroid Boys and Newport. Dell moving into Elliot, Elliot moving into Dell, fragments of himself never mixing, like oil and water.

Where he was from, he knew people who had never left the country, who had never been on holiday. People who grew up, left school, then settled down with a partner and stayed within the local confines of their hometowns for a lifetime. This life he had, which had panned into a revolving door of stages and bands and cities across the continent, rarely happened to people he knew. Not to kids from his part of Newport, not to a teenager from St Julians, not to anyone.

He had seen his music move souls, kids with their band name tattooed on their skin, supporters who told him that the tones of Astroid Boys had guided them out of dark places, had led them to friends and community. He had been to the edges of Europe, spent weekends spitting bars onstage to hundreds, and playing out festivals to thousands. And then he would come home, back to Newport, back to St Julians, back to school the next day and sit in a Geography lesson after playing Glastonbury or Newcastle. He was home, Elliot again. It was a splintering of him, 'the birth of two different kind of people', he says, 'was almost like leading a double life'.

When back in Newport he never spoke about what happened or what he saw on his weekends away, never mentioned the band and the music because, he says, 'of that mentality of what life is', in Newport and similar towns.

'If somebody is doing something a bit extraordinary, or out of the normal, playing shows or having fans, people are quick to take the stance of "Alright, mate, who do you think you are?"'

'I think that played into me keeping my head down,' he said, and when people would enquire about his endeavours, he would keep it brief, would say, 'I'm in a band, we play some tunes and we just played Glastonbury.'

'It did disconnect me from my life in Newport,' he said, because, 'it wasn't like I was around people who were doing the same thing. I felt quite alone.'

There was isolation on the road and at the shows too, the same sense of separation and blurring of boundaries between dream and reality, fiction and truth.

He was fourteen when they first started to hit the live circuit, the rest of the boys smuggling him into the early clubs and over-eighteens venues they played. By the time he was eighteen or nineteen, the venues got bigger and the music began to take them across Britain, to venues in Middlesbrough or Leeds or Norfolk, the arenas a meeting spot for an emerging cult following. Wherever they went, they would be swamped by supporters who sometimes treated them like demigods, who idolised their words, who gushed over their music, who queued for photos after the show and who assumed wealth and affluence had partnered the rise and popularity of their music. Outside of some venue in some faraway place, excited supporters would approach the boys, shaking and trembling, raining praise in their ears:

'You're killing it, boys.'

'Can you sign this?!'

'Ah, ya killing it, it's amazing.'

But supporters never knew that money was still tight in a band where everything was split five ways; they never knew that riches had not followed years of steady grind; never knew that sometimes they never sold enough merch to pay the van hire the next morning; that Dell had spent months writing *Broke*, unable to work, still living at home in Newport with his mother and his grandad.

And so Dell, standing outside of the venue with supporters, slightly uncomfortable at times, would think to himself, *But I'm no different to you, I'm just a kid . . . I'm just a normal kid, I live at home in Newport.*

When he got home, back to Newport, back to St Julians, he would be silent about it all.

'So many times, I felt like I was missing out on a childhood and an adolescence,' he says. 'I like getting up to things, I like being mischievous, I like breaking rules.'

He remembers a night around the time Astroid Boys inked their record deal with Sony. He was still in school, and it was Bonfire Night in Newport. He and a few of his friends from home had taken shrooms and were headed out to a park to light fireworks and watch them crackle and burst in the black sky above South Wales; young boys, not quite men, feeling out the edges of their world, an early adolescent rite of passage. The other boys were not yet in university, or on a career path, had few responsibilities, had nothing to lose, had no band that was teasing a breakout. But Dell's life was different. And so, while he walked through Newport, on the way to the park, he felt uneasy. With a record deal and a band and an album in the works and Class As in his system, he began to fret about consequences, visions of being confronted by the police and his career crumbling into dust, everything he had worked for slipping out of his grasp, six years fumbled and lost. Anxious about what could happen, his mind ticked over:

Is that going to end my career?

Is that going to change my life?

Is that going to take away the things I worked so hard for the past five years?

Shit, I've got things on the line here. If I get locked up, what are the label going to say about that?

Is that going to damage my reputation?

Eventually, he stopped and turned to the boys.

'You're all going to think I'm a pussy but I'm making a decision here,' he told them. He told them he was heading back to the house, that he felt uneasy, that he would listen out for the fireworks. And then he went home.

————

The band carried on for a while after Phil and Dell left. Astroid Boys was grinding to a halt. But Benji stayed on.

'I didn't want to let go,' he said, 'because in my head I was like, *We're on the cusp of something good here.*'

Prison changes a person. A version of you walks in, and at the end of a stretch, a different one leaves. When Benji was inside, all he could think about was freedom and writing music again. But when he left, in the winter of 2014, finally able to dive back into Rap and melody, there was a part of him that didn't want to.

How do you scramble for steady ground above the moving wheels of a tour bus?

Things moved fast when Benji came home. The band's hard work was beginning to bear fruit. They had *Bacon Dream* out in the world, and his verses on *CF10* needed writing and recording. He was on tag. He was in studio sessions. He was on the Benji's Back tour across the country. He was on stage in Southampton and Manchester and London in the afternoons. He was screaming his lyrics to kids who knew every word. And by evening, he was back in Cardiff for curfew. His world was moving again, and he needed to move with it.

'I was just wrapped up in a whirlwind,' he says, 'and never really had a moment to settle. And that eventually started to chew me up.'

He began drinking and using substances, and messing around with women: 'Self-control issues that I had,' he says, 'because nobody could tell me no.'

He was suffering, struggling to reckon with his vices in an industry that encourages abandon from its artists, that encourages them to get fucked up. He was coming apart in a job that hands you a crate of beer every night, puts you out in front of a crowd and needs you to act like a hooligan.

'That's a trap,' he said. 'I don't really know how to explain it. The words coming to my mind were *that wasn't fair on me*. But then I don't know if that's the right sentence, because I suppose it's me that has to be in control.

'But when I say it wasn't fair on me, what I feel wasn't fair was that I didn't know how dangerous that life I was living was until it was backfiring, till I started to upset people and take people for granted.

'Like, you know, me and Dell. We have a difficult relationship now because we got into so many heated discussions where I was often drinking. I probably didn't have the most polite way of saying things, so I think I deeply hurt his feelings all the time. And I did that with a number of other people.

'There's being drunk at the time, that's one problem. But the other problem is when you're drinking five days in a row. You just become quite a horrible bastard. You're drinking through hangovers, you're just grumpy. I just wasn't that pleasant for a long time, I know that.'

During the band's final stretch together, in those months when the wheels were coming off and an end of seven years was looming into view, Benji found out he was going to be a father.

'Phil wanted to get married,' he remembers, 'I was having a baby, Dell was getting a bit sick of the way he was being treated, by everybody, not just me . . . I think the boys were kinda like, "Let's just knock this on the head for a bit now."'

This chapter of their lives was ending. They had run their course. A season was closing out. But Benji clung tight, refusing to relent, even when it was only him of the three left. He wanted to keep moving with the roadshow, wanted to throw tours, remembers thinking to himself, *I've got a baby coming. This is all I really know.*

'I literally was like a dog with a bone, I wouldn't fucking let it go.'

In the winter of 2018, a year after *Broke* was released, an Astroid Boys line-up, headed up by Benji, without Phil and Dell, embarked on their final tour. Newcomers were brought in to replace the absent members, and Benji tried to crack on. They would start in Glasgow in October and end in Sheffield in January.

But midway through the tour, in the New Year, the *NME* reported that the band was set to go on indefinite hiatus. They reposted a Facebook post from Benji that read:

I'd like to first apologise for the confusion over the past few months regarding AB. Some of the key members have indeed left the band and there will be a hiatus from the end of this tour. I've not been handling the changes very well and I guess my mental health hit the ground.

I was pissed that the boys didn't want to make any more AB music. I wanted to keep AB going and was willing to do anything to make that happen. I made a mistake. I should have left with the others and saved the AB legacy but instead I booked more shows and let myself fall into a pit of depression.

I've had a good few weeks over Christmas and new year and I'm ready to smash these last few shows. I guess what I'm saying is that after this tour and the two local shows that have been agreed, I won't be playing any more AB shows or making any AB inspired music.

It's done! So if u want one more chance to vibe out to 'posted' 'dusted' 'dirt' 'minging' etc., etc. please buy tickets and help me say goodbye to the most exciting thing that I have ever been a part of.

By the end of January 2019, Astroid Boys was over.

16 THE RATED LEGEND
SOUTH LONDON

9 February 2019. Around 1.30 a.m.

Cadet is in the back of an Uber, riding a quiet stretch of village road in Wrinehill, where the borders of the West Midlands and North West England meet. He is with his DJ Skaps, his photographer Ed and another friend, Money. They are on the way to a show at nearby Keele University where Cadet has been booked to perform that night.

The road is open and dark and feels like the middle of nowhere. As they approach a bend, the headlights of a speeding red van appear out in front. The van is moving at twice the speed limit, its driver is drunk and travelling in the wrong lane. Somebody in the Uber yells, and then the van hits them head-on.

A statement from Shropshire Police read:

Following the collision, the male rear seat passenger of the car was treated by paramedics from West Midlands Ambulance Service at the scene, but sadly, despite their best efforts, the man was pronounced dead at the scene.

He has since been identified as Blaine Cameron Johnson, also known as Cadet, aged twenty-eight, from London.

———

Death freezes loved ones. The seconds and the minutes and the hours that follow can feel like a dream, a numbness carving that moment into clear memory. And even when the years pass, the flashes of where and who you were when you heard the news can remain fresh, a mark in the road where your old self left, and a new version of you, with a part of itself missing, staggered on.

Many were sleeping when the news came in, awoken by phone calls in the middle of the night, and then passing the message on to unaware family and friends. Some were working late shifts. Some were on holiday. Some got the news live from the scene via phone call. Some slept through to morning and only realised what had happened when they woke to a flood of messages. Some saw the official statement the family released via Cadet's Instagram at daybreak, and even then, didn't want to believe it, holding faith until they arrived at the family home in Clapham and saw relatives and close ones gathered on the steps.

The family and friends went into mourning, and after the news broke publicly, the wider community did too. There was a void. The Johnsons had lost one of their own. Britain had lost one of its most treasured and respected MCs, and so the family, as well as the close-knit scene from which he sprang and participated in, began to reckon with their grief.

How does South London mourn one of its own?

Music can be hard to understand and contextualise for those with loved ones who are artists. YouTube views and Spotify streams and chart numbers never show the full picture. They are figures on a screen that struggle to measure how a musician has reached out and touched the lives of those who listened. Krept wanted the family to see in the flesh just how much his cousin had touched the people, so later that afternoon, a message went out across social media that the next day, Sunday the 10th, there would be a gathering in Hyde Park at 3 p.m., a balloon release at 4 p.m., and all were invited.

Sunday was blue skies with streaks of white clouds stretched thin across the horizon. A cold London afternoon. In Hyde Park, by the Serpentine Lake, where the paddle boats dock, thousands gathered. They were in bloated puffer jackets and hoodies to shield from the winter. They were immediate family and close friends. They were old work colleagues and boys Cadet had known since the playpen. They were supporters who had travelled from across the country. They were small children with tears running down their cheeks. They were rappers and DJs. They were music-industry people. They were supporters embracing one another in tight hugs. They were groups of bikers revving and spinning their tyres on the pavement in tribute. They were the many lives his music had touched, and they were gathered here in the park, holding balloons in their fingers with messages of love scrawled across the rubber.

Some of his friends were shocked at the turnout, at how far his music had reached. Some walked through the crowds in a daze, still unable to register his passing. Many of his loved ones were in tears. The family were standing by the lake, facing the thousands. Then the crowd fell quiet, the gathered allowing space for the Johnsons to speak.

Cadet's Mum, Janice, told them, 'I'm just so glad that his music has just touched you in whatever way it's touched you, enough for you to come out and it just gives me just so great pleasure . . . My son's life was not in vain. He was not in vain. He was able to maybe touch your lives and influence you to do what and achieve whatever you want to be. Whatever.'

She continued, 'I need you men to express yourselves, express your feelings.'

Krept told them, 'I just wanna say that if you have any issues with anyone that you love or you're close to, please resolve it because I am so glad that me and him was able to resolve our situation before this happened, because if I didn't it would have ate me up for the rest of my life.'

Cadet's dad, Paul, was in a puffer jacket and a woolly hat. He had a ring on his pinkie finger, and standing looking out at the crowd, he was choked up. 'As I came to the park today, I can't believe . . . I can't believe all these people he's touched.'

Then his voice trailed off and his breath got shorter and for a moment it looked as if he was going to break into tears.

He steadied himself. 'Thank you,' he said finally.

Together, everyone counted down the balloon release from ten. Then:

Five . . .

Four . . .

Three . . .

Two . . .

One.

Arms slowly rose to the sky. And then a cheer. Thousands of balloons were let free. The crowd rejoiced and some shouted 'Brapp!' as they watched the floating tributes tilt in the breeze, climbing towards the clouds, painting the London skyline with notes of a boy remembered.

How does South London mourn one of its own?

Tech was living in Bournemouth and couldn't make it to London for the afternoon. He gathers with his family and friends in a local Bournemouth park. They hold a tribute of their own, and set off balloons into the blue skies.

How does South London mourn one of its own?

There is an Islamic burial, and there is a Christian church service. There is a Jamaican Nine Night. It is held in nearby Streatham. By doing so, they honour the many sides that made him whole.

How does South London mourn one of its own?

They release music in testimony to the man that he was. His twenty-eight years are remembered on song. Krept writes and releases 'Last Letter to Cadet'. Konan sings on the hook. Deno writes and releases 'First Days'. One of his best friends, SeeJay 100, writes and releases '6 Months'. Rapman writes and releases his own letter, and as the time passes, songs begin to flood in from other artists across the country: Big Tobz from East London, Shocka from North London, Clue from Clapham Junction, Lady Leshurr from Birmingham. Tech writes two tributes and waits for the right time to release them.

How does South London mourn one of its own?

A few weeks after his passing is Cadet's twenty-ninth birthday. He never liked to celebrate. But this one would be different. Krept, seeing the turnout at Hyde Park, thought they could put on a show to celebrate Cadet's life, legacy and music. Any money raised would go towards a charity project of the Johnson family's choosing.

When Krept raised the idea with artists, the response was overwhelming. And so he, and a small team, set about bringing The Rated Legend tribute show into reality. They had two weeks to put everything together. The wider scene pooled in to help. Krept put together a setlist of twenty-five artists, all of whom agreed to perform for free. The team at BBC 1Xtra helped them liaise with the relevant artist's management teams. YouTube Music stepped forward to provide a live link for the evening. Nando's covered food. Amaru liaised with brands. Pretty Little Thing, Puma and Foot Asylum all gave donations. Tobi, who managed South London rapper Ms Banks, pitched in on the set and stage design.

For a venue, they were recommended the 2,300-capacity O2 Forum in Kentish Town. But Krept thought they could go bigger. Instead, he pushed for the near 5,000-capacity Brixton Academy. Some were doubtful, but even though it was short notice, and stage shows are booked months, even years, in advance, the venue signed off on the show, even waiving production and crew fees. When the tickets went live, the show sold out in seconds, and Live Nation, who helped with promoting, said they have rarely seen tickets move so quickly.

And so, on 2 March, on a Saturday night in the city, a community made a pilgrimage to Brixton. Cadet had always wanted to play here, under the blue dome that juts into the South London sky. It was a mile or so from his side of Clapham, the closest major venue to where he was raised. This was not just a tribute but a homecoming.

The scene had never gathered like this before, more than twenty-five of the biggest artists and their teams meeting under one roof. To book them all on a normal night would have run into millions, and yet here they were. It felt like a day-long festival condensed into a few night-time hours, one superstar leaving the stage for another to take his place as the crowd screamed at every arrival.

From old-school to new-school rappers, from first-generation Grime MCs like Lethal B to new-age Drill artists like Unknown T, from UK Rap to Afroswing, Section Boyz to Fekky. Dave to Stormzy. From the corners of far North and East and West London to the many boroughs of South. From rappers he had grown up with to those he had schooled with and others he had met along the way. From Birmingham and from Manchester, from family lines stretching back to Jamaica and Nigeria, to Trinidad and Barbados and the

Ivory Coast and Eritrea and Ghana, here they were, gathered under the stage lights.

At this rare cross-fade in Black British MC culture, where Grime had peaked and UK Rap had grown dominant, when UK Drill was rumbling out from the roads and scattered kids of the diaspora had combined their influences into Afroswing, The Rated Legend Show, like Cadet's career, came to represent something bigger than this evening. It was a unity in sound and community. By the end of the event, they had raised £108,647.75, which was to be put back into the community.

He was weaved through the show. His name flashed in lights on the stage, and whenever an artist performed a song he had featured on, his voice boomed out of the sound system and into the arena. On a screen looming over the set, pictures of him from his twenty-eight years flashed on a looping carousel.

Krept and Konan took to the stage wearing black T-shirts with Cadet's face printed on the front. The picture that flashed behind them was a screenshot from Cadet's music video 'Gipset Flow', released during his second arrival into music. Konan stands to his left, and Krept is behind on the right, just like the two had been back in their Richmond College days together. Krept and Konan perform 'Wo Wo Wo' from their second album, and then when the music stops, Krept starts to speak. 'No longer underrated,' he says about his cousin, 'definitely died as a legend.'

A few moments pass, and then he shouts, 'WHO?' and by instinct the crowd chant, 'CADET CADET,' a callback to Cadet's famous catchphrase. Krept bows his head, and Konan shouts, 'WHO?' and the crowd repeat, 'CADET CADET,' thousands echoing his name under the blue-domed roof.

At the closing act, the family are invited onto stage. Mum, dad, sister, brother and nephew are all there. They wave at the applauding crowd. Cadet's friends arrive next, SeeJay 100 and a few others holding framed plaques with large silver discs encased inside. 'Advice' had gone silver, selling 200,000 copies, and because Cadet had sold out the arena, there was a commemorative plaque for that too.

When 'Advice' played, Deno roved across the stage, joined by the MCs and rappers who had performed, by the friends who had been sitting backstage, by the family holding the plaques and by the wailing five thousand. Some of Cadet's people are out in the audience, primary-school friends and college friends and faces that hadn't seen each other in years, and when they heard the soft knock of his silver-selling single, and heard everyone rapping the lyrics, some burst into tears. Others remained in the back, the moment still too difficult, too raw to confront.

On stage, confetti exploded from the rafters and rained down over the crowd and the performers. They pulled up the track a few times, taking it from the beginning, savouring the hour. When the encore finished, and the instrumental faded out, this large extended family of thousands took a moment. Cadet would have been twenty-nine today. They marked the milestone by singing him 'Happy Birthday', offering their praises to their brother, to a South London legend whose name will live on.

PART IV
BRAND NEW DAY

17 **THE SOUTH WALES VALLEYS**
SOUTH WALES

The Valleys run horizontally across the belly of South Wales. They rise from the coastal city plains of Cardiff and Newport and into Valley towns like Ebbw Vale and Caerphilly, then span west across the region: Merthyr into the Rhondda, Neath into the Swansea Valley; mountain peaks and deep valley lowlands, dipping and rising and scampering away from the Wales–England border until they breach the boundaries of the rural west, where the terrain peters out into garden counties and sprawling national parks.

They are the communities forged in the old industrial heartlands, the terraced towns carved into the hillsides of mountain rock, the villages spread like butter along the basins of valley floors. They were steel towns. They were mining villages. They still rest upon the tamed flames of the South Wales coalfield, and in the decades gone by, the Valley people quarried and mined the black gold that brought Britain its wealth, which built cities like Cardiff and tilted a nation's fortunes.

Theirs is a story of the coal industry waning and the mines gradually closing, towns and villages relenting to Margaret Thatcher's cold-winter reign, a story of working-class communities who once survived on one trade, one industry – pushed to the brink when the work went missing.

It is a story of communal pooling and working-class resistance through the 1980s, when Thatcher first unveiled plans to shutter the coal mines and tear down the mighty industrial trade unions representing the workers. In the year-long national miners' strike of

1984–5 – an attempted pushback against the proposed closures – the Valley towns never broke the picket line, even when social welfare was denied to those voluntarily out of work and the Conservative government cut family benefits for those on strike.

To get by and to keep everyone fed they set up soup kitchens and fundraisers. Russian miners sent food packages. The men went to the picket lines. Women ran the food centres and joined their fathers, their husbands, and their brothers at the rallies.

Tyrone O'Sullivan, a strike coordinator in the Cynon Valley, remembers the strike and the women's movement. He told *Wales Online*:

'We saw them growing, we saw them getting up and saying, "I am from South Wales and times are hard and it's costing,"' and, '"We are not up here to beg for food but to fight for a cause."'[1]

There is soul and community in the Valleys: a history of immigration from Ireland, of miners' halls and working men's clubs entrenched within the Folk and Blues circuits, hosting international singer-songwriters who played tones of solidarity for the globally oppressed.

But in Wales, Valley people are sometimes patronised and stereotyped by their own countrymen. In my time in the country, I heard the Valleys called 'bandit country' and 'slightly simple'. When I split a taxi to Cardiff with a few strangers on the way back from a festival in Newport, one warned me off, saying, 'I wouldn't go up *there*.'

Some of the Valley towns are still staggering back from the edge, some fifty years later still wrestling with the economic aftershocks of deindustrialisation. They exist now as predominantly white working-class communities out on the fringes of Britain, who some feel have been abandoned and forgotten. The roads have been rebuilt, but industry has not followed. Work has come and gone, but never really stayed. Unemployment has climbed above the national average.

Housing prices are depressed, and many are leaving, chasing employment out in the bigger cities. Today, Valley towns are often named among the most deprived places in the country.

From those cracks, Rap is beginning to emerge.

The Valleys are often spoken of as one. But every Valley has its way; every town its own sense of identity, its own story. Luke RV comes from one of these towns, Neath, far west of Cardiff and just east of Swansea, where the Vale of Neath descends to the coast.

He was twenty-five when we met in 2019. He had been in Cardiff for around two years, chasing a music dream, another link in a long chain of Valley migrants moving out of their hometowns and heading west into the capital to find work. His music is a mixing of alternative Rap and soulful crooning, a bleeding of the heart and a tender reporting on home. It speaks to Valley pain and Valley pride, is the restless notes from the margins of Britain, a kid from a small town tussling to find his own way in a world shaped decades before his arrival.

Rap arrived in Neath in waves, he remembers: the distorted tones of Kanye West sweeping the land after the release of album *808s & Heartbreak* in 2008; the vivid street diaries of North-West London rapper K Koke entering his ears after a heralded Fire in the Booth freestyle on BBC 1Xtra in 2010; each crash on the Valley shores bringing the sound in closer to home. The hybrid tones of Astroid Boys reached Neath after the release of *Bacon Dream* and *CF10*, the band's Metal influences fitting neatly among the legions of skater kids enamoured with Metal and Thrash. And though Luke was not one of them, he remembers being pulled into the band's orbit when he was young, stunned by their vast following and how they competed seamlessly with the artists and MCs out of London.

'They made people realise that you can perform to massive crowds and be from Wales,' he told me, 'know what I mean?'

Eventually, he began to travel into Cardiff to watch shows, driving down from Neath and attending events on his own, watching Astroid Boys and others in venues across the city. In those early days, he remained a stranger to the country's tight-knit music scene, so when a show finished, and if he had had a few drinks, he would sleep in his car until daybreak and head back to Neath in the morning. On some evenings, he would bring a change of clothes, wait out the morning and afternoon in his car and then wander out by himself to another show the next evening, tunnelling his way into the scene, gradually becoming part of a movement he had watched from afar.

He is a staple of this moment in South Wales now. Phil and other prominent MCs like Local are among his new friends. Artists he glimpsed from the sidelines have become collaborators. Strangers have become flatmates. When we met, he was living in a flat not too far from the city centre with a friend he had met on those early voyages into Cardiff; his friend Conrad, another Valley migrant from a small town in the Rhondda.

They released a song together called 'Coal' in early 2020 and shot the music video in Valley heartlands, in an extinct coal mine rooted among the hills and fields of the Rhondda Valley. Industry halted at the mine in 1983. By the 1990s it had fallen into disuse and was converted into the Rhondda Heritage Park, a tourist attraction that promises an insight into the life of a South Wales coal miner, a window into an era past. In the video they stumble among the empty steel walkways and concrete collieries, a former community stronghold frozen in time.

These are the legacies preserved and made permanent in Welsh Rap. The stories of Luke and Conrad form part of a new generation of artists from South Wales who follow the lineage of artists like Astroid Boys and Local and Newport MC Fernquest who came before them, working-class kids combing their Welsh realities into song.

And so the slow crumble and gradual splintering of Astroid Boys was not a burning up of the Rap and MC pastures in Wales, but instead a readying of the soil, a wildfire ripening the land for those who would come next. Their run across the country and the continent had primed a new generation to flower from their embers. It is a passing of the torch, a lighting of a new flame, the kids of the early-millennium youth clubs handing down tradition to the young of a new decade who had grown up in their wake. By doing so, the reporting on life in the margins continues. Luke RV is a signpost of that tradition at work, his story another chapter in the oral history of the working-class in South Wales.

———

I remember the mountains first. If you leave Cardiff by car and skate along the A470 road where the wide carriageways are flanked by the residential sprawl of the city's northern reaches, a Valley highland rises on the horizon and breaches the flat terrain like a blue whale out of ocean. It is a colossal mound coated in deep greens and browns by an unsteady climate, and peers down on the city like an angel from the heavens. For miles it splays across the car windshield, a celestial mass dominating the skyline and tugging at the eyesight. To see the Valley terrain for the first time is to stare at a land hand-carved by the gods.

'The Valleys', Luke tells me as he drives, 'go through Carmarthen all the way to Newport onto the coast.'

We were headed west, out of the capital and tracing the south coast. He wanted to take me back home, back to Neath and Port Talbot, to the last frontiers of Britain's industrial past and the cloaked enclaves of a South Wales Valley town. And as we drove out of the city, on towards home, into a Wales that once was – the coast some way out to our left, the mountains looming out ahead – Luke said, 'When you go just outside of Cardiff, you can see a city . . . and you can see the mountains in the background and the coastline to the left . . . It's like you've literally got every aspect you could want in one place.'

It was late December 2020, the Christmas period, a month or so after Wales had been lifted from the latest of a steady succession of national lockdowns during the COVID-19 pandemic. But he had maintained a close tie with home throughout, heading back to his town often, driving this same stretch of road west, capital to valley, British Wales to Welsh Wales, Cardiff to Neath Port Talbot.

He knew the route almost by instinct now, knew that after the A470 came the mass Coryton interchange and after the interchange came the M4, his white 4x4 eating the motorway, writhing across the belly of the map like a snake in the low grass. He was pulling on a vape as we drove, blowing smoke from his driver's side window, the car tyres swishing the tarmac, the M4 inching him towards home.

The M4 is a concrete stretch of no man's land that connects the many corners of South Wales, its junctions slipping off like veins into coastal towns and Valley villages, its six-lane dual carriageway barricaded by a green-tree guard of honour that blurs softly into shadow as you drive, breaking every so often and exposing an old mining town, an estate, a community hidden in the pits of a Valley floor. On days like this, when the roads are empty and the sky is in a dance between clear blue and rain clouds, it is a forty-five minute drive into Neath.

Around half an hour into our journey, a storm cloud beckoned and then burst over the road and rain rattled the windshield, winter tears spilling onto the M4.

'I woke up thinking what a nice day it's going to be today,' he said. '*That's* Wales.'

We drove in wet and rain, car wheels kicking up foam. Then on the final stretch into Neath Port Talbot, the rain stopped, and the skies cleared, and it was as if the heavens were welcoming him home. The incline petered out and the road levelled. The horizon opened up before us. And there was Port Talbot, industrial fields of factories and steelworks teetering on the edges of the coast. The blue water in the bay glinted in the sun and extended out into Swansea Bay. Factory chimneys pointed skywards like rows of long, skinny pipes, smoke puffing from their rims like halos, an industrial mirage shimmering on the water. And whenever Luke was driving back from London or from Cardiff or from elsewhere, and saw the sea spread out ahead, the bed of factories in the distance, he knew, *Ah, this feels like home.*

'It's so picturesque in a weird way,' he said pulling into town, sucking on his vape. 'It's like an ugly beauty.'

I remember the smell of steel first. When you enter Port Talbot, the bitter fumes of metal smoke creep through the crevices of your vehicle and settle without warning in your throat. It is a welcome for the senses. For Luke, the smell meant he was home.

Port Talbot and Neath are neighbouring sister towns pushed into coalition, along with other towns in the area including Briton Ferry and Pontardawe, as the Neath Port Talbot county borough. Port Talbot is home to the steelworks and the sea; a hybrid place, a Valley town on the coast. Neath lies further up in the Valleys and is where Luke lived as a boy. As we splintered from the M4, the coast and the steelworks of Port Talbot glimmering from my window, he could see from his window, mountains rising from the coastal plains, small towns of Neath Port Talbot borough delicately carved into their rock.

For nearly two decades, these towns had been all he had known, a sprawl of connected communities from the coast up to the edges of the Valleys. These are towns where the populations are a few thousand and everyone scrambles for jobs at the steelworks. Towns where people grow up and tend never to leave. Towns where locals never hang their washing out to dry because the steel in the air will tint their clothes orange. It is a final frontier of industrial Britain, a glimpse of a Wales that once was.

'Everybody I know works in the steelworks,' he says, 'or has worked for the steelworks.'

We drove through Port Talbot first, through the low-rise housing and quiet high street that snaked to the seafront, and he began to tell me about home.

He is the sum of many parts, of a grandmother who immigrated from Ireland, of parents who raised him in Neath with an older brother. Of a mother who loved Motown and Michael Jackson, and a father who could draw and be creative but who worked hard and took a trade as a welder and now teaches in Luke's old school.

He is the sum of a place where, after you left education, it was the steelworks all week, he says, then rugby on the weekend afternoons, and out with the boys on weekend evenings. Then the steelworks again. And repeat, and repeat.

He is the sum of a place where they felt Welsh and not British or European, where the Swansea–Cardiff South Wales football derby felt like the biggest rivalry in the world, and where the road signs are in a national language many cannot speak; of a place stranded between cities, the twinkle of Cardiff too far, the cabs into Swansea too expensive, the public transport not great, he says, and so 'it stops people from leaving'.

'When taxis are really expensive and there's nothing for miles, you stay in your area.'

Luke remembers how they began drinking too early, at thirteen and fourteen, in the fields or a nature reserve or a garden or the street, roaming without cause until the police turned up to give chase. When they turned fifteen and sixteen, and were afraid of dirtying their clothes, the boys would rent minibuses and head to rugby-club fundraisers deep in the Valleys, get hammered with the other schools and then head back in the morning.

By eighteen he was burned out and tired of drinking, but remembers how for others the show still went on, house parties stretching for days, people out on a Friday and home on a Monday morning because 'there's nothing to do'. Remembers walking to school once on an early Tuesday and hearing music still pumping from the walls of a house he was passing, a party that had no reason to end.

These are the small-town experiences folded into his music, the Wales that he knew, the notes of the unnoticed. On his song 'No One's Looking', he half-raps, half-sings of life in the shadows, of childhood days drinking in fields and scampering from blue lights. And as his voice drifts over gloomy drums, vocals moving over grieving keys, there is a sorrow that rumbles from his soul, a longing for more; a love for his home and a bittersweet reflection on the encounters that have moulded him. It is a mournful mural to Neath Port Talbot. There are tears in his tributes.

We were driving along the seafront now, running by the water, could see handfuls of people wandering the winter beaches. The steelworks on the horizon were closer now, smoke still rising like halos, fires burning in the furnaces, blinking orange and amber in the afternoon sky. A coastal town in a British winter feels like the very edges of the earth.

Here, among these valleys and these roads, the water and the sand and the blue expanse are a constant in any upbringing.

'When was the last time you went beach?' he asked me. 'I've been so often that I didn't even realise that is a thing that people didn't do.'

When they were young, he would swim in the water, and wade back to shore with sludge covering his skin, only recently realising that he was swimming in steel residue. When they were older, he spent days on the beach, camping out on the sand with friends, lighting a fire and then drinking until they found something else to do. Most recently he shot a music video on the sands, the scenes overlooking the sea, home always a part of him and his art.

The seafront hasn't changed much since he was seventeen, since everyone would drive their first cars up and down the strip all day, revving their engines in an adolescent fluttering of feathers. The beaches are still packed in the summer, and as we drive along the mile road, we skate past the local attractions, the adventure golf course and the aqua-splash centre, the surf school and the leisure centre, a cinema that had shuttered and a Burger King that had been franchised but never opened, its interior bare and barren. Nothing changes quickly out here in the margins.

'Things don't really change, full stop,' he said.

But he said, 'It's nice to come back. I always say to myself, when I'm back it's like putting the world on pause.'

The rain had started again.

'Yeah, it'll start and stop a few times,' he said, 'the rain does lag up here.'

We drove away from the seafront and the steelworks and out towards Neath. It was late afternoon now and a quiet dusk was beginning to feel its way in, the half-blood sun receding gently, its encore washing the town in a red-amber sunset.

The main road through Neath is lined with two-storied terraced housing, some converted into small shops and flatlets. Then there were the local institutions fixed into the town's core, and dotted along the road: bingo halls and a Lidl, a pub where Luke had his sixteenth birthday and a terraced house that converts into a chip shop during the daytime, the resident selling food from his front window. Along the small high street, Welsh flags flap from tentpoles. Then the road began to incline as we edged into the Valleys. We passed his old school and his old college and all the elements that had marked his two decades here.

'Growing up I never thought I was poor,' he said, 'and I wasn't poor, put it that way. But I thought we had it good.'

Then he went off to university in Swansea and began to meet kids from across Britain. Kids from private schools, kids who came from money, kids whose families owned big businesses, and then he began to realise, 'Oh my god. I was in my own bubble.

'I didn't know what a private school was. There was no private schools around here. What? You pay to go to school? That don't seem fair.'

In a small town you don't think about the outside, he told me. In his small town he was popular growing up, was one of the boys and never wanted to ruin that reputation, never wanted to be the talking point because, he says, 'If you're doing something, everyone's got something to say.'

He played chess as a kid, played for a club and then quit when the boys found out because back then he cared what people would say. He held a similar passion for music and Rap. For a while he had been writing lyrics. But he never released them, and though he had always wanted to, didn't think he ever would.

But he remembers when things began to jar, when he started to feel like he wanted more than the world he had seen. He was around twenty-one. Home was starting to wear on him, the routine after-noons and weekends out with the boys, smoking and chilling and bickering about small bits of money no longer filling his soul. One afternoon, he was sat on his own in a car park, had been there all day, rolling up and smoking, gnawing frustrations creeping in. Eventually he remembers asking himself, *What the fuck am I doing?*

In that moment, he realised, 'there was so many things that I want to do and I'm not doing them, and I don't believe in myself enough to do them'.

In that moment, he made a change, decided that he would try music and Rap and see where it took him, thought, *Fuck it, I don't care what anyone has to say, to be honest*; thought, *I'm just going to give it a go, at least, then I can look myself in the mirror and say I'd at least give it a go.*

And now driving through Neath he said, 'I didn't feel like I fitted.'

'I do love it here, and all my friends and my family are here. But it's just . . . I don't feel fulfilled, and I think that's important, know what I mean? If you're really enjoying your lifestyle then all the power to you, I'm not trying to be like "it's the wrong one". It's definitely not, I just know I weren't enjoying it like that. To be honest I don't even know what it is I'm trying to accomplish, but even just doing what I'm doing, I'm enjoying that now, know what I mean?'

He started by ripping instrumentals from YouTube and releasing songs on SoundCloud, then taking trips to Cardiff for shows. And then things began to move. His first gig was in a Newport nightclub, opening for K Koke. All his friends came down from Neath to support him. Now he is three projects deep, has released one a year to a steadily growing audience: the album *Going Nowhere* in 2020 following EPs *Valley Boy* in 2019 and *Purgatory* in 2018. And during that span he has emerged as one of Wales's Rap scene's most promising artists.

'Since I started, I haven't looked back,' he said. 'It's been like a weird obsession. That's what I wanna do now, I don't really care about going out, I just want to crack on with the music, really.'

A few days before he drove me out here, he'd been back in Neath. His car was being valeted. He waited out the time by standing on the side of the road, watching the traffic drift by. After some time, he realised that almost every face that had cruised past was a face he knew or recognised in some capacity. And now, as we were leaving the town, heading deeper into the Valleys, he said that it was 'mad to think that's where my life was, was in that'.

We were taking the back roads away from Neath and home towards Cardiff. Luke had driven deeper into the Valleys, away from his past life and everything he had known. We were in rural territory now. The towns faded away as the road beneath us rose up, estates and terraced housing petering out into a thin road bordered by miles and miles of roaming green fields. The region was soaked in a gentle evening dusk. On the road, the 4x4 revved on the tarmac, pleading with the gravel for grip. Then the incline gave way and the road evened out, and ahead of us, leaning into view, was an expanse of mountain ranges echoing far into the distance, vast ridges climbing and falling for as far as our eyes could travel. The breadth of the view brought us to silence.

Every so often, we would pass a horse grazing by the road, or the silhouette of a car would flash on a bend out in front and a stranger in his car would skate by, his headlights glazing our eyes. But for the most part, it was just us out there, the car moving quietly over the tarmac, two men suspended in a rural twilight zone, drifting through the back ends of the South Wales Valleys.

'These are the roads where many of the Valleys meet,' he told me, where communities are burrowed deep into the basin floors and masked from view on the faces of the descending valley slopes. And though there were times he would drive up here with his friends, park up, rumble music from a speaker and have a smoke, he never comes out here as much as he should because, he says, 'you know when you've just got it on your doorstep you don't do it'.

Maybe he would start driving out here more often, he said. Maybe he would rent a drone and shoot a music video.

Maybe.

Maybe.

For Astroid Boys' last headline show in Cardiff, Luke was among the audience. He had one song out at the time, on SoundCloud under the name 'LRV'. He was still a stranger to the dominant figures of the scene. He was watching on at what could be, watching as a band who had inspired many gave their final, stunted farewell.

Their passing of the baton to artists like Luke represented a shift in British Rap. A genre that had for so long filtered into inner cities and communities on racial and cultural lines was now blossoming in the far corners of Britain in a union defined more by class.

Luke was different to the rest of the boys I met on my encounters in South Wales: he was not from an inner city, not from Splott or Rumney or Newport, was not the son of Black immigrants or connected to Garage and Jungle and the Sound System culture that birthed Grime and paved the way for UK Rap. His voice was one specific to a post-industrial, 98 per cent white, working-class town, to the Welsh Wales Denis Balsom spoke of, to the Valley character and spirit that in many ways so greatly differed to ethnic pockets in the largest cities in the country.

His music carries a perspective often unheard. He, a proud Welshman, who by his interactions with Rap, had picked up genres with roots in London, and before that the Caribbean and America and Africa. By doing so, he has found a voice of his own. This breaching of terrain, this meeting of community, has seen British Rap present the broadest look into Britain as it exists today.

In our day driving through the Valleys, Luke spoke on subjects not raised by Phil and Benji and Dell, or by the rest of the boys I had met. During our long drive, he told me about the frustrations of growing up in the Valleys, with a strong sense of Welsh identity but being labelled British.

'We never really felt British, know what I mean?'

He told me about the growing cries for an independent Wales in the aftermath of the pandemic, about how the Welsh were the guinea pigs of English colonialism, how you can't drive into the north of the country without passing through England first, and about how the

Welsh language was physically beaten out of school kids in the nine-teenth century. Some schools used the Welsh not, a wooden tablet hung around the neck of any child heard speaking the language. A child would wear the tablet until somebody else was caught speaking Welsh. Whoever was wearing it at the end of the school day would be beaten or punished.

He told me about the lingering effects on his generation today, how many of them attended Welsh primary schools as kids, but never became fluent and are now stuck in a limbo of the tongue.

'It's not that we'd rather be all English, we'd rather be able to speak the Welsh,' he said. 'It feels a bit embarrassing to be Welsh but to not have that under your belt . . . Wales isn't regarded like Ireland is, and I think that irks people in Wales. It's got a culture and heritage and the language and all of these things that make a country unique, but it's just regarded as England, really.'

It's why his music sounds how it sounds, bleeds with soul and paints sonic murals of home; why he so often speaks about coming from a place no one can see.

'Music's not political,' he told me, 'but it's a big representation of political decisions.'

Lemfreck, a musician from Newport, echoed those thoughts. He told me that in the heavy stems and tones of Luke's music, 'you hear the thoughts and the views of everyone from places like that'.

Lemfreck was a Valley kid of sorts too, a hybrid in South Wales, who moved from Pill out to St Julians and then from St Julians to the Valley town of Abergavenny in the Vale of Usk. The stories he brought back from the region are of the same stock and strain.

'Go to where Luke's from and they forget about them,' he said. 'Go to where I'm from and they forget about us.'

He told me about a friend of his back in Abergavenny. A few years back, after Lemfreck had enrolled in university, one of only a few boys he knew who had done so, he was back in town, visiting friends. He was around eighteen. A group of them had been out drinking together on the Saturday and had woken up hungover. A friend of his, who still lived in the town, began pouring himself a morning pint, drank it, and then poured another. And another. And another. And after a while Lemfreck turned to him and said, 'Yo, bro, that's like your fifth pint.'

He remembers his friend saying, 'I'm on the dole anyway, I ain't got a job to go to on Monday, so I might as well keep going.'

When they saw him the next day, he was still drinking.

He told me, 'Honestly, man, when you're eighteen not a lot hurts you,' but, 'I felt that in my soul, man . . . It's been something that's really stuck with me. I wake up and I think I need to have a purpose; my day needs to have a purpose . . . Because I don't ever want to feel like I might as well keep going because I ain't got nothing else to do.'

The legacies of neglect and the loss of hope has fuelled them, has spurred on musicians who refuse to be cast as victims despite all that has happened in the Valleys. They are from places where people are moving through their lives the best way they can. And now those stories of home are leaking out to the world on the tongues of this new breed of Welsh musicians and rappers.

'It's like, what do you do?' Lemfreck said. 'Are you gonna sit and moan and sit in the negativity that is being forgotten, or are you going to push for people to notice you, d'ya know what I mean? That's some of my driving factors. I'm not leaving this earth without people knowing what I'm on or where I'm from or what I do. I'm not doing that.'

Luke and I had reached the motorway, back on even territory, had clambered down from the altitudes. It was dark now, a winter evening, the headlights of oncoming traffic flashing and trailing past in the windshield. Luke was affirming the empowering mantras that Lemfreck had spoken. He believed in what was possible.

'I used to think it was a weakness coming from Neath because nobody knows where it is, nobody wants to be from there,' he says. 'But now I think it's more of an advantage really, because I can sell something nobody else is selling . . . It doesn't matter where you are geographically; the journey is not necessarily a geographical journey.'

In the period before lockdown, he had played his first show abroad, had been paid to fly over and perform in Ireland, at The Academy in the heart of Dublin, opening up for North London rapper Benny Banks. It was around the same time he had watched Local's first headline show. The entire scene showed out that evening at the Welsh Club. Jaykae graced the stage as a special guest and the audience knew every word to every Local song. The artists in attendance were amazed. 'That was the moment in my head it clicked,' Luke says.

He believed in what was possible now.

And then his own hour came. His EP, *Valley Boy*, was nominated for the 2020 Welsh Music Prize. He lost out to Cardiff rapper Deyah, and the pandemic robbed him of a suit-and-gown ceremony. But the nomination was reward for his work. They played his songs on national radio, and he finally had something tangible he could take back to his mam and tell her about.

By the early evening the roads were in total darkness. The conversation had slowed. A day driving and talking for hours wears on your senses, slowly fatigues your mind. So we drove on, comfortable in our silence, music from the stereo infusing the white space. We hurtled along the M4, driving back across the country. Every so often a well-lit patch of motorway gave way to streaks of total darkness, as if somebody had shot out the streetlights with a pistol.

'It's amazing in Wales,' Luke said. 'Biggest exporter of electricity, but hasn't got any lights.'

Then we were in silence again, on cruise control back to the city, humming along the road, the Valleys far back in the distance, his future somewhere out ahead.

Then the music stopped. His phone was ringing. It was Conrad, Luke's housemate. His voice came through the speakers.

'Have you seen the news, mate?' he said.

'What's the news?'

'You might wanna let him [me] know, we're going back into lockdown.'

'Tonight? Is it?'

'Yeah.'

Then the phone went dead, and we kept driving.

18 HILLFIELDS: FRONTLINE

WEST MIDLANDS

'Me live ah Hillfield, me live ah deh battlefield.
Come test me pon the frontline.'

ASHER BANTON, HILLZ FM

The frontline in Hillfields runs from Primrose Hill Street to King William Street and begins at the foot of a rise. Hillfields is secluded territory, an insular community just north of the A4053 ring road that fences in Coventry city centre. Primrose Hill Street unofficially marks its borders. At its outer frontier, there is a faded Hillfields welcome sign bolted into a patch of rambling green grass, and across the road is the local school, the shiny new blocks of Sidney Stringer Academy where kids from these grounds have schooled for generations.

A few streets away sits the Coventry Refugee and Migrant Centre, the landing strip the school kids and many of their parents and grandparents have passed through, decade after decade, generation after generation, loose threads of far continents grounding in the old country. The centre hints at the spirit of Hillfields and the frontline, immigration and distant settlers branding this walled corner of Coventry.

Walk the heavy pavement up Primrose Hill Street, past Sidney Stringer and past the Kasbah nightclub, past the kebab house, and the grocers with vegetable stalls folding out onto the paving. Walk as the road creeps, the hill levels, orange clay terraced housing lining the way, Primrose Hill Street turning over to Victoria Street and Victoria Street opening into King William Street and the frontline.

Frontlines are roads that sit at the core of a community. In Black and marginalised working-class towns and regions in Britain, they are the focal points that define an area, a street or high road that represents the beating heart of a place and its people. History is written into the frontlines. Many have been meeting spots for large-scale protests when a community rises in resistance, and then, when things boiled over, have been the stage for riots too. These distinct roads are scattered across the country. In Brixton, Railton Road was named the frontline. In Peckham it is the high street. There is a frontline in Handsworth, a frontline in Pill, Newport, frontlines in Lewisham, South London, and a frontline in St Paul's, Bristol.

On the Hillfields frontline, haunting tower blocks loom over the road like the erect tombs of guardian angels. Frontline is where people live among rows of shops, in and out of Kurdish bakeries and Halal meat grocers, Caribbean food places and Middle Eastern dinner spots, chicken-shop hangouts and barbershops, a youth centre for the kids, a Paddy Power for the gamblers.

The strip ebbs and flows with the moving tides of the day: quiet in the morning and teeming in the afternoon, when Sidney Stringer shuts and flocks of teenagers adorn the kerbs. Some still remain at nightfall. In the summertime there are communal gatherings, and when winter comes, Santa Claus giveaways out on the square. Frontline is the soul of a working-class suburb, the strip buried into the local psyche. When they came aground in Britain, immigrants and asylum seekers drifting in from wherever, frontline became their home away from distant homes.

Hillfields is what they call a transient community. Rebirth is in the bones of the concrete. It has layers of immigration deep-set in its spirit, fossils of foreign communities who walked the long rise onto the strip and slipped into the towers and the terraced housing just off the mains. The Irish came to Hillfields first. Then Punjabi, South Asian and Caribbean people after the war, turning over the ground, moving in and out of the terraces and then the high-rises, pushing their prints into the land and rebuilding a ruined city, reimagining the face of a changing Coventry – just like they had done in Birmingham and West Brom and Walsall and the Black Country.

Like those regions, Coventry was once a manufacturing place. For large runs of the twentieth century, the city sat at the heart of Britain's car-manufacturing industry. Factories were scattered across the city: hundreds of working sites owned by the world's largest car manufacturers and manned by local workers pushing Jaguars and Minis and Rovers and Singer Motors from droning conveyor belts out onto the roads. Hillfields was home to over twenty of these factories.

But the city was blitzed in the war, targeted for its munitions and engine factories. During a long November night in 1940, German planes raided over skies, flinging bombs like grains of sand, the heavy explosions lighting the darkness. Some feel that Winston Churchill and the UK government sacrificed the city; that when UK intelligence cracked German code, and realised it was Coventry and not London to be targeted for heavy bombing, they remained quiet, never sending through warning, because doing so would have alerted the Germans to the scrambling of their code. The raid devastated the city: 75 per cent of factories were damaged. Thousands of homes were rubbled. Hundreds were killed. Coventry was cracked into pieces, and till this day, many still remember the alleged betrayal.

In the years after the war, tower blocks flowered on the city skyline. Hillfields was marked as an 'Area of Comprehensive Development' by the local council, with over half of its homes declared unfit to live in. Many of the terraces came down and, in their place, giant post-war council blocks went up, a tightly woven constellation of ten-storey flats like Unity House on Cross Street and Selina Dixon House on Weston Street, Paul Stacey House on Castle Street and Phoenix House on Queen Street. Two seventeen-storey blocks rose above the concrete tips and marked themselves on the Coventry skyline – Thomas King House on Wellington Street and Pioneer House on Cross Street, the angels looming over the frontline.

This was housing made for a booming industrial city. But by the 1980s, amid two long recessions, Coventry and Hillfields were in decline. Car manufacturing was cheaper in Japan and elsewhere abroad. Manufacturers shut down. Stringer closed their five Hillfields factories, and the working-class communities buckled under the strain. Almost one in three were unemployed.[1] Hillfields was among the most deprived areas in an already struggling city, and the promise of those manufacturing boom years was swallowed by darkness. Another story of a West Midlands revival gone wrong.

Music howled from the blackness. Song is how generations made sense of their surroundings, their testimonies climbing out from the night, giving wider Britain a distinct peek at what lay within itself. The music came in waves: 2-Tone originators The Specials released 'Ghost Town' in 1981. The genre's name was a nod to the mixed roots of the band, Ska blended with Punk Rock, Blacks among whites, Jamaicans among British, the Coventry inner city in one voice.

'Ghost Town' captured the mood of the era, speaking of mounting unemployment and angst, of a loss of hope and a worrying violence, the vocals mourning over organ chords and wailing brass. Lead vocalist Neville Staple was from Hillfields by way of Jamaica. 'Government leaving the youth on the shelf,' he muttered. 'No job to be found in this country.' The song was a premonition of the anger rising out of the economic and social crisis. In the same summer 'Ghost Town' went to number 1, riots began to blaze across Britain, including the unrest in Handsworth.

The Specials were an indicator of something, of Hillfields speaking, the tower blocks shedding their stories. The tradition continued through the eighties. Second-generation Jamaicans, born and raised on the frontline and schooled at Sidney Stringer, blared Reggae on Pirate Radio stations from the peaks of Pioneer House, and threw a carnival every summer down in the shades of the concrete forest.

A decade later, in 1995, twelve local kids starred in *Blazed*, a short Channel 4 drama set and written about the area. In one scene, old-school Hip Hop booms out of a car stereo as one of the characters cruises the frontline, past boys hanging on the street, the towers standing guard overhead. 'Making money is the only pleasure in this deadbeat place, man,' he says to a friend in the passenger seat. 'Let's gets serious, make some serious money. Get out of Coventry money.'

They are voices standing on the shoulders of the past, signposting the troubles of a region still not whole, music making its way out, a tradition continued. By the new millennium, Grime was blooming in the WATCH centre, a youth club on frontline. Masses of teenagers held court over cyphers and evolving instrumentals, bringing life in one of the city's most deprived areas into colour; a new generation of Hillfields kids feeding the land with their stories.

They are part of a wider heritage at work. Black music genres moving across the strip like high tide, then receding, and dissolving into the ether, leaving room for the next genre to emerge: 2-Tone and Reggae into Pirate Radio and Carnival. Hip Hop into Grime, Grime into Road Rap, and today, in the early stages of a new decade, UK Rap and Drill emerging out of the concrete. East and West African kids whose families have walked the long rise into Hillfields like migrants always have done, falling in step, using music to speak on what the frontline and Coventry had made of them.

Pa Salieu is one of those kids, a boy who came from afar and settled like a pine seed in the cracks among the tower blocks. Hillfields is his home away from home. The frontline is in his soul and his sound. His debut mixtape *Send Them to Coventry* is a tribute to the sums that made him whole, a fifteen-song diary account of his Hillfields upbringing. The first lines of the tape's first verse crystallise his experience: 'Look, my name is Pa and I'm from Hillset / Bust gun, dodge slugs, got touched, skipped death.'

But throughout there is acknowledgement of his roots and a restless look at the immigrant experience. 'I come from warriors / I know my past,' he says on 'B***K', 'I'm another lost soul in the Wild West world.'

He came from elsewhere, born in Slough during the summer of 1997 to Gambian parents. Slough was a holding spot, not home. His parents were young immigrants: they needed to work, they needed to bring in money. They sacrificed to do so. They sent him back home to Gambia as an infant to live with his grandparents. A son pulled away from his parents, and his siblings, shifted back across the continent to the well from which his family sprang.

Before you can make sense of Pa and his music, and the cold nights on the frontline, you must understand his connection to Gambia and home. They named him Pa Salieu after his dad's eldest brother. *That* Pa Salieu was a police officer in Gambia, a man everyone in the family looked up to, who made money and found good work and a good career. He was killed in a motorcycle accident while on duty. The family passed the name onto his nephew.

You must understand that his dad's family were from the city Serekunda and his mother from Bundung, both in a crook of land by the coast. In this region of Gambia, among his family, raised by his grandparents, he grew up climbing the mango trees in the farms and fields behind the house, roaming among the chickens in the compound.

Family and community-building were sitting at his roots, buried in him in the small mosque his grandad built, attended by locals. Buried in him in the afternoons when lunchtime came and the family set out big plates on the floor, then called the neighbours to come and eat. A close community sharing food and family, space and prayer.

You must understand that music was a tradition long before it was a past-time and then a career. His mother is from a people and a tribe who carry music in their spirit, pulling songs from the dust. Melody is a folklore of the family line. His aunt is a Folk singer who performed across the world. Pa grew up listening to her at weddings and naming ceremonies, or videotapes of her performing in America, the music passing down the ways of their people, just like his name had been passed onto him.

He lived like this for years, among the dust and the farms, the mosque and the fields, Gambia ground into his essence until any trace of Slough and Britain had been dissolved. A child of the West African coast and strong family.

Then his mother sent for him. He was around eight years old. He left home, returning to his family back across the continents, to his mum, dad, his siblings, to his birthplace in a foreign land. He arrived with music inside him.

Britain was different than he remembered. It was concrete tower blocks in Coventry. It was snow. It was frontline. It was a new primary school where the kids taunted him about his accent until a parent pulled his mother aside and whispered that the environment was not safe for him, that 'you need to get your son out of here'.

In secondary school at Sidney Stringer at the bottom of the hill, it was more of the same. More taunts about his dark skin tone. More taunts about his accent. He fought those who teased him, a rebellious streak showing itself as he grew into his teenage years.

'I can't run away from my accent,' he told a magazine once, 'most people would try and hide it – but that's your DNA, that's your instrument.'[2]

Through his teenage years and into adulthood, he wrestled with the English language, attempting to bridge a disconnect between his imagination and the words that would leave his mouth in jittering stutters and snap sentences.

'It's a problem,' he says, 'because what's in my head . . . everything starts coming . . . bare shit at once.'

The strain further scarred his school experience. He found it hard to pull his thoughts out into words, and as a result, felt the teachers cast him as unintelligent.

'I never felt stupid, but I felt like I can't speak to people.'

School for him was laced with memories of being left out, days spent in exclusion blocks after fighting with other kids. Sometimes groups would fight among racial lines. It's a reality some of the children growing up in Hillfields face, first- and second-generation immigrants who are not wholly of this place.

The duality of Coventry and Gambia sit at the heart of Pa's identity and music. He represents a shift in the dynamics of Black sound and presence in the wider West Midlands. Unlike the Grime kids in Birmingham before him, he does not trace his family line back to Jamaica and the Caribbean and Windrush grandparents, or to ancestors rebuilding West Midlands' cities, or generations of family moulding Black music on tower-block roofs and Pirate Radio airwaves.

He is not a generation removed from *home*. He knew Gambia before he knew Britain, and that rearing sits on his tongue, threading itself through his music.

At the conclusion of 'B***K' from *Send Them to Coventry*, a sample of Gambian Folk pulls into earshot before the song closes. It's his aunty, who goes by Chuche Njie. Speaking about the song in an interview, he said, 'I wanted to say I'm unapologetically Black, I'm unapologetically African. Don't be ashamed of being Black. This is pride, this is my intent.'[3] Gambia is always with him, even when he is apart.

In that way, Hillfields is different from the wider West Midlands. Kids in Hillfields hold two worlds within them, continental plates converging on the frontline. Pa Salieu is among the latest generation of fused kids, a product of two worlds. They are from Gambia, Somalia, Iraq and Afghanistan. Children of another home. Children of Coventry. Hillfields is sculpted around this tension.

In the afternoons Pa was excluded from lessons, Susie Murphy would find him wandering the hallways of Sidney Stringer. She works for the Positive Youth Foundation, a registered charity whose purpose is to raise the aspirations and life chances of young people facing challenging circumstances in Hillfields and wider Coventry. They work out of a youth centre that is hidden like a bunker behind the seventeen-storey Thomas King House off the frontline.

We are sat in the main hall, orange tones throbbing from the wallpaper, the centre silent in the dead afternoon of a school day. The foundation has been going around ten years, ever since the founder Rashid Bhayat bought some footballs, went out into the local area and started putting on football sessions for hundreds of kids. Today PYF have evolved into a thirty-person-strong organisation, reaching their hands deep into the inner cities of Coventry, helping guide the lives of kids needing support. They are a north star in a challenging time and have two offices: a base in the city centre, and this one here in Hillfields.

In the afternoon hours after school, the doors will breach, and the hall will flood with local kids making the most of the youth centre, recording in the studio, speaking with the youth leaders. For the younger kids, there are boxing, football and basketball sessions down the hill at Sidney Stringer. For the older ones, there are employment and further-education programmes. And for new refugees and asylum seekers, who have found home in Hillfields, there are integration and settlement schemes, aiming to ease the transition into a new country.

'Do they know where to get cheap clothes in town?' Susie says. 'Do they want a boyfriend? Have they got a phone? It's about not forgetting that they're young people.'

Families that arrive in Hillfields sometimes acclimatise to the country in a staggered pattern. The youngest kids, malleable in tongue, often pick up English quickly. Some are born here, and ease like water into their surroundings. Their parents often sit at the other end of the spectrum, may not pick up English at all, and are easily identified as new arrivals.

Somewhere between the two is a grey area, kids like Pa, raised in Britain from a relatively young age, but who arrived with an embedded first language and accent and a dipping understanding of English.

'They don't qualify as newly arrived young people with English as a second language,' Susie says, 'but they equally struggle to keep up with their peers who have been here for a long time.'

In this isolating state of limbo across Hillfields, where three-quarters of households do not consider English their first language, and 25 per cent have no members with English as a first language at all, young people often fall through the cracks, arriving too young to be considered for linguistic help, but old enough to have forged permanent lingual connections with home.

And there are more obstacles. Many of the kids growing up in the area are battling issues beyond their years. The same problems linger from decades before: the area is among the most deprived in the country, named in the top 5 per cent across England in 2019. At Sidney Stringer there are more than 400 pupils eligible for free school meals, a figure that stands at 40.4 per cent of its total students,[4] almost double the national average of 22.5 per cent.[5] There are high levels of poverty and unemployment, issues around youth violence as well as overcrowded households. And though some of the tower blocks have come down over time, the area ranks lowest in the city for access to green spaces.

A resident who took part in a community study about the West Midlands Violence Reduction unit described Hillfields as 'an anxious place with so much anger and stress levels in the area'. While a teacher in a local school said 'that these children have lived way more trauma in their five years than I've lived in my whole life. And they're just used to it. This is just how they live their life.'[6]

Susie told me of how young kids at the foundation had been stopped and searched by the police as early as aged eight, and so how now, when police officers make a rare visit into the centre, the kids walk out straight away. She told me how these kids witness homelessness and prostitution on the street, and sometimes have family members in and out of prison.

She also said that kids can walk the heavily surveilled frontline and pass five shops selling chicken and chips. How there are fifty-seven nationalities signed up to the centre, many of whom don't have English as a first language. And how in the thick of these issues, they can be lured into making money by dangerous avenues.

'So that notion that we need to look out for the fifteen-, sixteen-, seventeen-year-old kids?' she says, 'Way late. They're exposed to things eight, nine, ten and go under the radar because no one's looking at the kids in primary [school].'

Among a strongly bonded community, young kids are walking tightropes. Pa was among them. When PYF found him wandering the halls at school, they would pull him aside into classrooms, engaging him with creativity, an outcast finding another home away from home. But he still bears many of the scars the community warn of.

The tower blocks are what he remembers. Gambia replaced by Hillfields and Coventry, the concrete a barricade on the horizon, stopping you from seeing beyond the ends. When he was growing up, his mum worked as a cleaner and was regularly out of the home. So, he helped out, going with her on cleaning jobs to split the workload, and raising his younger siblings, walking his brother and sister to school, passing needles on the frontline as they went.

By his teens he was trapping, wandering down a dark road. When his grandparents passed, he took to the streets to get by. He can tell you about graveyard shifts; about standing out on the street in the dead of night; about trap houses and needles and shootings; about funerals; about friends lost to mental institutions and friends lost to prison, not eligible for parole until 2035. In those dangerous times he would occasionally write his experiences into a notebook, processing what was happening, the lined page a diffuser for heavy days. Sitting in a trap house, waiting for a sale, he would write. The day an addict tried to rob him in town, stabbing Pa with a needle, he wrote. Then he woke up the next morning and read over what was there, thinking, *Ah shit, I appreciate I'm here, you know.*

He tried legitimate work. There were two warehouse jobs and a short stint at Nando's. But a criminal record for carrying a knife made finding and keeping work difficult. And when you ask him about it, he will tell you how on that occasion, he was studying art in college and had accidentally carried out one of the knives from his lesson. A case of bad luck. 'I get caught with a knife,' he says, 'now it's hard to get a job . . . so nigga, I'm trapping, I'm trapping . . . I'm trapped. I felt trapped.'

On other occasions, he carried something, he says, 'not to rob random civilians. But me, I know what the ends is like and I'm not dying easy. I'm not dying easy. On my whole life, I'm not dying easy, know what I'm saying?

'You're not out to harm no one but you can't lack, bro. People get shot left, right . . . people getting shot up . . . I tried with the working thing but circumstance, innit. I had to do what I had to to survive. If it's gonna fuck my shit up, I'd rather survive than . . .'

So he stayed with what he knew, and it was in this period he found music. In his school days he stole an MP3 player from his cousin, and listened to the few songs it held on loop: Vybz Kartel classics like 'Touch Ah Button' and other Dancehall anthems keeping him company. A few years later, in his shotting days, his life drifting down a dangerous road, he went to sell weed to a man in Stoke-on-Trent. The man had a studio in the house, and Pa began to record there.

Something happened to him in the studio. Something moved inside him. Standing before the microphone, the gap between imagination and words melted. The stutter was lifted. Words slipped out with clarity. It was like he was free. The studio became an obsession. Some days, his friends Shinks and Ricky would find him on the strip and say, 'Let's go Stoke-on-Trent.' Then he would be gone, music a relief from the frontline.

The results of his studio sessions surfaced on the internet in drips – rough freestyles on his Instagram, two videos on GRM Daily in 2018, a BBC 1Xtra freestyle where he raps over a sample from The Specials. Neville Staple, who had written about the 'Ghost Town' of Coventry decades ago, makes a cameo in the music video. It was the early stems of a music career. A light in the fog offering a chance at escape.

'I didn't feel it was going to help me. I just wanted to feel free.'

But the streets were still there. In September 2018, his close friend Fidel Glasgow, also known as AP, was murdered outside a nightclub in the city centre. Family mourned, and tributes were paid. Fidel was Neville Staple's grandson. In a Facebook post, Neville said, 'My beautiful daughter Melanie and wife Christine Sugary, all the family and myself are still shocked by this tragedy, but would like to thank you all for the kindness and messages we have received.'

Before his passing, AP had started his own clothing line, Money Moves, and pushed Pa to take a serious turn at rapping.

'For him to have so much belief in me, he saw something in the future.'

His friend motivated Pa to double down on his own craft and continue to record. His first music video dropped the day AP passed.

'It's all not for nothing,' Pa says. 'You really do live through people; you're living through your ancestors; you're living through so much.'

After AP passed, Pa was on edge. Another close friend passed a few months later, and he began to feel like people were dying around him. In a February 2019 freestyle on Mixtape Madness, those haunting thoughts were shaped into song. He vented visions of his own death:

> I had a dream that I'm dead up
> Head-top red up
> Must've got blown by a two-barrel [shotgun]
> How did I end up and slip like this?

Eight months after its release, outside a pub in Coventry's city centre, Pa was shot in the head with the same type of gun he had rapped about. When the shot went off, he turned his head on instinct, knowing *I'd rather get shot in the head than my face,* otherwise *I wouldn't be here.* More than twenty pellets pierced his skin. Fighting to keep his eyes open, he moved down the stairs, bleeding everywhere, and called an ambulance, guided by a quiet voice in his head with a defiance in its tone, telling him, *Fuck that. This has just started. Ain't nothing gonna stop me, no way.*

He went into intensive care. He went into surgery. His mum thought he'd died. He woke up with nineteen pellets embedded beneath his skin and was discharged from hospital after more than a week or so. A survivor.

The shooting forced him to a fork in the road. His mum, a daughter of Gambia in a foreign land, had sacrificed for her children, had lost a job because he was in hospital, had seen her eldest son almost swallowed whole by the ends. He had a choice. He could go back to what was, follow a dangerous path and maybe never emerge out the other end. Or he could bet the small odds on music, put his pain into song and pray for salvation.

He went back into the studio and staked out a Rap dream.

These experiences are folded into his music. His single 'Frontline', released a few months after the shooting, weaves the threads of the strip and Hillfields into three-minute union. The instrumental lays a canvas with sirens wailing over a murmuring synth and the steady knock of the bass. It's a distinctly Coventry soundscape, the dark underside of a ghost town. Pa stalks across the terrain, pushing out memories of days lived on the edge, in a corner of Coventry where Class As were sold and packaged, weapons were drawn and used, lives glowed like sky lanterns and then went out.

He wasn't the first to rap about the frontline. There were other rappers, from generations past who did the same. Rap group C.O.V shot large portions of their 2004 '4 My City' video on the strip, boys of decades gone, dressed in baggy jeans and swollen hoodies, stumbling through the same minefields Pa and his friends did years later. After C.O.V there was Chess, who released two frontline freestyles in 2012. And Shakavellie, who joined Pa on 'Active', featured the road in his music videos.

Pa's video was shot on the strip, with his boys wrapped in puffer jackets and tracksuits. The towers stand to attention overhead, the grey concrete settling into the grey of the Coventry sky. Pa appears confident in stance. A strong Gambian inflection colours his rhymes as his voice carries clearly, a symbol of the continual immigration that has defined, and still defines the area. By holding Gambia with him on record, a culture and community is cemented, its migration paths catalogued, and a place still known as *the arrival doors of Coventry* set in stone. Forty years on from The Specials, the song was Hillfields speaking again, the frontline emitting its stories.

'Frontline' was Pa's breakout moment. Like Jaykae with 'Toothache', Pa caught a wave as he showed an enclosed West Midlands community to the eyes and ears of the country. It flooded the internet and the radio and social media, pushing him to the vanguard of an emerging generation of British rappers. 'Frontline' and *Send Them to Coventry* were folded into the canon of West Midlands Rap and MC culture, continuing the legacy of the likes of Vader and Despa and Jaykae and Dapz and Lady Leshurr and the rest of the Grime generation who came before him.

This tradition is a reaping and sowing. Pa's music pulls from the river of Black music in the West Midlands, making room for him to change his life. Throughout 2020 and 2021, he began to grace magazine covers; modelling looks in tribute to his friend AP. When the lockdown lifted, he began to get booked for festivals and dates abroad. His debut tour was put in place, and he moved down to London, he travelled the country and, when in the countryside, even saw the seaside and mountains for the first time. Music was a gateway, a bridge from one life into another, a road that climbed out over the tower blocks in the ends and allowed him to finally look out at what lay beyond.

When we sat down in a London private member's club by the Thames it was the winter of 2021 and his life, on the outside anyway, was changing. Traumas still ate at him. But in just over a year, he had moved between two extremes, the memories of the shooting and the ride to the hospital where he sat saying his prayers still fresh, now offset by the kind of visibility and fame few experience: legions of devoted supporters in Britain and back home in Gambia, millions of views on YouTube, and his first live bookings, doing two festivals in one day. He was gliding in the slipstream of 'Frontline', and another song 'My Family' with BackRoad Gee, a rapper from London by way of Congo. His stock was rising. I saw Pa at an awards show. I watched him on TV. I heard his songs on the radio and in raves. He released *Send Them to Coventry*, and he won the prestigious BBC Sound of 2021, the broadcaster crowning him as one of 'Britain's most exciting musical talents'. All of this, because he chose to share his story.

'Pain is beauty,' he told me, 'and they'll hear nuttin but our pain.'

When we met, he was a few weeks out from going on tour and was about to go into rehearsals. In person he is gentle, and quiet, smiles frequently, speaks with hunger, and a deep-rooted ambition to give back to his homelands.

But talking could still be difficult for him. Recently, he had been interviewed on a popular YouTube channel, and when he tried to speak about some of these things, he stuttered and mumbled, struggling to pull his thoughts out into the open. The experience irked him.

Still, his message was being heard. He was just back from Barcelona, having left Britain for the first time since he was a kid. When in Barcelona, he met kids like him, who grew up on frontlines in the city's most deprived areas. In his music, they had found a sense of comfort, a loud expression of the experiences that had been eating at them.

'Frustration was coming out,' he told me, 'they were telling me their frustration.'

'Frontline' was beginning to mean more than just Coventry.

The community in Hillfields goes on. In the same month I sat with Pa, I went up to Hillfields again to visit some of the youth centres. I was in the WATCH centre on the frontline, the home of Hillz FM, the local community radio station. The DJs are from Hillfields by way of Jamaica and South Africa and Dagenham and Ireland and more. They have Reggae shows and Bollywood shows, community talk shows and Jazz and Funk shows, shows that have been broadcast in Polish, Punjabi, Kurdish, Urdu and Iranian, and when I sit in the lobby, Afrobeats is echoing out of the speakers.

The station has been here for years, born out of the youth project in the same building, and run by the same staff members. Some of the staff have seen different waves of immigration shape the evolution of Black music in Britain. They remember when it was Pirate Radio from the flats of Thomas King House, and then Grime sets here in the centre and out on the square. Change being the only constant in the arrival doors of Coventry.

Most recently, the area has seen a wave of Polish, Czech and Slovak immigrants arriving, sitting alongside the Irish, Caribbean, Somalis, Eritreans and Gambians. As always, the station and community will adapt to their needs.

It is 11 November, Armistice Day, a day of remembrance for those who fought and died for Britain in the war. Here in Coventry, where some feel the damages of war were heavier, the remembrance takes on special meaning. At 11 a.m., the radio goes dead. Airwaves cut. There is a two-minute silence held in tribute to the fallen. The city and its residents still remember what happened here, more than seven decades ago, and how they are still rising out from the ash. When two minutes have passed, the station whirs back into motion, and music pours out into Hillfields again.

Later that afternoon, school breaks and Armistice Day activities continue. The kids flood into the youth project. They are undertaking a project called 'Rap for Peace', where the youth leaders use lyrics and rap to teach about the war's impact in Coventry. As they arrive, old C.O.V Rap videos are playing on a screen in the corner, the frontline in the new millennium flashing across the monitor. And as a schoolgirl walks in and notices what is playing, she says, 'Oh, my dad's in this video!' and then sits down to point him out. The future of Hillfields remains connected to its past. Its stories and families are remembered in song.

————

Pa's November 2021 Afrikan Rebel Tour was scheduled to take him across the country. Seven dates. Seven cities. Bristol then Manchester, London then Leeds, before a homecoming Coventry show at the Kasbah, a venue at the foot of the frontline marking the entrance into Hillfields. But around a month before he hit the road, the Coventry show was cancelled. In a statement posted to social media, Pa wrote:

Sadly due to reasons beyond my control, the authorities have decided that I can't play my Coventry show next month. This after already being cut out of certain City of Culture activities this year is just too disappointing. I feel like I'm being let down by the city I love . . . Why do they fear us?

A homecoming was deferred. An extra date in Birmingham was added in its place. And so, on a cold evening in November, a few weeks after Armistice Day, he was twenty miles away from Hillfields, on stage at the O2 Institute in Birmingham city centre. The air was heavy with the sweat of a few hundred people. A sound system and a live band was booming out into the darkness. Pink and white strobe lights roam across the arena. A cameraman sweeps across the stage, cementing the moment.

Pa has been performing for around half an hour. Some of his boys stand behind him throughout, teasing the crowd into frenzy as the songs play. Pa stalks the stage, walking slowly but with confidence, a bond deepening between himself and the supporters who he had shared his clearest and most personal thoughts with. Here, he could be himself. Here, he never stuttered, or jumbled sentences as he spoke. It was like he was in the studio for the first time. This was freedom.

When the evening begins to reach its high point, Pa stops in the middle of the stage and looks out over the few hundred gathered. 'Shall we take them back to Coventry?' he says, 'We're on the frontline right now.' From the sound system and the band, the sirens and drums of 'Frontline' begin to wail. The strobe lights blinker and the crowd roar in excitement. Pa holds the mic to his face, ready to catch the drop as the instrumental guides him in. He steadies himself, opens his mouth, and when he speaks, his words come out clear.

19 STREATHAM VALE TO THE WORLD

SOUTH LONDON

South London folklore is written in the tarmac of a quiet North London side road in Camden.

There are teenagers, around two hundred of them, clustered in the middle of the street. The side road is locked off. Cars can't enter. The young ones had the winter evening jumping like a block party.

They are swarming around a boy. He is eighteen years old, in the centre of a storm he spoke into existence. The crowd tug at his arms and jacket, shrieking and screaming in his presence. Hands and fingers thrust phones in his face, their flashlights beaming in the darkness, casting him under a spotlight. The flock snap pictures and selfies, pulled into his orbit, desperate to claim a piece of history as their own.

He tries to push through the crowd, moving through the bodies, the screams and hands and iPhones falling towards his face.

'Oh my God,' the boy, David Omoregie, eventually mumbles to himself, jostling for space, 'this is mad.'

British Rap was changing, MC culture in Britain mutating into something new as an emergent generation sought to hand-craft the sounds of their forebears into something they could call their own. When change came, South London sat at the heart of the evolution.

Among the high tides of the Grime and UK Rap boom, young sons and daughters of the ends began to experiment and grow.

Section Boyz from the deep South blended Trap and UK Rap and Grime into a style they called Section Sound, crawling inside instrumentals and pushing out a new, South London mutation, their experimental flow patterns and ad-libs becoming a guiding light for teenagers-turned-rappers in wider Britain.

And from the estates around Brixton and Brixton Hill, boys who had grown up on UK Rap opened their ears to the contemporary music of Midwestern America, the booming sounds of Chicago Drill and Chief Keef seeping into South London through the steady veins of YouTube. Collectives like 150 in Brixton and 67 in Brixton Hill sprang out of local street gangs who began using the genre to air out and document the experiences of a new generation of the young and vulnerable growing up on the roads. Songs like 'Skeng Man' by 67 and 'Look Like You' by 150 were a testament to this contemporary borrowing and influencing from the diaspora, the deep, haunting baselines typical of Chicago Drill now rumbling out across the streets of South London and the wider UK.

As Drill bedded in, producers and rappers began to reassemble the sound: the instrumentals growing faster and fanning out, the punchlines creeping in, ad-libs occupying the empty space between each bar, and references unique to British life coating their lyrics as this new hybrid became the style defining its generation.

By 2016, UK Drill was a sound detached from the Chicago version, folding itself in under the umbrella of Black British MC culture. The instrumentals were pinned on sliding 808s and rappers bouncing and turning over them like dirt bikes over gravel, using the pounding bass as a vessel for the sometimes bleak accounts of life.

It was a continuation of UK Rap. Many Drill artists began as UK rappers before the new genres snatched their attention. There was a bond to Grime too, a resonance with the earlier scene's sound in tempo. Drill artists were raised under the haze of Grime's 2014 emergence, and some listened to and were inspired by the older MCs they saw having success in their local area. Both UK Drill and

Grime hovered around 140 bpm, with the rappers and MCs flowing double-time over the instrumentals.

And so UK Drill and a new generation of UK rappers came out of familiar surroundings: 150 out of Brixton, where PDC and Roadside Gs and many rappers and MCs freestyled in the summer days in Brockwell Park. K-Trap came out of the deep South, the Central Hill Estate in Norwood where Krept was raised. A group named Zone 2 came out of Peckham, once home to Giggs; another, Moscow17 out of Walworth Road. Further afield, Drill artists and groups emerged from the Broadwater Farm estate in Tottenham, Hackney in East London, in Ladbroke Grove and the Mozart Estate off Harrow Road; Handsworth and Lozells and Hillfields in the Midlands; Butetown in Cardiff.

They were kids on the receiving end of Tory austerity, some of their experiences a consequence of cleaved youth service budgets and poverty and the surging youth violence that had followed. By translating these experiences into music, they were unknowingly following a tradition set in place long before they were born, Black kids coming out of working-class communities, pushing their day-to-day experiences into music, just like Smiley Culture and So Solid Crew and Giggs and Krept and Konan and Cadet and Stormzy had done before them.

They were who and what came next, utilising the infrastructure and platforms built and mapped out by the generations before to push their songs into the world, to wade into the charts and change the lives of the artists and producers who followed its tide.

David Omoregie, in the years stretching 2015 to 2019, was among this uprising, a unicorn of sorts, a UK rapper emerging in a generation dominated by Drill artists. He sat distinctly aside from UK Drill, choosing a more traditional style of UK Rap, but was seemingly shaped by the same social, economic and political forces that had created it. Together, they were among a new era of rappers out of

South London, whose presence and music deepened the legacy and history of Black communities in the region as their sounds continued to pull away from the homelands their parents and grandparents and great-grandparents travelled from.

He emerged on YouTube, a young boy with a story to share. In May 2010, at London's Victoria Station, Dave's older brother Christopher was involved in the group murder of fifteen-year-old Sofyen Belamouadden. Twenty teenagers were arrested, and by use of the contentious legal doctrine Joint Enterprise, which can make a group liable for a crime committed by one of its members, all were charged with murder. At the time it was reportedly one of the largest Joint Enterprise cases ever brought to court in England and Wales. The trial went on for two years, was covered heavily throughout British media, and by the time the final conviction had been settled in October 2012, Chris had been sentenced to life in prison.

Three years later, Dave was sixteen. Struggling to process the feelings rising from problems at home, he emptied himself into Rap. Dave's first freestyle proper appeared on the YouTube Channel BL@CKBOX in May 2015, recording the freestyle at their studio in Essex over a haunting Eminem instrumental. In the video, a Gucci hat leans off his forehead, and when he opens his mouth, four silver teeth glint out at the world.

Over four minutes, he tells his South London story. A boy on the edge, his older brother incarcerated for murder and his family coming apart in the aftermath. There are pills to cope with the pain, there's his grandmother's passing and the toll the loss has on his mother. There is anger, and shock and prison visits and a sixteen-year-old boy relieving his burdens, an intensity as he stares down the microphone, barking his words, the bars flowing out in a simmering rage.

Dave's South London was a three-bedroom house on a quiet road in Streatham. Streatham is South-West London, SW16, a middle ground rooted between the region's central communities of Brixton and Battersea and Clapham, and the outer zones of Norbury and Thornton Heath and Croydon in the deep South. You can walk the 1.8 miles of Streatham High Road, which some residents claim to be the longest in Europe, and watch the city turn.

The edges of Brixton Hill bleed over into Streatham proper, red double-deckers steaming down the street, heading south to Pollards Hill and West Croydon and Old Coulsdon. On the main strip of the High Road the continents brush fingers: a Somali barbershop teeming in the late afternoon. A Sudanese market store, a Polish supermarket, and a Lebanese food spot. Salons with Black women braiding hair and East Asian women giving pedicures. School kids in uniform gathered in the Morley's Chicken shop, and Deliveroo drivers huddled in packs outside local restaurants. Then the road continues to stretch, past the low-rise tower blocks edging the street, past the big greens of Streatham Common with families holding BBQs on the grass. Past the war memorials and the internet cafés and Streatham ice rink and the pubs and the Cash Converters and the new-build flats hinting at a creeping gentrification, until you reach the William Hill down by Norbury, where Croydon opens its jaws and South London fans out into its deep, concreted suburbs.

David was raised here, the youngest of three boys. A mum who immigrated from Nigeria, a dad who immigrated from Nigeria too. They are Edo people, from Benin City in the south of the country. He wears that family line in places you can't see, in his surname Omoregie, and his middle name Orobosa, subtle hints at a home beyond Streatham. But he grew up a South yout.

His dad wasn't around, and his mum was a nurse, leaving in the early hours and returning late in the night. Then his brother Chris got life and his other brother Ben went to jail for robbery a few years later. He spent a lot of time with friends as a result, boys born of the city. You can hear it in his music, an identity shaped in these corners of the country where varying Black and ethnic communities have fused together and reshaped the land, redesigned the language, redefined what it means to be British. Here, they have birthed an identity of their own.

And so, in this distant son of Nigeria, raised under the veils of Streatham, you can hear Jamaican patois as he raps, natural references to patties and dumplings and Dancehall anthems. Black Caribbean culture, which had been threaded through South London for more than five decades, was now threaded through him also. When you hear him rap in the BL@CKBOX freestyle, there is little hint of Nigeria on his tongue. Instead, there are casual slips of Arabic and fading cockney, and a distance between his parents' generation, who arrived in London, and his, who were raised here:

'Bruv I've been to them graveyards.
I've been to the pen for my bros
And bruv I've seen what a skeng does to mugs in the south,
Like I've seen a shank leave a nigga's guts hanging out
Seen big straps make a whip crash, no whiplash.
Big money-maker, big man look like a kid akh'[1]

This was a language distinct to Britain, patois blended with English, English blended with Arabic, the many influences of Britain's immigrant communities folding into one, and coming out from one of the region's own.

He found music in his early teens. He was around eleven when his brothers went to prison, the aftershocks rocking both him and his mother. His brothers were moved between prisons all over the country, and he would go and visit them. His mum struggled, and he can remember how 'a lot of the time when my mum was going into rooms when I was younger, it was this thing about her: "That woman there, her sons are in prison." My mum definitely felt the stigma.'[2]

She kept Dave locked indoors, and on school days, his brothers would ring to make sure he had arrived home safely. At home he began to find himself, watching Japanese anime, spending hours drawing and listening to music, losing himself in films scores by Steve Jablonsky and Hans Zimmer. At school he liked playing the piano, so when he turned fourteen his mum bought him a digital keyboard, and he taught himself how to play. He and his friend Kyle would choose a piece like 'Hallelujah' by Leonard Cohen, or the soundtracks to films like *Inception* and *Interstellar*, find the sheet music or tutorials online, and then learn to play them. Sometimes he'd play piano for four or five hours every night. Eventually he reached a Grade 7 level, and, when he got good enough, he stopped playing others' works and began to create his own melodies.

But his early music hints at more than a reclusive life in the sealed walls of home. There is a desperate hunger for money, a hope that pounds and notes would bring his life into balance; and there are the risks he seemingly took to meet that end. In his BL@CKBOX he raps with a sorrowful intensity about hustling, about street politics, and everything that comes with it: shootings and stabbings and fraud in the bleakest ends of life in the city.

'For half dark, half light, get it for a calm price,
Hanging out the passy, like Heath Ledger in *The Dark Knight*
What the fuck's a one-on-one?
Fighting fucking punch to punch,
I'll boot you in your face bruv,
I won't ever watch my darg fight'

Rap was something that had been with him 'since the dawn of time'. His brother used to rap, and Dave grew up on MCs like Devlin and Kano from East London, who rhymed their words cleanly, never wasting a metaphor or a bar. There was Youngs Teflon, who featured on the *Lost Tapes of Brixton* DVD many summers ago, and the producer Carns Hill. They were pioneers for Dave, both from Brixton, who on their records together would sample films like *Karate Kid* and *Transformers*.

Dave wrote his first bar at around eleven years old, something about Newcastle football club and relegation. By the time he began to rap properly, British Rap was rising, entering its golden age. He was the first generation to grow up with the genre as a realistic pursuit, seeing Skepta and Stormzy, Giggs, Fredo and AJ Tracey make a career from writing.

When he was on his way to college, making the two-hour round trip to Richmond College, the same institution attended by Cadet and Krept, he would play the song 'Diamonds' by older Streatham rapper Pak-Man, and stew in the restless and rugged ambitions of this South-West London street anthem, his mind dreaming about the day his brother would touch road. He wanted to help get him up on his feet.

What came out of him at the BL@CKBOX studio in Essex was a culmination of these things, the memories and wounds and highlights of his sixteen years here. South London and Streatham was in him, and with this rare gift of his, he would walk both onto the world stage.

More freestyles followed throughout 2015. There was a freestyle on YouTube channel Street Starz where he is rapping under nightfall, moving over another Eminem instrumental, spitting at pace, his friends stood at his side, sometimes finishing a bar for him when the sentences ran too long and he needed to catch breath. There was another on BL@CKBOX, an under-eighteen cypher, where he lists the prisons he has visited: Cookham Wood in Kent, HMP Elmley on the Isle of Sheppey, Feltham in Hounslow, Swinfen Hall in

Staffordshire, High Down in Surrey and Ford in Sussex, Wandsworth and Thameside and Brixton in South London. And then there was an SBTV Warm Up Session shot on the balcony of the company's central London offices.

'Feeling like I can't breathe, life in South London's hard,' he raps, staring into the camera, heavy emotion in his voice.

It was on these platforms that his voice began to echo out across the country, a career forged on the networks and culture established by generations of British rappers and community-builders that came before him. The infrastructure, carved over many decades, as well as the heightened popularity surrounding the genres, allowed Dave, and other artists from his cohort a smoother and quicker transition into established music careers.

It meant that in 2016, just a year into his career proper, three of his first five singles landed in the Top 70 on the singles charts as a contained buzz begun to move out towards the country's open ears. His videos scaled to views in the hundreds of thousands and then millions. Among those singles was a Grime collaboration with AJ Tracey named 'Thiago Silva', after the Brazilian footballer. They shot the video in Paris, where Thiago Silva was then playing football for Paris Saint-Germain. They don PSG tops in the video. It became his first song to breach Middle England.

Some months later, when I saw him perform it at the SBTV Summer Cookout to a watching audience of a few hundred, he sprinted through his verse, unable to catch his breath, until there was no air left in his lungs and he had to stop and restart the song from the beginning: his career moving so fast that he hadn't yet had the time to fine-tune and learn the live arena.

Elsewhere, there was the piano-led, melodic single titled 'Samantha', with another rising star J Hus. 'Wanna Know', a song from his 2016 debut EP *Six Paths*, was remixed by Drake, pulling his music into a global view and further altering the course of his career and life. By the end of 2016, he was throwing his first headline show in Camden, leaving the venue and walking out into the North London night mobbed by his new supporters, cameras thrust in and around his face, a boy caught in a changing world.

A few days after his show in Camden, he sat in his manager's central London apartment. I had come to interview him for *VICE*. He sat at the piano, fingers tracing over the keys as he tried to explain an instrumental to me. Whenever he played the wrong key, or the melody bent out of tune, he would start again, trying to recreate what he had heard in his head. Obsessed.

There was a stillness about those fleeting moments, an anchoring in a life that was changing. I was watching a young boy from South London leave one world and enter territories new and unfamiliar. He had just sold out his headline show and seen supporters clamour around him as if he were a prophet. In the past year he had shared his heart and family pain on videos and freestyles with millions of views, his stark social commentary giving voice to those living and surviving and running into dead ends in the far sides of cities. Now, he was learning how to craft songs that would carry into setlists as well as car stereos and summer festivals. 'Wanna Know', one of his first attempts at striking that balance, saw a remix and the Drake co-sign. He had started to travel across continents, drove a rental Benz around LA, performed on stage at the Royal Opera House in central London. He was in interviews and photoshoots. His songs were on the radio and lighting up streaming platforms. He was famous. Many were labelling him the great hope of the genre, and his life was changing quicker than any British rapper's life had before him.

But he was still visiting his brothers in prison, making music so that they could hear him, so that he could motivate them. They heard him on the radio first, and were now watching him on TV. Recently, he had gone into a prison to give a presentation and have a discussion with some prisoners, speaking on how a negative situation could be turned into a positive.

'There are a lot of people in prison who are misunderstood,' he told me. 'And people overlook them and forget about them because they don't understand. It's good to go out and let people know that I understand, I'm coming from a place where the same things were around me.'

He was still topping up his Oyster card at the train station in Streatham. He was still with the same boys from South who he grew up with, and who first appeared in his early music videos. He still worked through the nights and slept through the afternoons, like many teenagers do. He still loved anime. He hadn't put an album out yet. He was on the edge of two converging realities, fame and a music career pulling him away from what he had known. He was barely an adult. He was still only eighteen. He was still Streatham. He was still South London.

———

Dave's presence and rise were a signal of something shifting in the earth, a forecasting that UK Rap and Grime surfacing in mainstream Britain was not a peaking of a genre, but instead a beginning.

As the year turned into 2017, more applause began to arrive as word of a rare gem out of Streatham Vale began to spread. He released his second EP *Game Over* and charted at 13 in the UK Albums Chart. He made an appearance on BBC One, performing on *Later . . . with Jools Holland*, was nominated for the BBC Sound of 2017 list and was the subject of a bidding war between Britain's major labels. He rejected their advances and decided to plough the independent route, following a path set by Stormzy and Skepta before him. He was nominated for the GRM Daily Rated Awards, and won Best Newcomer at the 2017 MOBO Awards, following a long line of rappers and MCs from out of South London.

Rappers are not vessels or voices for communities by default. These are titles earned by trust and faith, by those who reckon with the weight of their responsibility and use their expanded platform to bring the frustrations their people have held within, the injustices their communities have faced, to the public ear. Every era has a handful of these people, young men and women whose vocalisations of their life experiences, whose heritage and perspective strike a note with the masses raised in the communities they come from. Dave was among these anointed, an eighteen-year-old boy out of Streatham Vale, shouldering the weight of his home.

In 2017, he released the seven-minute-long song 'Question Time'. It was released in a defining and harrowing crisis point in the history of contemporary Britain. A year before, the country had voted to pull out of the European Union. A reported quarter of a million NHS workers marched on Westminster, protesting an underfunded NHS and further proposed cuts to the health service. Throughout the track, he speaks of how his mum had been a nurse for decades, how she even took cleaning jobs in the evening and still found it difficult to get by. The National Health Service, the heart of the nation, was coming to its knees, he said, with workers underpaid and overworked, local services understaffed, and its running overseen by upper-class senior politicians.

The fourth verse tilts towards West London, addressing the Grenfell Tower fire, a high-rise council block in the Royal Borough of Kensington and Chelsea that caught fire in the dead of night. The tower block burned for sixty hours. Seventy-two people died. Many of the deceased were immigrants and working-class people who were failed by the Conservative-led local council who had prioritised costs over the safety of the residents' and the building.

In the verse he speaks of the horrors he had heard, about families who choked on smoke, about those panicking at the wail of the sirens and the cracking and popping of a burning building, about the muffled screams and the fear of a man who died after jumping from the sixteenth floor to escape.

Across the country, Black, immigrant, minority and working-class communities were in mourning and anger, grief and shock. As Dave's star was rising, he absorbed these frustrations, barking questions at the incumbent Conservative government, more specifically the Prime Minister, who had reigned over the chaos.

'Question Time' was followed the year after by his single 'Funky Friday', with West London rapper Fredo. It was an example of the balance Dave was attempting to strike, offsetting deeply personal and political songs with anthems that can live on in raves and dances and radio. It debuted at number 1 on the UK Singles Chart, and was what many considered to be the first authentic number 1 record of the genre, going on to sell over 1.2 million records. A moment for British Rap, and an indication of the rare air Dave had walked into, becoming one of the most popular musicians in the country in the space of a few years.

———

A psychodrama is a course of therapy that sees patients dig into past events and memories, bringing the forming moments and traumas of their lives into light, and by doing so, hoping to heal and make sense of them. Dave's brother Chris underwent a course in prison. The course shaped the making of Dave's debut album, a concept piece titled after the therapy course. Healing and trauma were the template for his first real offering.

Psychodrama the album is autobiographical, taking his new listeners back to his beginnings. It is deeply local, deeply South London, deeply Streatham. There are sly references to the 118 bus that cuts down the high road from Brixton, and to Mitcham Lane that connects Streatham and Tooting. After, he takes listeners behind the frontline, into a place where teenagers are on stolen peds, where teenagers are growing up in poverty, where teenagers are selling cannabis and then cocaine, teenagers with an urge to kill other teenagers, teenagers who, among it all, still have to be indoors by curfew. Deep in his diaries he hints at how life in South London scarred him, depressive episodes that bordered on suicidal thoughts. They were broke growing up, but went to school with the rich, he tells us, and how among these polar extremes a tension was fostered, unhinging them, daring young boys to gamble their freedoms for a wealth they could see waiting on the other side of the fence.

On release, *Psychodrama* debuted at number 1 on the UK Albums Chart in March 2019, and a new prince of the genre was crowned. It was labelled as the defining British Rap album of its time, political and personal, bringing the wider country closer to the social issues and environments some Black and working-class kids were springing from. A nationwide tour accompanied its release, and he stopped in Dublin and Glasgow and Nottingham and Leeds and Liverpool and Sheffield and Manchester and Birmingham and Leicester and Norwich and Bristol and Bournemouth, before ending with two nights in Brixton, just two months after he had appeared at the same venue to celebrate the life of Cadet.

After came a North American and a European and an Australian tour as the world opened up to his and their sound. He took South London on the road, to Germany, Copenhagen, New York, Toronto, Chicago and Sydney, touching venues in far continents.

*

By early 2020, he was back on home soil, South London, for the fortieth BRIT Awards. The O2 Arena was sold out, and over three million people were tuning in from home. Dave had been nominated for four awards: Best New Artist, British Male Solo Artist, Song of the Year for 'Location' and Album of the Year.

American vocalist Billie Eilish was presenting the award for Album of the Year. Among the nominees were Stormzy, from nearby Norbury, soul singer Michael Kiwanuka and pop artists Harry Styles and Lewis Capaldi. When Eilish held the microphone in one palm and looked down at her placard, the arena fell silent, tense.

'And the winner is,' she said, before pausing again, 'Dave, *Psychodrama*.'

The dam on the silence broke and the O2 filled with cheers and screams. 'Streatham' began to play out from the big speakers, honouring the winner. On the floor, Dave's managers and his friends shook him with excitement as a dazed smile crossed his face. Then his mum stood from her seat and wrapped her arms around her son, hugging him with a deep joy.

He walked to the stage in a blue tracksuit and white trainers, looking almost shaky on his legs, trying to take in what had happened. The bass of 'Streatham' crowned his arrival. He gripped the microphone in one hand. He thanked God and his mum and his family and his team, then stuttered slightly, trying to gather himself, the moment almost overwhelming him. After a few moments, he steadied, and spoke clearly. He gave a nod to the incarcerated: 'I want to say everyone that I know that's inside doing their time, hold it down, I love you guys.'

And he had a message, too, for everyone coming from where he comes from, for 'young kings and queens' growing up in South and North London, West and East London, Birmingham and Manchester, trying to chase their dreams. His life was a testimony.

He was just like them he said, a boy born of the ends. And like him, they could do anything with their lives.

As his speech closed, he raised the award to the sky.

'Thank you so much,' he said, 'Streatham Vale to the world.'

PART V
SPIRIT

20 **AFTERLIVES**

SOUTH WALES

For so long he had been Dell of Astroid Boys. But he wanted change now. He wanted to honour his roots. So he reformed his producer tag. Dell became Douvelle19 – the number an ode to his old postcode in St Julians, Newport.

Five years had passed. It was 2020. Douvelle19 was twenty-six now. He was living in Cardiff, in a terraced house with a few of his childhood boys from Newport. They were in the student area, near the centre of the city, not far from the towering lecture halls of Cardiff University, the crowded student pubs, the sprawling greens of Bute Park and the fading concrete walls of Cardiff Castle.

It was a lads' house. In the front room, a large flatscreen TV balanced on a stand and a game of FIFA had been paused. Four bedrooms were spread across two floors, with Dell's master room on the first floor overlooking the main road. He could look out over the street and watch the students drift by like the seasons, at night seeing their shadows pool on the pavement, students shuffling along the road, alone into the darkness.

There was a large desk facing his double windows. On top of it was a huge Mac desktop screen. In the weekdays, he opened up his production software on here and made sample production packs, a trade that had become his wage. His room was now his office.

Sitting here today, Dell was reflecting on his past with Astroid Boys. For him, the band had meant flirting with the kind of surreal sensations only a musician can know, precious moments on a stage with your boys, a backing band and an audience singing your music. But it had meant anxiety also, and exhaustion and a quiet unease that shadowed him through his late teens. For this next chapter of his life, he hoped to pull out the best bits of his old life, and leave the anxieties. For him, this new chapter could be the same, this new chapter could be different too.

He and Phil are friends still. They went out to Cyprus together last year and rode mopeds along the island roads. They saw Phil's family. They ate. They went to the beach. Then, some time after they came home, Phil sent over the early iterations of a solo Rap album. Dell made notes, then sat with him to give earnest feedback. The bond is still there, but no music has been made together, yet.

'I wouldn't mind making a tune with him but at the moment we're still kind of letting that be and letting it all simmer.'

How does it feel? How does it feel to come out the other end, whole?

The answers are on his bedroom wall, stuck onto the plaster. He pointed them out for me, the big moments and the small milestones that had made him. There were photos of his sister and his mother. Photos of his dad with a record collection. Photos of his dad with his grandfather. Photos of Dell as a kid, and photos of Dell as a man. Photos of him with friends on weekend trips to festivals, friends from Cardiff and Newport and elsewhere. He had his people.

There were plaques of the Astroid Boys artwork covers too, of *Bacon Dream* and *CF10* and *Broke*. He hasn't listened to the album much since it came out.

'It is what you make it, I think,' he said on the experience in a band. 'I can either dwell on how hard it was, or appreciate how hard it was, and thank it.'

There were posters of a new chapter too, artwork for the club night he had been throwing in Cardiff. He called the night Locally Sauced. The idea was to put on an event that was in South Wales, and made by South Wales, to bring something to life with the fruits of home.

And so, the DJs on the line-up were all from South Wales. The artwork was made by an artist from Cardiff, and the venues were in Cardiff. He sold out a 150-capacity place for the launch, and then a 330-capacity place for the follow-up. When the nightclubs are running again, he'll eventually aim higher.

'I don't feel washed,' he said, 'I feel like I'm still going, I feel like I'm still raring to go really.'

On the wall was all of him, all of who he was, all what he came from. A son of Newport and St Julians and Greece and South Wales, the son of the migrations and ancestral wanderings that move and beat through the blood of the region. A son of Astroid Boys. A son of Grime and Metal and Rap and Drum & Bass. A son of the middle ground in which they meet. He was a son of the Urban Circle and the youth centres. Dell was a son of everything that had come before him in South Wales, and the son of everything that will be.

Benji rose at 4 a.m. most mornings. Half an hour later he was out the door. By 5 a.m. he was at work, and soon after that, the streets still dark, Cardiff still quiet, he was on the road. Since Astroid Boys had run aground, he had been working as a milkman, delivering wholesale to the petrol stations and shops and schools across South Wales.

Riding in his van, *The Joe Rogan Experience* keeping him company, he moved from business to business, nurseries to hospitals, making his drop-offs. His routes trawled through Cardiff and Newport, and through the South Wales Valleys.

Some mornings, when the skies were clear, he watched the sun break through dark purple skies, no cars on the road, no traffic, no stress, no pressure, just him and his van, a Cardiff boy, in 2020, finally at peace.

Being out on the road gave him a feeling nothing else could. When he was in his van at sunrise making his deliveries, or out in his car, heading someplace, he could feel it, could feel his mind going quiet, could feel the thoughts fading away; the waves on the water easing to ripples and the ripples into gentle calm.

'I've only been driving for a year,' he said, 'but I think it saved my life, man, it's just so relaxing.'

Some days he would drive out to the rural countryside with his missus and have lunch in a small pub or a nice restaurant. On other days they would drive out to the mountains and hike the trails. He said, 'We're blessed in Cardiff really. We've got the Brecon Beacons [mountain range], just like a half-hour drive north. The coast is all along us. We've literally got everything right within a short driving distance, so it's nice to just get a spliff and go exploring.'

He had recently turned thirty-one, a landmark in his new state of renewal. Since the band had split and the tours ceased, he had stared deep into himself and slowly revved the cold motor of change. Benji was growing up. Gone were the benders and the destructive drinking, the crippling depression that had haunted him in Astroid Boys' twilight. The darkness was fading, receding quietly into the backwaters of time.

The previous night, a still Saturday, he sat on his own with a quiet drink by the telly and watched heavyweight champion Anthony Joshua knock out Kubrat Pulev in the ninth round. The next day, his alarm would wake him at 4 a.m. and he would climb into his van for his sunrise crawl across South Wales, the day breaking in, the horizon bruising crimson on the lonely roads.

He was levelling out. He was maturing. He was untangling from the mess and madness of his twenties. He was a thirty-one-year-old father now with a baby daughter and a stable job and a steady relationship.

In the time since the band's flame had gone cold, he was, he says, 'working pay cheque to pay cheque'. But for him, these had been the happiest and most humbling days of his life.

We were parked up by the riverfront in Newport town centre, at a parking bay overlooking the grey expanse of River Usk. Christmas was cresting on the city, and from his car, a sharp convertible, the Usk was swallowing the rainfall, the brown water driving out towards the Severn Estuary and the Bristol Channel. Along this little stretch of waterfront, he made some of his earliest appearances on camera, a young kid in a black tracksuit, freestyling and battling other teenagers.

Some days he jogged this route, he said, and recently realised that if you were to run this quarter of the riverfront in a loop, crossing the footbridge in his far corner, running down past the rising new-build homes and Newport County football ground, and then cross again at the red rungs of Newport Bridge, the distance was a perfect 1.5 km lap.

'. . . so two laps is three kilometres,' he was saying, 'and four is . . .' and so on and so on.

It was peaceful. It was rhythm. It was stability.

The time that had passed had given him space to reflect on things. The band was what it was. Maybe things could have been different. Maybe not. Maybe life sets you on a road and you go with it into the quiet dark and emerge out to a new dawn breaking. Given this time again, there were things he would change, people he would treat differently, money he would spend more wisely. Sometimes, back then, big sums would drop into his bank account, and he would burn the notes away within a year.

'Nobody told me to save money, bro, and that's sad,' he said, 'I could've been doing a lot better for myself realistically . . . but I guess that's how I wanted to live, to live fast.'

There were things he wouldn't change, too, tours he would still go on, countries he would still travel to, places he would still see. Sometimes, rich kids came into the Astroid Boys following, he says, 'turning up to our shows dressed like fucking flames, and I'm dressed in rags because I'm still skint'. They would invite the band for after-parties, and Benji would turn up to their massive mansions in the countryside, thinking, *Jeez, I never would have seen these places, I would have still been going to council flats around St Mellons and fucking Trowbridge.*

And now he was saying, 'There's not a city in the UK that I haven't passed out in. I've got friends in every country in Europe, I can go anywhere and catch up with people. That's been really good, I've made the world a little bit smaller for myself . . . especially for kids like us, who weren't necessarily expected do anything beyond average coming from where we come from, and what we come from.'

He went on:

'All of us coming from our own little hardships . . . We didn't even know how hard each other had it. Everyone's problem was the worst in the world to them, but when you get a little perspective you real-ise, we all needed each other, and we should all have been a bit more careful with each other. Everyone had their issues, man.'

Maybe a break is what they needed. Maybe he needed time away from the relentless grind of the music industry. A break from back-to-back-to-back tours on two or three hours' sleep a night. A break from the stage, and the supporters guided by your every word. A break from caring about YouTube views and likes and stacking your sense of self-worth by how they swing. A break from an industry that can break you, that can bring out the worst version of yourself. Maybe that's not who he is any more. Maybe that's who he never was. Maybe this is him.

———

What happens after the boats of your boyhood ambitions float away on the water until the headsails become specks and the specks melt into the expanse of blue? Surrendering a part of who you were is never easy. Some take the loss hard, like the slow passing of a family member, grieve for weeks that become years, and never quite recover from the promise and the echoes of what could have been.

For Phil, the first few months after Astroid Boys were dark. He came back to Cardiff skint and unsettled. For the first time in years, he had no tours, no band deadlines, no focus to swing for in his eyeline. He was unsure of what would come next. He was free, and he was lost.

What would come next was a series of rogue jobs to get him back on his feet and earning some money. What would come were shifts in a warehouse, sanding down thirty-foot-long racing boats from morning till evening. And he didn't have a car, so he ran the five miles to the lot every morning. And he was sanding by hand, so his palms and fingers bled every day. Then he would come home, soak in a bath, head to bed and start over when he woke.

What would come next was a questioning of faith, a feeling that honouring what God had asked him to do felt like the worst thing in the world. He felt like he had made a mistake. He felt like he was in a drought. There were legal dramas with the label. There were legal dramas with management. And under the weight of it all, Phil ended up getting ill, coming down with an abscess in his throat that had to be drained, leaving him out of action for months.

'It was rock bottom,' he says, 'and I had my faith as well, so I was like, "I don't know what to do any more."'

But after the job sanding boats came a breakthrough. He found work at a T-shirt factory. He helped out his dad selling diesel. He began speaking in schools and in prisons, started a Punk band, and recorded a separate solo Rap album. He saved some money from his jobs. He sold his flat and bought a house. Then he bought a ring. He took his girlfriend to New York and proposed to her one evening under the Brooklyn Bridge. They were married in 2019.

————

Phil can tell you about one of his first encounters with music as a boy. Sian Evans, the frontwoman of early-millennium Electronic group Kosheen, was dating his uncle. A single she featured on with DJ Fresh titled 'Louder' sold 120,000 copies in its first week. She had platinum and gold albums to her name. She had toured across Europe and Australia. She was part of an exclusive ring of Welsh artists alongside only Dame Shirley Bassey of Splott and Sir Tom Jones to have mounted the UK charts summit. She was a titan of her time.

When Phil met Sian, he was around six years old. He was stood side of stage at one of her shows, leaping in the air and watching her perform the Kosheen classic 'Hide U', a platinum-selling anthem spun around an Amen breakbeat. When the show finished and the lights dimmed, she came offstage, saw a young Phil standing by, and asked him, 'What do you want to do when you get older?'

'I wanna do this,' he told her.

Noting that he was serious, she passed down some advice that would give him stability for the decades ahead, told him, 'Don't touch drugs or don't touch alcohol, or you won't remember all the great memories.'

She wrote out the message on a plain napkin and then sealed it with a kiss. Phil framed the message on his bedroom wall, a star among his gallery of posters and pictures.

While on the road with Astroid Boys for those long years, he never drank, and he never smoked. He never crushed pills into fine powder or inhaled any substance that would tilt him off-balance.

Those golden memories are diarised in his mind. He remembers the faces out in the crowd, the hundreds of shows they played, the stages they graced. Remembers their steady incline, remembers everything, every mosh pit and memory connected to *Bacon Dream*, and *CF10* and *Broke*.

Shortly after he was married, Phil and his wife went to Boomtown festival in the South Downs. Together they walked among the sets and the stages, stopping at Rage Against the Machine and Lauryn Hill, swinging between the darkest Metal and the purest Hip Hop, a palette in eternal flux.

And while they wandered, he would get stopped by people. They were old Astroid Boys fans who remembered him from the shows. And because Phil never drank and never smoked, their faces crystallised back into memory. Kids who he had seen out in the crowd at their gigs. Kids who he had skated with in the cities till 4 a.m. Kids who he remembers sitting and eating chicken and chips with after a show. Kids who had bounced in rage and rapture on his cue. Kids who were grown now, their many faces reminding him of a childhood dream realised.

21 THE BLACK POUND

WEST MIDLANDS

n the early stretches of 2020, Despa found an office space in a complex not far from the city centre. Then the pandemic hit and Birmingham retreated into lockdown. As the world burned, he spent hours and days and weeks building up the space from scratch, assembling work desks, cleaning and bringing in furnishing until the place began to take after the vision he had in his mind.

BE83 Studios opened later that year and a boyhood pipe dream was realised. There was an office space and, next door, a studio, where artists could come and record. Those early Darlaston dreams of his own music label were bearing out into reality. BE83 Music was up and running with a management wing, a label, a publishing arm and now its own permanent home with a studio. A No Limit poster was hung on one wall and a framed image of Steve Jobs on another. Those who had shaped him, even from afar, with him now as he took the next step in his journey.

There was more good news, too. Despa and BE83 inked a global distribution deal with Sony Music's leading independent music distributor and label services company, The Orchard.

'Birmingham is a city overflowing with talent that has often lacked music business infrastructure,' he said in the official press release, 'This new partnership between BE83 and The Orchard is enabling us to scale up our business and deliver on this vision to take the Midlands' sound around the world.'

Timothy Youdeowei at The Orchard noted Despa as somebody with high aspirations and said, 'Despa has shown himself to be a highly skilled emerging music mogul, independently building a full-service entertainment company, which we are now proud to have partnered with globally.'

And so Despa and BE83 began a new chapter. Employees were interviewed and hired. The studio opened and business rolled in.

This establishing of infrastructure, which was happening in cities across the country, was an indicator of British MCs' continued rise. UK Rap and UK Drill are at the onset of a global spread. Artists like Dave and Stormzy and Central Cee have become globally established, popular artists.

The influence of the sound is showing up in communities across the world. In the working-class suburbs of Western Sydney, Samoan Rap group OneFour have fashioned Australian Drill from the slang, flow patterns and instrumentals of UK Drill. They cite their exposure to Grime legends like Skepta as inspiration for their music careers.

The same is happening in regions across Italy, Amsterdam and Spain too. Brazil has its own thriving Grime scene, which blends the sound with the native Baile Funk. And in New York, the mecca of Hip Hop, rappers have borrowed heavily from UK Drill, with artists like the late Pop Smoke working, at times, almost exclusively with British producers, taking influence from the sound to propel the rise of their own local Brooklyn Drill sound. The diaspora's Rap boomerang, for the first time, is working in reverse.

As these sounds have spread, the language, traditions and culture of Black Britain has spread with them. The future, for now at least, looks bright.

But there are long-term worries. Things aren't as they once were in the regions that birthed these sounds. Across South London, Black communities are being uprooted, a cold and expensive city squeezing out its working-class residents as gentrification continues to erode away the family lines etched into communities around Brixton and

Clapham, Croydon and Peckham. One Friday evening I walk along a high street in Crystal Palace with a friend who has lived in the area his whole life. He tells me that when the 2008 recession hit, this place was empty, the shops all boarded up, and if you weren't from around the way, you wouldn't come up here past a certain time. But after the recession was over, gentrification began to set in, reforming this corner of South London. And so on this evening, one of the last in summer, we see a string of coffee shops and vegan restaurants and tapas bars. The ends had changed, and sometimes it felt like the community who had built the place were being locked out from that transition.

In South Wales, the youth centres that held safe ground for a generation of kids have begun to fade and close. In 2020, a YMCA report titled 'Out of Service' noted that during the past decade, youth services in Wales have had their funding cut by almost 40 per cent, a loss of £19 million. In Cardiff, the figure was 64 per cent.[1] This is the consequence of local councils in Wales suffocating under the mounting pressures of the UK government's austerity programme. In an attempt to leave balance sheets and budgets in the black, councillors have shed and cleaved funding for youth services and libraries and community halls.

The fallout is felt on the ground. A generation suffers in the wake of these decisions. A member of a youth programme in Cardiff told me about how the 'city used to have twenty-two standalone youth centres, in every geographical area. And then they went [down] to five. Just bosh. In the stroke of a pen. We're feeling that now.'

When I sat with Jamie Winchester, a mentor to Dell and Phil more than a decade back in the Urban Circle youth centre, he tells me that they, like everywhere else, have felt the strain under the cuts. He told me how the shuttering of a space or a reduction in hours and contact time changes things out in the community, altering the paths of those who need them most.

'When you've got a consistent connection with a group of young people,' Jamie said, 'you can really work on it and gel with one another. They know they're gonna be there Wednesday to Friday. They get used to you. You might be the only stability in their life. You might be the only role models in that young person's life. And that happens a lot.

'If I say we're doing a course for three months, and on Wednesday and Friday we're gonna be here at two till five, and if I ain't there because things are getting cut . . . first of all I've let you down and I've reminded you of the other elder in your life that has let you down. That's bigger than all of it, because then you start thinking, *Who can I trust?*

'It's like you and your partner. If they're consistently good to each other it's great. But if you're on and off on and off, you don't know where you bluddy stand, do ya? Same as this.'

The young and the vulnerable increasingly have no other place to turn for support.

Communal loss is being felt in the West Midlands, too. In early 2021, Winston Mendez, aka Major, whose studio was the fulcrum of Birmingham's Black music scene, passed away. The city gathered at his funeral, the young, the old, the rappers, the managers, the DJs, the Grime MCs, the Drill artists massing to pay their respects. Many felt lost without his studio, not sure where to record.

DJ Big Mikee mourned his friend. 'God Bless Major's soul, man, rest in peace,' he told me, 'he's left a massive gap there now and no one has filled it. No one ain't filled that gap . . . Him passing away has left a massive hole but it's also an opportunity for somebody who's got them sort of skills to step in and take that opportunity.'

It brought into focus the importance of establishments like BE83, and the need for the music scene in the region to build a deeper infrastructure and eventually become self-sufficient. They form part of a wider ecosystem of Black business in the West Midlands, a foundation in a community that is piecing together a road for the next generation to walk on.

Cipher, a rapper turned entrepreneur and community leader, explained the importance to me.

'We've lost so many spaces in the Black community in this city,' he said. 'Go to all of the towns. You go to Walsall, West Bromwich, you go to Dudley, go to Coventry, we've lost space. London. Speak to any Black community in London, North, East, South or West, we've lost spaces. And because we've lost the spaces or we've lost the ownership of spaces, we've actually lost control of things. We don't have a place where we can gather.

'I think it's wrong that Black people in the Black community don't have spaces to be themselves, to practise the art they want to practise, to practise the culture they want to practise, to practise the lifestyle they want to practise.'

But there is resistance. Cipher was a mentor of Despa's. He had lived through the many iterations of Black music in the West Midlands, starting on Pirate Radio in the 1980s, releasing Hip Hop with seminal music group Moorish Delta 7 in the 1990s and 2000s, walked the narrow road of unity through the gang era and shot videos in both areas to include the separate sides. He saw Reggae and Jungle, Garage and Grime blossom and then evolve. More than thirty years on, he is cemented as a pioneer and a driving figure in the community.

I meet him in the Legacy Centre, a large community space he runs in the heart of Newtown. Formerly known as The Drum arts centre, an entertainment and educational resource for the Black community, it closed in 2016. Three years later, Cipher and partners acquired the space, and reopened it for the people.

The day we meet, the centre is hosting the monthly Black Pound

Day Market. Black Pound Day falls on the first Saturday of every month. The national initiative, founded by So Solid Crew member Swiss, encourages the community to consciously shop with Black-owned businesses on the designated day. In partnership, with Cipher, the two have erected the market as a focal point for the community in Birmingham. Set up in the main hall are Black businesses and vendors from across the West Midlands, and as far as London and Bristol. Reggae and old-school Garage and R&B ring out from the speakers, as traders and customers pass goods and money and smiles back and forth. Families fan out across dining tables, and in a corner, a mum, a sister and a daughter dance to 'Candy'. It felt like a large family gathering.

'Sacred spaces are very, very important,' he told me. 'If you go into a mosque on a Friday or Jewish synagogue on a Saturday or a church on a Sunday, or a gurdwara on Sunday, those are sacred spaces. You go into those spaces and you feel a certain way, and you know the people in that space feel comfortable in that space. Culture is very similar.

'Right now, our community know they can come here, it's a safe space for them. No one ain't looking at them different because they're Black African or Caribbean. No one's judging the food that they eat. No one's judging nothing.'

BE83 is an example of this, too. The day I stop by, Despa is sat a desk, working. A few of his friends-turned-colleagues are lounging on bean bags and crouched over laptops. Dapz is talking with his day-to-day manager. There is a meeting ongoing in the boardroom, the muffled tones of a Zoom call drifting through the walls. Friends arrive at the front door, and a few teenagers stop by to use the studio. For BE83, it is business as usual.

From this new institution, music is finding its way into the world. Jaykae, managed by Despa, began releasing songs like 'Chop' and

'1,000 Nights' with vocalist Jorja Smith from Walsall in anticipation of his debut album; Dapz too with 'Shinobi Part II' and 'Beautiful'. Remtrex released a mixtape and then went back inside, incarcerated on remand for almost two years. In early 2022, he announced his release with a new song, 'Fresh Out on Bail'.

Shortly after, Despa's daughter, Ayaana, arrives from school, and sits in a chair scrolling an iPad, while Despa and friends debate music and plot out music videos and release schedules. Eventually, she folds some white paper into a paper aeroplane and begins throwing it through the room. It lands at a chair next to Dapz. And then on the desk by Despa, then towards whoever else is around and still at work. Smiling, they pick it up and throw it back, its makeshift wings slicing the air, and crash-landing on the carpet. On one occasion, the plane lands by her feet. She picks it up in her fingers. In bold lettering, on the side of the wing, she has written 'BE83'. Then she extends her arm back, and throws it forward, tossing the plane through the house her father has built.

BLAINE CAMERON JOHNSON FOOTBALL CLUB

SOUTH LONDON

How does South London remember one of its own?

It's been around three years since Cadet passed and they are all coping in their own ways. Some still listen to his music, loading up their most cherished songs from *The Commitment* and playing them on repeat. Some kept old messages and voice notes and play them from time to time when they want to feel close to him.

For others it took a while before they could listen to songs and music videos without breaking down in public. They live in their own little memories of him instead, keep pictures of him on their fridges and watch his old interviews every now and then, or see him in their dreams sometimes, smiling.

His family and his friends have tried to keep his name and legacy alive. With the money raised from the show in Brixton, the family set up The Cadet Trust and began funding youth projects in Lambeth and wider South London.

Krept and a few others gathered his unreleased material, phoned artists for feature verses and put out a debut album, *The Rated Legend*, released in April 2020 via Cadet's label Underrated Legends.

When Stormzy headlined Glastonbury in 2019, becoming the first British rapper and the first Black British solo act to do so, he walked onto stage in a stab-proof vest with a Union flag embroidered on the front. At one point during his set, with around a hundred thousand people gathered in a festival field in Somerset, and a million more watching from home, the stage lights drop into red. Across the screen crawls the many towns of The 7 and the deep waters of South London: Thornton Heath, Selhurst, Croydon, South Norwood, West Norwood and his own home, Norbury.

Later, he pays homage to the artists of his era, a new generation taking British Rap and Black British music into territories uncharted. In a moment of quiet he reads out fifty-two names: artists, MCs, singers and rappers, and as he is about to finish, he extends his arm into the night and points towards the heavens:

'Rest in peace my brother Cadet as well,' he says, the hundred thousand swelling in cheers. 'We love you, Cadet. My guy.'

Cadet's picture flashes onto the screen. The caption reads: *In Loving Memory of Blaine 'Cadet' Johnson. Rest in Eternal Paradise.*

How does South London remember one of its own?

They remember him every Sunday on recreation grounds across South London and Surrey. In 2019, Adam, who Cadet worked with at The Listening Company, decides on a whim to set up a football team.

'I don't know why,' he will say. 'I just don't know why; maybe it was like a therapy or something? I don't know. I've got to do something, innit.'

He reaches out to the Surrey FA and sets up a meeting. At the meeting, out in Leatherhead, a panel of four ask him about the potential running of the team, not knowing that Adam, who goes along with another friend Jason, has no players, no kit, no sponsor, no home ground. When asked about funding, he says they'll self-fund, that they have a pot of £200 ready to go. The panel have doubts, but they give Adam a shot. He registers the team as 'BCJ', short for Blaine Cameron Johnson football club, and then posts the surprise news into the group chat with Matt and Ashley and a few of the other boys who also worked with Cadet. They will compete in the Leatherhead and District Sunday Football League.

To make a first-team squad, they scramble together brothers and friends and younger cousins. They find a home pitch in Epsom, just outside of South London, and play in black and purple kits. Matt is the manager. Ashley and Adam round out a wider management team. The team fund everything themselves, putting their money together to carry on the legacy of their friend.

The first season is tough. In that first year they only win two games, and before they can really settle into things, the COVID-19 pandemic and the subsequent lockdowns cut the football season short.

The second season is better. They finish third, this time only losing two games all season. They reach the semi-final of the cup, too, desperate to bring home a trophy in Cadet's honour. But they lose. Some of the boys take it hard, and for months struggle to shake the disappointment. But it doesn't overshadow the season entirely. At one home match, after they score, a woman runs onto the field and jumps on the goal-scorer, Darnell. It is Cadet's mum, Janice. When the rest of the team realise, they pile on and celebrate with her in a loud moment of joy.

They are in their third season now. And every Sunday morning, at around 9 a.m., a squad of around fifteen of them, ages ranging from mid-teens to thirty-plus, gather on a football pitch and pull on a jersey to represent a piece of South London who still lives on. Some think about him whenever they pull on that shirt. Before kick-off, they huddle in a circle, and on the count of three chant 'BCJ' before walking onto the field. They are cheered on by a contingent of about ten people, made up of some of the players' mums and partners and small children and friends who follow the team home and away.

In the winter months, when the season is played, they take his name across the region. Blaine Cameron Johnson is celebrated on the football pitches across outer South London and Surrey. They take his name to edges of South London, out by Chessington, in a big green field with misty winter rain dusting the mud, and orange leaves rusting on the trees in the distance. Huddling in a circle, they put their hands in and bellow 'BCJ' loud, their collective voices echoing across the park. Then they charge into battle, going into the trenches on a cold Sunday morning for something bigger than them.

On Remembrance Sunday, they play in Camberley, Surrey, a town defined by the Deepcut army barracks. As you drive through dense forest, towards the playing field, you pass veterans in blue and black army blazers, medals and ribbons fastened to their pockets as they walk the road towards the cemeteries and churches, their wives and daughters and grandchildren trailing behind them. You pass social clubs and lamp posts and other establishments all decorated in large red poppies.

When the team reaches the field, some of the kids who have come out to watch BCJ with their parents remark how this place is nothing like South London; that they even saw cows grazing in the fields. At kick-off, the teams gather around the centre circle for a two-minute silence to remember the fallen. Both have lost something, and someone.

Other games are more strained. At a home match in Epsom, still in the depths of winter, patches of sunlight come out over the trees and perched clouds glow a gloomy blue. The mood on the pitch has grown tense. Matt and Ashley watch from the sidelines as tackles stray over the edge of fair play and twenty-two men in the contained white lines begin to grow agitated. The game pauses as the morning threatens to boil over and the teams square up to one another. Afterwards, Matt takes the team aside. He is angry. He reminds them what and who they are representing out there, that yes, the game can be competitive, but they must never cross a line into violence, that this is bigger than all of them, that 'this is my bredrin's team. We have to carry ourselves like men.'

This is how the season goes on. Some games won, some games lost, their purpose for playing always remaining the same. They play in Wimbledon and in Sutton and in Merton, their friendship group bumping up against another. They honour his name wherever they travel. Sometimes on the drive back, they will turn his music on in the car and let it play loud, or sit on the train back into South London, and reminisce on Sky TV days.

Matt, Ashley and Adam would love to scale the team up one day, get some coaching badges, start a BCJ academy and help wayward kids out of South toe the line. But for now, they keep playing, weekend after weekend, showing up for Cadet the best way they can.

On a Sunday in late February the winter begins to break. They are in Kingston, and blue skies are pulled out over tower blocks and terraced housing. In the park, families are taking walks with buggies and dogs, South London smelling spring on the horizon. BCJ are 4–0 up and coasting, the boys' approach, play and tactics singing in a magnetic harmony. Adam and Matt are on the touchline, laughing with friends and some of the loyal supporters who have made the trip. The youngest members of the team are standing at their side, bantering with each other about parties and ends. Some of them would have been eleven, twelve and thirteen when Cadet was on his rise, watching his videos in school. And now they are here, grown, in light and laughter with some of his closest friends, all gathered together in this weekly ritual of quiet celebration.

This is how they remember one of their own.

Cadet carried their South London stories into the light. And now he is gone, South London continues his march, carrying his name and his song across their many green fields of home.

ACKNOWLEDGEMENTS

Many hands went into the making of this book. I want to thank my first editor, Alexa Von Hirschberg, for believing in my writing and what was, at the time, scraps of a book. Your words filled me with confidence, and the advice you gave was invaluable in shaping the work and my craft. Thank you to my agent, Emma Finn, for seeing and believing in the book from such an early stage. Thank you to Mo at Faber, for guiding me through the process. And thank you to the rest of the Faber team too: Hannah, Dan, Sam, Joanna, David, Jess, Anna and everyone else. Thank you to Simon Pemberton for the cover illustration.

Thank you, Mum, for dropping book after book in my lap as a kid. Thank you to my brother Ukeme too, whose confidence in me kept me going at times that I wavered. Thank you, Priscilla, for all of your support and encouragement, for coming with me on one of my very first reporting trips when I was shooting in the dark, and for listening to me talk through every interview thereafter before a word had even been committed to the page. RIEP Hannah Britton, God bless your soul. And thank you to Dad for passing on a love of music and literature.

To all my long-time friends who made this book possible – both directly and indirectly. To Mo for sharing a love of music – I still remember you, Ukeme and myself crowded around your bedroom speaker listening to the copy of *Walk in Da Park* you'd copped from HMV in the week it came out. Thank you to Ash. SBTV was a life changing time for me. Our endless conversations about craft, music and purpose shaped the man and writer I am today. To Ivan as well, your drive inspires me. To all my friends, thank you for every song we shared over Bluetooth, for every rave, house party, hall party, birthday party, BBQ, music debate and car ride. You all allowed me to not just listen to the music I love, but to experience it too. All of those experiences and memories are threaded throughout the spirit of this book.

Shout out to my early readers. Thank you to Calum Jacobs, a great friend and a great mind. Thank you for the hours and hours of voice-notes we racked up over the past few years. Thank you for the Sly Murkage mixtapes, for your South London memories, and all of the doors you opened for me in the region. Thank you for listening to pieces of the book before anybody else had read it, and thank you for always championing my writing. For all of that and everything else, I'm forever grateful.

Thank you to Tice Cin – for your time, for your feedback, for your friendship. I can honestly say that the book is better because of your eyes, and your care. Thank you to Ciaran Thapar – I'm deeply appreciative of all the writing and publishing wisdom you've passed on over these past few years. Your book and work have been a beacon. Thank you to Dan Hancox for reading early chapters too, and to Sam Knight for the jewels on how to construct, structure and write narrative nonfiction.

Shout out to the rest of my writing people, my creative friends and community. Your words, books and art have lifted me: Christian Adofo, Yomi Sode, the 10K family, Musa Okwonga, Caleb Azumah Nelson, Candice Carty-Williams, Que, Jason Okundaye, Paul Gibbins, Marco Grey, Mabdulle, Lawrence Burney, Seth Pereira, Yemi Abiade, Jesse Bernard, Guy Gunaratne, Sofia Akel and everyone else.

Thank you to my various journalism editors who have taught and guided me over the years, especially Robin at *CLASH*, and Ben and Laura at the *Guardian*.

I'm thankful to have been inside the building, watching as this golden era of British Rap has blossomed. For that I have to thank the various people and places who gave me the opportunity to work and make a living in this scene. Thank you to Link Up TV for giving me my first ever music writing opportunities way back in my uni days. And thank you to Rashid for your generous access to quotes for this book. Thank you and much love to my SBTV family. The first ideas of the book were born in my eighteen months there. What a time in my life that was. I'll always treasure it. RIEP Jamal Edwards, may your legacy live on.

To all my South Wales people, thank you so much. Thank you to Phil for allowing me to share your story here. The same to Dell, I'm deeply appreciative. That extends to Benji and Luke too. Thank you to everyone who spoke to me in Wales, helping build and refine the history contained in this book: Jamie Winchester for the history of music and community work in South Wales and Newport. Thank you to Mace, Lemfreck, Keith Murrell, the Grassroots youth project, Butetown Community Centre, Liara Burussi and Monkey. And thank you to Jean Jenkins at Cardiff University for your invaluable insights into the South Wales Valleys.

Thank you to all my South London people. RIEP Blaine 'Cadet' Johnson. Your music and message changed the lives of many. Thank you so much to Chandler and Janice, and the Johnson family for allowing this to happen. I'm eternally grateful to Amaru for your help in making this part of the book possible. Thank you to all of Cadet's friends, collaborators and supporters who spoke candidly with me: Tech, Wonda, Aaron (Grievous), Harleigh, Adam, Ashley, Matt. Shout out BCJFC for letting me follow you around South London and Surrey for the season. Good luck with everything. Thank you to everyone from South who generously shared memories of growing up in the area, as well as vividly recollecting the music cultures you were a part of: Joey of Pixel TV, Chris the Capo, Joe Walker and Cookie Crew.

And thank you to all my West Midlands people. A massive thank you to Despa for allowing me into your life. The book started with that first trip to Birmingham many, many years ago. Thank you to Casey for opening so many doors for me along the way, for the introductions, and for giving me an understanding of the Black British experience in Birmingham. Thank you to Cecil Morris of PCRL, to Cipha of The Legacy Centre, to Big Mikee, Vader, Dapz on the Map, Hitman and Trilla. Many of you allowed me into your homes. Speaking with you all has enriched my life massively. Free Pa Salieu, and thank you for allowing me to share parts of your story here. There is greatness in your next chapter. Thank you to Hamish as well. Thank you to everyone in Hillfields and Coventry who made me feel welcome in the city: Kate and the rest of the Hillz FM team, as well as Susie and the Positive Youth Foundation. The work you all do is incredible.

And finally, thank you to everyone who has played a part in creating and building the genres documented in this book. Your creativity, your music and your persistence has given my life fulfilment, purpose, and an untold amount of joy. For that, I'm eternally grateful.

Thank God, always.

NOTES

INTRODUCTION

1 *Giggs: The Landlord Headline Show* [video], Link Up TV, 14 November 2016.

1 BABYLON

1 Thomas Fair, '"Thrive, No Matter What": Stories from the Windrush Generation', *BirminghamLive*, 27 October 2021.
2 Fair.

2 HANDSWORTH SONGS

1 Section 4 of the 1824 Vagrancy Act.
2 Kieran Connell, 'Riots Don't Happen Without a Reason', *Guardian*, 10 August 2011.
3 Connell.
4 *Handsworth Songs*, dir. John Akomfrah, Black Audio Film Collective, 1986.
5 'Pirate Radio Operator Sentenced', BBC News, 24 January 2004.

3 LONDON UNDERGROUND

1 'Going Underground: The Windrush Arrivals' Subterranean Dormitories', BBC News, 21 June 2018.
2 'Sam King: Notting Hill Carnival Founder and First Black Southwark Mayor Dies', BBC News, 18 June 2016.
3 Leah Sinclair, 'Windrush History Explored At Clapham South Shelter', *The Voice*, 14 June 2018.

4 JUNCTION BOYS

1 Tania Branigan, 'Clubbers Shot at Top Group's Party', *Guardian*, 2 November 2001.
2 Fiachra Gibbons, 'Minister Labelled Racist after Attack on Rap "Idiots"', *Guardian*, 6 January 2003.

3 'Rappers Under Fire', *NME*, 6 January 2003.
4 *This Is So Solid*, dir. David Upshal, Lion Television, 2002.

5 MIDDLE ENGLAND

1 Rhonda Byrne, *The Secret*, 2006.

6 THE DOCKS

1 Daniel Evans, 'Welshness in "British Wales": Negotiating National Identity at the Margins', *Nations and Nationalism*, 25:1, 2019.
2 Natalie Crockett, 'Newport Faces Battle to Get Out of Recession – Report', *South Wales Argus*, 19 January 2010.
3 Urban Circle Newport, founded by Dennis McKenzie, Ali Boksh, Loren Henry and others.

7 DIRTY SOUTH

1 Office for National Statistics, Census 2001, 29 April 2001 and Census 1991, 21 April 1991.

9 CF10

1 'In-depth: The Black Spots of Unemployment', *Alt.Cardiff*, 13 December 2013.
2 'Astroid Boys Interview with Major Magazine of Death', Astroid Boys WordPress [About/ethos page], 23 August 2011.
3 *Generation Grime* [documentary], BBC Radio 4, 2017.
4 *Generation Grime*.

11 BROKE

1 *Shreds: Murder in the Dock* [documentary], BBC Radio Wales, 2019.
2 *Shreds*.
3 *Generation Grime*.

12 THE 7

1 *Cadet Interview: In-depth Interview about Relationship with Krept, His Come Up So Far and more!*, DJDUBLTV, 22 December 2016.

13 A BRITISH DREAM

1 *Risky Roadz: 0121*, Amazon Music, 25 June 2021.

14 HIS LIGHT

1 *Cadet Interview: Lack Of Label Interest, Is Drill Music Escalating Violence, The Pressure To Succeed*, Amaru Don TV, 23 April 2018.

17 THE SOUTH WALES VALLEYS

1 'Women's Role in the Miners' Strike, 25 Years On', Wales Online, 7 March 2009.

18 HILLFIELDS: FRONTLINE

1 Hansard HC vol. 75, cols 540–604, 15 March 1985.
2 Felicity Martin, 'Pa Salieu Is the Breakout Coventry Star on the Frontline of UK Rap', *DUMMY Magazine*, 30 June 2020.
3 Pa Salieu, *Send Them to Coventry*, Warner Music UK, 2020.
4 Department for Education, 'Sidney Stringer Academy', Get Information about Schools (GIAS), April 2023.
5 Department for Education, 'Schools, Pupils and Their Characteristics', 9 June 2022.
6 Aleksandra Kazlowska et al., *West Midlands Violence Reduction Unit: The Place-Based Evaluation*, University of Opportunity, March 2021.

19 STREATHAM VALE TO THE WORLD

1 *DAVE*, BL@CKBOX, s. 6, ep. 24/65 [video], 10 May 2015.
2 Alistair Foster, 'Dave: My Rap Success Has Given Mum "Bragging Rights"', *Evening Standard*, 26 June 2019.

21 THE BLACK POUND

1 YMCA, *Out of Service: A Report Examining Local Authority Expenditure on Youth Services in England and Wales*, 5 January 2020.

SELECT BIBLIOGRAPHY

FILM/DOCUMENTARY

A Beautiful Tragedy, dir. David Kinsella and Anna Sirota, 2008

Battersea Junction – Stories from Winstanley and York Road Estates, digital:works, 2018

Black Crusader Sound @ Hillfields Carnival, Coventry, UK – 1991, [online video], Saffron Saffron, 5 December 2016, <https://youtu.be/pa1UuCoeVEw?si=E4Z1M10LENQC2yOL>, accessed 2022.

Butetown, 1960s, [online video], Archif ITV Cymru/Wales @ LlGC | ITV Cymru/Wales Archive @ NLW, 2 December 2014, <https://youtu.be/9tfu8bNdFUI?si=d4q4kjBLCMbc7G1M>, accessed 2020

Bombin', Channel 4, dir. Dick Fontaine, 1987

Cardiff manor DVD (part 1) coming soon, [online video], Astroid Boys, 2009, <https://youtu.be/DWep7Drq48o?si=w6_jhotI9FjJqRMD>, accessed 2020

Casablanca Beats, Ali n' Productions, 2021

'Champion Sound' – Documentary on the history of Reggae sound systems in Coventry, UK (2010), [online video], Saffron Saffron, 12 December 2016, <https://youtu.be/kRydM-pOGPg?si=IxD6EiqDJT0gTzu5>, accessed 2022

Children Underground, Childhope International, dir. Edel Belzberg, 2001

Conqueror Sound System, [online video], 1984, 15th FLoor Productions, 17 Jul 2015, <https://youtu.be/bNciAoF0G7M?si=fox6AJ56BcKAnL-7>, accessed 2021

Kabul, City in the Wind, Silk Road Film Salon, dir. Abozar Amjnu, 2018

Les Misérables, Srab Films, Rectangle Productions, Lyly Films, dir. Ladj Ly, 2019

Lost Tapes Of Brixton: VOL.1 – Clash In The Park, [online video], Apex, 16 Mar 2017, <https://youtu.be/nAO3RUUCtXk?si=UqKOvSdOEC13nWfd>, accessed 2022

Nothing Compares, Showtime Documentary Films, dir. Kathryn Ferguson, 2022

Peckham and Wooly Road before the #zone2 #Moscow Beef (2004) Block Patrol DVD, [online video], Big Ego Media, 31 December 2020, <https://youtu.be/5-GVmhPSozg?si=nqQcOM5snSCnAEV4>, accessed 2022

SELECT BIBLIOGRAPHY

Powerhill Crew/Bass Developers/Vortex Crew – Serious FM 93.3 Birmingham UK, [online video], Original Vybe Promotions, 14 August 2015, <https://youtu.be/rlnyA1Fr_js?si=bCgCvqV1qKatZVeG>, accessed 2021.

Small Axe, Turbine Studios, 2020

(SN1) GIGGS, KYZE & REV (187) EXCLUSIVE ONTOP FM SET, [online video], SOUTHLONDONBOROUGHZ, 15 December 2020, <https://youtu.be/_xgsSq0DfAA?si=eZX3BrXwcoCmHiyP>, accessed 2022

Southern Hospitality 2 DVD2, [online video], CHAMBER, 25 January 2019, <https://youtu.be/YDyb3mm8XQ0?si=9XxiLudm_4TAPPBk>, accessed 2022

Style Wars, Public Art Films, 1983

Sunderland Till I Die, Fulwell 73, 2018

Unsafe Convictions, BBC Panorama, 1992

Vintage Documentary: Blues Parties & the closure of Black night clubs in London, UK – 1980, [online video], Saffron Saffron, 24 November 2019, <https://youtu.be/vownU4oXEyA?si=o_MCjRqK2qcR6jDi>, accessed 2021

Where the Houses Used to Be, Thames Television, dir. Carlos Pasini, 1971

ARTICLES/JOURNALISM

'A Community of Communities? Similarity and Difference in Welsh Rural Community Studies', Graham Day, *Economic and Social Review*, July 1998

'Focus: When Britain Loved Rastafari', discoversociety, 1 July 2014

'Full triangulated account for the 2011 "riots" in Clapham', Beyond Contagion, 2018

'Ghost Town racism and resistance – The Specials play Coventry 1981', History is Made at Night – The Politics of Dancing and Musicking, 23 February 2019

'Lost Cities: How Cardiff's Thriving Multicultural Hub Was Crushed', Chris Sullivan, *Byline Times*, 5 August, 2020

'Port Talbot struggles to see a life beyond steel', Karl West, *Guardian*, 2 April 2016

'Post-war High-Rise in Birmingham I: "Saucer City"', Municipal Dreams, 19 May 2015

'Providence House: from mods to rappers, a haven for London's "little rogues"', Yvonne Roberts, *Guardian*, 4 May 2014

'Riot Recovery: Why Clapham Junction Remains Divided Three Years On', Will Martindale, *Huffington Post*, 8 August 2014

'The regeneration of Cardiff Bay has "lost its way" according to Cardiff's council leader', Sion Barry, Wales Online, 30 March 2018

'When The Cops Come They Don't Just Come In Ones Or Twos – Dennis Bovell Talks', Ransom Note, 19 August 2018

SELECT BIBLIOGRAPHY

MUSIC

Berwyn, '017 FREESTYLE', Heritage, 2020

Bis X Blanco X Active X MizOrMac, 'Kennington Where It Started' #HarlemSpartans, The Drop 36, 15 January 2017

Blood Orange ft Skepta, 'High Street', Domino Recording Co Ltd, 2013

Bru-C ft Bou, 'Streetside', CRUCAST, 2021

Bugzy Malone, *M.E.N II*, B. Somebody, 2019

Che Lingo, 'South', 7Wallace, 2020

DC, 'Neighbourhood', Universal Music operations Limited, 2021

Headie One, 'Both', Relentless Records, 2019

J Hus, 'Spirit', Black Butter Limited, 2017

Jorja Smith, 'Blue Lights', FAMM, 2018

Kano, *Made in the Manor*, Parlophone Records Limited, 2016

K-Trap, 'Warm', Thousand8, 2021

LAY DEM ANTHEM, [online video], SkoresOfficial, 8 August 2008, <https://youtu.be/1v3nby8Ff_8?si=U2SrN9Zx8fN5edIJ>, accessed 2022

Local, 'Village Side', Richard Sheppard, 2019

Meekz, 'Like Me', Young Entrepreneurs Music, 2020

M1llionz, *Lagga*, M1llionz, 2020

MizOrMac, *Return Of The Mac*, MizOrMac, 2020

Nines, 'Outro', Warner Records, 2020

Potter Payper, *Training Day 3*, Potter Payper, 2020

Skepta, 'D.T.I (Pirate Station Anthem)', Dice Recordings, 2003

SL, *Gentleman*, SL, 2017

SR, *Welcome to Brixton*, SR, 2020

Starvz, *Diff Boy (Street Version Remix)*, Starvz, 2019

Swiss, 'Cry', UK NOIZE, 2019

Teeway, 'Feeling It', OVO Records, 2019

TrueMendous | Warm Up Sessions [S6.EP26]: SBTV, SBTV, 7 January 2013

Wretch 32 & Avelino ft Youngs Teflon, 'GMO', Renowned Records, 2015

Wretch 32 ft KayyKayy, 'Anxiety', Universal Music Operations Limited, 2021

MUSIC BOOKS

Hanif Abdurraqib, *A Little Devil in America: In Praise of Black Performance*, Allen Lane, 2021

Jeff Chang, *Can't Stop Won't Stop: A History of the Hip-Hop Generation*, Picador, 2005

Kevin le Gendre, *Don't Stop the Carnival: Black British Music*, Peepal Tree Press, 2018

SELECT BIBLIOGRAPHY

NARRATIVE NON-FICTION

James Baldwin, *Notes of a Native Son*, Beacon Press, 1955

Katherine Boo, *Behind the Beautiful Forevers: Life, Death, and Hope in a Mumbai Undercity*, Random House, 2013

Robert S. Boynton, *The New New Journalism: Conversations With America's Best Nonfiction Writers on Their Craft*, Vintage Books, 2005

Jessica Bruder, *Nomadland: Surviving America in the Twenty-First Century*, W. W. Norton & Co., 2017

Truman Capote, *In Cold Blood: A True Account of a Multiple Murder and Its Consequences*, Random House, 1966

Matthew Desmond, *Evicted: Poverty and Profit in the American City*, Crown, 2016

Joan Didion, *Slouching Towards Bethlehem*, Farrar, Straus and Giroux, 1968

David Finkel, *Thank you For Your Service*, Farrar, Straus and Giroux, 2013

Amy Goldstein, *Janesville: An American Story*, Simon & Schuster, 2017

Calum Jacobs, *A New Formation: How Black Footballers Shaped the Modern Game*, Cornerstone, 2022

Alex Kotlowitz, *There Are No Children Here: The Story of Two Boys Growing Up in the Other America,* Bantam Doubleday Dell Publishing Group, 1992

Michael Paternitii, *Love and Other Ways of Dying: Essays*, The Dial Press, 2015

Johnny Pitts, *Afropean: Notes from Black Europe*, Penguin, 2020

James Rebanks, *The Shepherd's Life: A Tale of the Lake District*, Allen Lane, 2016

Eli Saslow, *Ten Letters: The Stories Americans Tell Their President*, Doubleday, 2011

Gary Smith, *Beyond the Game: The Collected Sportswriting of Gary Smith*, Grove Press/Atlantic Monthly Press, 2001

Gay Talese, *The Bridge: The Building of the Verrazano-Narrows Bridge*, Bloomsbury USA, 2014

Ciaran Thapar: *Cut Short: Youth Violence, Loss and Hope in the City*, Viking, 2021

Wright Thompson, *The Cost of These Dreams: Sports Stories and Other Serious Business*, Penguin, 2019

J. D. Vance, *Hillbilly Elegy: A Memoir of a Family and Culture in Crisis*, Harper Press, 2016

FICTION/POETRY

Ify Adenuga, *Endless Fortune*, Boy Better Know, 2020

Graeme Armstrong, *The Young Team*, Picador, 2020

Malika Booker, *Pepper Seed*, Peepal Tree Press, 2013

Kayo Chingonyi, *More Fiya: A New Collection of Black British Poetry*, Canongate, 2022

SELECT BIBLIOGRAPHY

Caleb Femi, *Poor*, Penguin, 2020
Seamus Heaney, *Field Work*, Faber & Faber, 1979
Tayari Jones, *An American Marriage*, Algonquin Books, 2018
Tommy Orange, *There There*, Alfred A. Knopf, 2018
Sam Selvon, *The Lonely Londoners*, Allan Wingate, 1956
Irwin Shaw, *The Young Lions*, Random House, 1948
Warsan Shire, *Bless the Daughter Raised by a Voice in Her Head*, Vintage, 2022
Yomi Sode, *Manorism*, Penguin, October 2022
Ocean Vuong, *On Earth We're Briefly Gorgeous*, Penguin Press, 2019
Jacqueline Woodson, *Another Brooklyn*, Amistad Press, 2016

EXHIBITIONS

War Inna Babylon: The Community's Struggle for Truths a Rights, Institute of Contemporary Arts, 2021